Sweetness and Blood

HOW SURFING SPREAD FROM
HAWAII AND CALIFORNIA
TO THE REST OF THE WORLD, WITH
SOME UNEXPECTED RESULTS

MICHAEL SCOTT MOORE

RODALE

Rodale books may be purchased for business or promotional use or for special sales.
For information, please write to: Special Markets Department, Rodale Inc.,
733 Third Avenue, New York, NY 10017.

Printed in the United States of America
Rodale Inc. makes every effort to use acid-free ∞, recycled paper ♻.

Book design by Joanna Williams
Photo credits: **Page 1** George Freeth aquaplaning © San Diego Historical Society; **page 33**
Kuta, Bali 2002, Thomson Reuters; **page 67** Uwe Drath and friends, Westerland Beach, Sylt,
c.1954, courtesy of Uwe Drath; **page 95** Pierre Chalaud and Abboud "Mamoune" Kabbour,
Morocco, courtesy of Pierre Chalaud; **page 137** John Webber's image of Captain Cook landing
at Kealakekua Bay, Hawaii, courtesy of the Captain Cook Society; **page 171** Dorian Paskowitz
at the Gaza border, 2007, AP/WIDE WORLD PHOTOS; **pages 217 and 249** Calle 70, Havana,
2009, and the author's surfboard, Porto Allegre, São Tomé, 2008, Michael Scott Moore; **page
283** "Big Wavers" surf club, Oiso, Japan, c.1964, courtesy of Osamu Sakata.

Portions of this book have appeared in *The Atlantic Monthly, The Los Angeles Times,
The Financial Times, Miller-McCune,* and Spiegel International Online.

Library of Congress Cataloging-in-Publication Data is on file with the publisher.

ISBN-10 1–60529–427–6
ISBN-13 978–1–60529–427–8

Distributed to the trade by Macmillan
2   4   6   8   10   9   7   5   3   1   hardcover

We inspire and enable people to improve their lives and the world around them
For more of our products visit **rodalestore.com** or call 800-848-4735

FOR MY MOTHER

CONTENTS

IN OTHER WORDS, THE HIGH AND THE LOW,
THE HISTORIC AND THE MODERN, WERE BUILT
ON THE BANKS OF THE SAME RIVER.

Peter Carey, *Wrong About Japan*

AUTHOR'S APOLOGY

AS A HISTORY of surfing, this book isn't definitive. It completely shortchanges—among other major forces—Dale Velzy, Mary Ann Hawkins, Greg Noll, and most of Australia. What I've tried to assemble is a folk history of surfing, a personal sketch for any curious reader of how the modern sport moved around the world and mingled with cultures that either have nothing to do with Hawaii or have strong reasons to resist pop silliness from the first world. The result is a story of hippies, soldiers, nutcases, and colonialism, a checkered history of the spread of Western culture in the years after World War II.

"Dude, you should have gone to Brazil," people told me. Or, "Are there really good waves in Gaza?"—as if the point were to search for beautiful surf. No, no, no. I left out major wave-riding nations like Mexico, France, and South Africa because most surfers know about them. Wherever possible I chose offbeat nearby countries (Cuba, Germany, São Tomé and Príncipe) to give the general reader an idea of how surfing reached each general part of the world and still, I hope, offer the dedicated surf historian something new—about how the sport mingled with Communism, or how it wound up in the North Sea.

The travel—spread over several years—starts with Chapter 2. Chapter 1 is really a prologue, a highly subjective but (I hope) still interesting review of the basic facts. I set out on this book as a landlocked scribbler, living as a journalist in Berlin. But I'd never stopped being a surfer, and I'd lived too long thinking the material I grew up with, the relentless superficial glare of southern California, had no value for a writer. Even pop culture has a human history, and modern surfing happens to be as American as baseball or jazz. By that I don't mean to claim it for America—surfing, almost as much as soccer, is a world sport—but I do want to provide ammunition against the eternal domestic bigots who say certain (ever-shifting, normally coastal) parts of America somehow don't belong; or against Europeans who think everything exported by America is bad; or against Northeastern snobs who think surfing isn't worth their time. Those three groups of people would never care to be caught together at a dinner party, but to me they're partners in ignorance.

Anyway, this isn't *Endless Summer*. It's not a pleasure trip, or a search for the ultimate stoke. When a surfer takes off on a wave, there are two possible results, and my book is about them both.

1

CALIFORNIA
AND **HAWAII**:
AS CIVILIZATION
ADVANCES

WHEN I WAS YOUNG, the George Freeth memorial in Redondo Beach, California, was a salt-bitten bust of a lifeguard who gazed with the stoicism you'd expect from an early surf hero into the deep mysteries of a concrete parking garage. His back was to the Redondo Pier. Most locals jogged or skated past the sculpture without examining the plaque, which read, disingenuously, FIRST SURFER IN THE UNITED STATES, then related the story of how Freeth was paid by the Los Angeles real estate and streetcar magnate Henry Huntington in 1907 to lure people to ride the Red Line tram to Redondo Beach on sunny afternoons and watch a new kind of athlete trim the waves. "George Freeth was advertised as 'The Man Who Can Walk On Water,'" according to the plaque. "Thousands of people came here on the big red cars to watch this astounding feat. George would mount his big 8-foot-long, solid wood, 200-pound surfboard far out in the surf. He would wait for a suitable wave, catch it, and to the amazement of all, ride onto the beach while standing upright."

I remember passing the sculpture on my bike as a kid.[1] Redondo Beach was, and still is, a glamour-resistant Los Angeles suburb. In the early '80s the beach was drab and blighted with rusting Coppertone trash cans and piles of seaweed. So I wondered why it would have occurred to people in 1907 to come here and watch a man do something so normal: "ride onto the beach while standing upright." Big deal. Could he do aerials? The surfers I saw in magazines—Martin Potter, Mark Occhilupo, Shaun Tomson—could all do aerials.

At the time I was a new and not very good surfer who walked to the beach some mornings before school with a lanky mathematician named Tim who had a dark sense of humor and an oversized Adam's apple. Tim, with his brilliant technical mind and his nerdy leather briefcase, didn't feel welcome at Mira Costa High. He tested out before graduation, I think during his junior year. Other kids who surfed, the California punks and spoiled rich sons of industry, floated in the lineup in expensive, colorful wetsuits and set a tone of cool neither of us could match. But Tim wanted to surf in contests. He pushed himself in the water the way he pushed himself in class, and under his influence I learned to appreciate the magisterial command of pros like Tom Curren and Mark Foo; the aggro wave-whacking styles of Occhilupo and Brad Gerlach; and the clever innovations of guys like Cheyne Horan, who won surf titles on boards he'd invented himself.

By then surfing was too far along for me to imagine any individual as the "first surfer" in America. Surfing was too obvious. It was an ancient sport in Hawaii; how come it took until 1907 to reach America? Didn't native Californians—the Chumash, the Ohlone—surf? (Actually, no.) But my teenage skepticism was justified. Freeth was only the first *celebrity* surfer in California. The first men on record to surf North America were three Hawaiian princes who noticed that waves at the San Lorenzo River mouth in Santa Cruz

---

[1] In the summer of 2008 thieves knocked the original bronze bust of Freeth off its plinth, probably to sell for scrap.

were up to snuff. In the late nineteenth century, Jonah Kuhio Kalaniana'ole, heir to the Hawaiian throne, and his brothers David and Edward attended a military school in San Mateo, over the hill from Santa Cruz. They shaped their own boards from local redwoods and hauled them out to the beach one day in 1885 for a little fun. "The young Hawaiian princes were in the water," wrote a local paper, "enjoying it hugely and giving interesting exhibitions of surfboard swimming as practiced in their native islands."

There's also the story from Richard Henry Dana's *Two Years Before the Mast* about Hawaiian crewmen from a ship called the *Ayacucho*, which met Dana's ship near Santa Barbara in 1835. It was Dana's first California landing. A rowboat full of his shipmates was waiting in high evening surf for a chance to row in when a launch from the *Ayacucho* "came alongside of us, with a crew of dusky Sandwich-Islanders, talking and hallooing in their outlandish tongue. They knew that we were novices in this kind of boating," so they showed the *haoles* how it was done. The Hawaiians had had outrigger practice, and outriggers are close ancestors of surfboards. Dana then sets down the earliest English description of riding California surf. "We pulled strongly in, and as soon as we felt that the sea had got hold of us, and was carrying us in with the speed of a race-horse, we threw the oars as far from the boat as we could," imitating the Hawaiians, "and took hold of the gunwales, ready to spring out and seize her when she struck, the officer using his utmost strength, with his steering-oar, to keep her stern out. We were shot up upon the beach, and seizing the boat, ran her up high and dry, and, picking up our oars, stood by her, ready for the captain to come down."

I agree with other people who have stumbled across this scene and found it hard to imagine surf-experienced Hawaiians passing "perfect Rincon or Malibu" in masted ships and not improvising a board—or just diving in—for a session of some kind in the water. "A surfer is a surfer," wrote Ben Marcus (the surf writer, not the novelist), "and a wave is a wave."

But George Freeth helped rescue stand-up surfing from the Christianized sickness of nineteenth-century Hawaiian culture and brought it to Redondo Beach. Like African music that crossed in ships to America and became the blues, and then jazz, and then rock, surfing would merge with the American landscape and become something new. After the pop explosion of the '60s there would be no stopping it. I'd been vaguely aware of the sport's imperial march in the years since I took it up, when stickers for Body Glove wetsuits and Quiksilver board shorts plastered on road signs and school desks were part of the provincial mood of Redondo, Manhattan, and Hermosa Beach—collectively known as the South Bay, a coastal suburb of Los Angeles—but it wasn't until I saw the Quiksilver store in Paris and watched surfers in Munich, where people surf Isar River canals, that I noticed with a measure of dread that "surfing" is a big-business American export, up there with cowboys and Hollywood.

Munich doesn't just have a plashing corner of the English Garden where you can put your board in the water and impress your girlfriend. It has a small but thriving surf *scene,* with dreadlocked German teenagers, local attitude, and an annual contest sponsored by Quiksilver. It's as if European kids can't think of their own way to rebel. And finding this scene made me wonder whether the migration of surfing from the Pacific to the four corners of the earth is good or bad—a symptom of the universal delights of a simple Polynesian sport or a warning that California has conquered the world.

Not to piss off Australians. Surfing by now is no less "Australian" than it is "Californian," in the sense that it's really Hawaiian. The sport is a national pastime in Australia because most of the white population lives along the coast. Broadcasters there can report on big waves and shark attacks without the irritating reflex in American TV to treat surf culture as a quaint activity in some province ludicrously distant from New York. The sport also has deep Australian roots. After Duke Kahanamoku gave a surf exhibition at a Sydney beach in 1915, "on a make-shift board [made] out of sugar pine," lifeguards and hobbyists took up surfing on redwood boards and kayaklike surf skis, the way Californians did just after Freeth. In the 1950s surfing was still a trundling curiosity in Australia until a hipper, faster version arrived from California (with the "Malibu chip" board), and it's the spread of modern surfing I'm curious about, the strange propulsion of it from America to just about everywhere.

The sport's early roots are older than writing in Hawaii and therefore untraceable. But it goes back hundreds if not thousands of years. Some historians think it grew out of the way tired Polynesian fishermen ended long outrigger rides: Instead of paddling in to shore, they learned to catch the rolling surf, like their descendants on the *Ayacucho*. Canoe or outrigger surfing was normal across Polynesia, and bodysurfing as well as bodyboarding was known not just in the South Pacific but also in places as remote from each other as Africa and Peru. The Hawaiian habit of riding surf may have started in Tahiti, which is the source of early Hawaiian culture; in fact, some Tahitians could even stand on their boards. But stand-up surfing—on long, coral-smoothed koa or breadfruit slabs—evolved in Hawaii, where it became a universal recreation practiced by men as well as women, peasants as well as kings.

The sport belonged to the islands like poi and roasted pig. It was a feature of the Makahiki new year festival, when people stopped work and even postponed wars to offer tributes to Lono, the fertility god responsible for sun, rain, storms, and abundant fish. Hawaiian tradition said Lono had once walked the earth, and the people hoped he would come again. To keep his cult alive, high priests in a procession of boats paraded a carving of the god around each island, clockwise, once a year, and Lono's surrogate rearrival was lauded in every district with tributes of taro, sweet potatoes, dry fish, slaughtered pigs, and fabrics. A clever class of tax collectors made sure this booty was loaded onto "tax canoes" and sent reverently out to sea. Meanwhile, people held surf contests, canoe races, boxing matches, lava-sledding contests (sliding down lava rock on slabs of wood), and elaborate feasts.

Makahiki celebrations lasted from mid-October to early February. They coincided with the end of harvest and the cycles of the moon—and, conveniently, with Hawaii's big-wave season. Unlike modern contests, which are judged on style, ancient surf contests were races: Rivals caught the same wave and raced to a buoy anchored in the shallows. The stakes in a contest might be a fishing net, a pig, a bride, a canoe, or lifelong servitude. Hawaiians would bet just as heavily on someone else's performance as on their own. "It was common for a man to lose everything he owned when betting on a favorite surfer," wrote Duke Kahanamoku. But commoners didn't surf against chiefs. When Hawaiian chiefs were in the water, it was taboo to paddle out. Male and female chiefs had retinues of servants who chanted encouraging songs from the beach, and Ben Finney and James Houston report in their short history *Surfing* that for royal contests, the servants would bake a dog in an underground oven so the athletes could paddle in for a snack.

No one knows whether Hawaiians chased big surf. They had no fin technology, meaning their flat-bottomed boards would have spun away on a towering face. A few chiefs, like Kamehameha I, were good at "canoe-leaping," which involved catching a swell in a canoe piloted by someone else, then jumping with your board into the wave. The only point to this maneuver, I think, is to catch a wave you can't paddle after with your own two arms, meaning Kamehameha and his "favorite wife, Ka'ahumanu," may have gone canoe-leaping in fairly big surf. I'm not saying that even the best ancient surfers dropped in on sixty-foot Haleiwa surf with a canoe and a wiliwili board; but canoe-leaping seems to anticipate tow-in surfing, the modern sport's big technical innovation of the 1990s. Tow-in surfers strap their feet to fiberglass boards and get hauled like water-skiers behind noisy spitting Jet Skis into waves once thought impossible to catch.

The point is that while Tahitians were struggling to stand on their bodyboards and Peruvians rode surf boats made of woven reeds, Hawaiians were leaping from outriggers and even surfing on their heads. They'd refined the sport of stand-up surfing into a ritual unique in the world by the time James Cook arrived in 1778 and '79.

Cook's first two voyages to Australia and Polynesia had been scientific and charting expeditions that carried him around the southern rim of the Pacific. On the third voyage, sponsored by the Earl of Sandwich, he cut north. He discovered a new island called Atooi and noted that it belonged to a chain, but kept moving. The earl and his other sponsors wanted him to find the nonexistent Northwest Passage. But ice thwarted Cook's mission near Alaska. On his way home he decided to stop at the Atooi archipelago to replenish his ships. The *Discovery* and *Resolution*—both colliers, designed for shipping coal, with shallow drafts and big cargo holds—missed Atooi (Kauai) but landed on "Mowee" in late 1778, then moved on to a big island called "Owhyhee." They circled this landmass with great care, stopping now and then to trade with islanders who came off in canoes. By the time the ships laid anchor at Kealakekua Bay, in January 1779, Cook and his men were well known. Word may have spread that this pale character in gaudy clothes who had arrived at the height of Makahiki and then circled the island, clockwise, in an exotic Yorkshire collier—flying white sheets that resembled the banners flown by priests during their annual procession—was, well, Lono himself. A painting by one of Cook's men shows a fleet of outriggers and canoes crowding Kealakekua Bay to greet the Second Coming. One man paddles a surfboard.

Impersonating a god may have helped Cook the way it had helped Cortés in Mexico, or else honoring him as a god may have been strategic for the Hawaiians around Kealakekua Bay. At any rate, they were happy to resupply his tax canoes. Cook and his men stayed in Hawaii for about three weeks, and his lieutenant, James King, set down a passage in his log in early 1779 that isn't the first Western description of stand-up surfing but must count as the most colorful.

A wave, King wrote,

sends them in with a most astonishing Velocity, & the great art
is to guide the plank so as always to keep it in a proper direction
on the top of the Swell. . . . On first seeing this very dangerous
diversion I did not conceive it possible but that some of them
must be dashed to mummy against the sharp rocks, but just
before they reach the shore, if they are very near, they quit their
plank, & dive under till the Surf is broke, when the piece of
plank is sent many yards by the force of the Surf from the
beach. . . . By such like exercises, these men may be said to be
almost amphibious.

After three weeks, Cook set out again in search of the Northwest
Passage. This time, the *Resolution* broke a mast in a storm before it
even cleared the island and had to return. The natives were confused.
Makahiki was over. Why was Lono back? With a broken mast? From
his own storm? Asking for help?

In Mark Twain's account of Cook's first landing, ten to fifteen
thousand Hawaiians greeted him as a god on the beach. They bowed
low and led him to a sacred temple, where priests roasted a putrid
hog and did him the high honor of smearing chewed coconut on his
face. On his return, he was greeted with less unquestioning trust.
The Hawaiians grudged him the benefit of the doubt, but there were
petty squabbles, and one islander stole a cutter from the *Resolution*.
Cook decided to kidnap a chief as collateral. This shockingly human
behavior—standard practice for a British explorer, but not for a Polynesian god—alarmed the Hawaiians. An eruption of violence on the
beach forced the British back to their ships. Cook and his men fired
pistols. They were used to watching islanders scatter at the sound of
exploding gunpowder. This time a few Hawaiians fell dead, but
others attacked, and one chief caught Lono's arm and bent him
brusquely backward—not to hurt him, since gods were invincible to

men, but to stop his mischief. Cook groaned in pain. "He groans!" the Hawaiians shouted. "He is not a god!" They slaughtered him instantly in the surf.

Four crewmen died with Cook, but his ships returned to Britain with a new archipelago on the navigation maps. The captain's heart "was hung up in a native hut, where it was found and eaten by three children," according to Twain, "who mistook it for the heart of a dog."

The arrival of Europeans would break the Hawaiian system of *kapu,* or taboo. When mortal strangers started transgressing ancient laws without punishment, confusion set in, and the people quit honoring their gods. By 1819 they didn't even bother with Makahiki. Missionaries from America came in 1820 with a new religion and fresh ideas of shame. They were earnest New England fusspots who dressed the natives in suits, taught them to read, and sent them to church. Missionaries mistrusted local pagan customs, including this odd, naked, water-walking ritual that seemed to empty villages and slay productivity whenever the surf was good. On Maui, old surfboards were chopped up to make desks and chairs for the schoolhouses. Meanwhile Hawaiians died by the thousands of imported disease.

If we believe the low estimates of Cook's men that four hundred thousand Hawaiians were alive in the islands in 1778, within 125 years the population had collapsed by 90 percent. A census in 1890 counted 40,612 natives, who nevertheless outnumbered whites missionaries and their children by almost seven to one. By then Hawaii was a constitutional monarchy with a Western-style legislature. The islanders learned to wear starchy suits and remembered surfing as a peculiar habit of their grandparents. To shore up their rights, they organized an independence movement under Queen Lili'uokalani, who announced a new constitution in 1893. The unjust "bayonet constitution" from six years earlier, she said, amounted to "a revolutionary movement inaugurated by those of foreign blood, or American blood."

The coup to dethrone Lili'uokalani is interesting because it was the first time the US government ever reached for land beyond North

America. In those days the frontier had just closed; Frederick Jackson Turner argued in 1893 that the lack of new land would change the American character, which had been forged on the edge of the wilderness as a blend of "coarseness and strength combined with acuteness and acquisitiveness; that practical inventive turn of mind, quick to find expedients, . . . that restless, nervous energy; that dominant individualism." That restless energy now hopped the Pacific.

Hawaiian plantations were so profitable for American businessmen that a number of them had lobbied Washington for decades to annex the islands and end the problem of import tariffs. But there was no compelling legal excuse to put the islanders under American command until Queen Lili'uokalani declared that her people should have the right to vote and run for office on an equal footing with foreign landholders. Her constitution would have granted suffrage to forty thousand native islanders and some twenty-seven thousand Asian laborers, regardless of money or land. That was unacceptable to the plantation owners, who would have been outnumbered. So a small group of American ministers and businessmen, backed by an American warship full of marines, dethroned Lili'uokalani without killing a soul and ended centuries of native royal droit in a cloud of rhetoric about the "public safety" and the "love of liberty." A reluctant Sanford Dole—son of a missionary, patriarch of the family that would later sell pineapples to Americans in cans—led the so-called "republic of Hawaii" until Washington annexed it as a territory in 1898.

Was Westernization good for Hawaii? Missionaries gave the natives an alphabet; they did the meddling but meticulous work of teaching them to read and write not just in English, but also in their own language. They laid a foundation for intelligent (Western-style) self-government and started a century-long process of transformation that would end with statehood for Hawaii in 1959 as a member of the wealthiest nation in the history of the world.

The transformation, though, came at the expense of a culture. Sydney Possuelo, a Brazilian *sertanista* who once made first-contact missions on behalf of his government to meet still-isolated Amazonian tribes, explained to *Scientific American* in 2007 why he was against continuing in that line of work. "They come into contact with you and start to die off like flies," he said. "One year later they are slack, emaciated, bowing their heads and begging for food and money by the roadside, more and more dependent on you and on the state. . . . Everything, everything, everything plays against them. They become so subordinate to us, for we break up their education, their health, their means of work, their mythical system. They become outcasts. For how long? Well, some of them have been outcasts for 500 years. Please name to me a single tribe in the last 500 years that became better off after contact. There is none!"

Nevertheless, the American men of God in Hawaii had progress to report after only a generation. "The decline and discontinuance of the use of the surf-board," wrote the leader of the Calvinist mission to the islands, Hiram Bingham I, in 1847, "as civilization advances, may be accounted for by the increase in modesty, industry and religion, without supposing, as some have affected to believe, that missionaries caused oppressive enactments against it." The passage is a defense of missionary behavior, and it may be true that the Calvinists never made rules against surfing. Bingham's writing about the sport, his descriptions of naked Hawaiians breaking through the rolling surf on long planks using their arms "as a pair of oars," then selecting a sizable swell and swinging around to ride shoreward "with railroad speed," are precise rather than outraged, shot with the fastidious interest of a man who considered himself a strong swimmer in open water but at risk in rocky shore break. The missionaries, frankly, were scared by good waves. They also noticed with some concern for the natives' souls that men and women surfed together, and sometimes wound up humping afterward in grass huts. But mainly the Calvinists just couldn't see the point. They'd come to Hawaii to enlighten the heathens, and to give them something to do.

୧୧୧୧୧୧୧୧୧୧୧୧୧୧୧୧୧୧

People think of Duke Kahanamoku, not George Freeth, as the father of surfing. Duke took the sport around the world as an elegant showman and appeared in Hollywood films (*Lord Jim, Mr. Roberts, Isle of Sunken Gold*) after winning gold medals in 1912 and 1920 as an Olympic swimmer. By the 1950s he was the only surfer with celebrity status in the American suburbs. But he was seven years younger than Freeth. They both started as "beach boys" at Waikiki around 1900, when the sport was known as a curiosity of the South Seas, something as odd and quaint as those big rings of rock used for cash in New Guinea. Duke and Freeth would have grown up seeing old lithographs of their ancestors riding surfboards, but surfing itself had "totally disappeared throughout the Islands," wrote Duke in his autobiography, "except for a few isolated spots on Kauai, Maui and Oahu, and even there only a handful of men took boards into the sea."

Freeth, who was half Irish and part Hawaiian, taught himself to surf in about 1901. An uncle gave him a heavy, sixteen-foot *olo* board, the kind once ridden by chiefs. The olo was too big for Freeth, so he sawed it in half. Soon the sport became a fashion on Waikiki. After a Beaux-Arts resort called the Moana Hotel opened on the beach, a crowd of local kids would take rich tourists on canoe rides and teach them to surf on boards. The group included haoles like Freeth, a number of women, and five or six Kahanamoku brothers. "A group of us, mostly Hawaiian boys," wrote Duke, "used to gather at a *hau* tree on Waikiki Beach and discuss boards, waves, the delights of surfing, and the latest thing in experiments. It was a poor man's club, but it was made up of dedicated surfers." This tradition hasn't died out. You can still take lessons on Waikiki from a beach boy. In fact the long easy waves on Oahu's south shore may be the most forgiving on the planet for greenhorn surfers. They complement the waves on Oahu's

North Shore, which become, during the winter, the planet's most forbidding. Island slang for this opposition is "town and country": town for the civilized surf at Waikiki, blighted by tourist hotels; country for the proving grounds in the north.

In 1907 Jack London and his wife sailed to Hawaii in a homemade boat. London took a surf lesson from Freeth and wrote home about a half-successful venture into the waves of Waikiki in a widely noticed article in *Woman's Home Companion* that became a chapter in his travelogue *The Cruise of the Snark*. He described Freeth in such appalling overwritten prose that it's clear he never got to know him. "And suddenly, out there where a big smoker lifts skyward, rising like a sea-god from out of the welter of spume and churning white, on the giddy, toppling, overhanging and downfalling, precarious crest appears the dark head of a man. Swiftly he rises through the rushing white. His black shoulders, his chest, his loins, his limbs—all is abruptly projected on one's vision. . . . He is a Mercury—a brown Mercury." And so on.

To be fair, no one seems to have known Freeth well. He was handsome, generous, charismatic, in many ways public, but remote. He never married. He died young with no kids. He would almost qualify as a romantic loner, but he understood publicity well enough to ask both London and another literary surf enthusiast, Alexander Hume Ford, for letters of introduction in California. They obliged, and by July 1907 Freeth was bound for San Francisco.

GEORGE FREETH OFF TO COAST, blared the Honolulu *Pacific Commercial Advertiser* on its front page. WILL ILLUSTRATE HAWAIIAN SURFRIDING TO PEOPLE IN CALIFORNIA. The article contained almost the full content of his obituary, although Freeth was only twenty-three when it was published.

At the time when Freeth first took up surf riding there had been very few here for many years who had been able to perform the trick of standing on a surfboard, and coming in to the shore on the crest of a wave. The white man who could do it was exceptional. Freeth determined that if the old natives had been able to do the trick there was no reason that he could not do the same. In a short time he mastered the feat and then went further. The older inhabitants told of natives in the early days who stood on their heads when they came in. Freeth soon proved that this could be done at the present time as well as before.

Redondo Beach in 1907 was declining as an industrial harbor. The inland city of Los Angeles had chosen a port to the south, San Pedro, to handle its cargo. Most of the coastline was still a stretch of damp and windswept dunes where wealthy men like Henry Huntington wanted to set up resorts. "When I studied the place, and saw its attractions, the beautiful topography it possessed, those terraces rising in harmonious degrees from the sea, I determined," he wrote with a real estate man's instinct for anticlimax, "that it presented such features as should make it the great resort of this region."

Huntington had competition. In 1904 a cigarette mogul named Abbot Kinney had announced plans to build a gimmicky village north of Redondo with a network of canals and bridges and a flock of Italian-style gondoliers who would pole tourists around in front of kitschy mock-European storefronts. He called it the Venice of America. Critics called it Kinney's Folly. It would come with a saltwater plunge—a public pool, fed by the sea, under an arched glass ceiling—and a Coney Island–style pier loaded with rides.

In 1905 Huntington countered this vision of Oz with a three-story pavilion in Redondo Beach, tens of thousands of square feet of seaside pleasure decked out with Moorish arches and flag-topped golden domes. There's no trace of it now, but for a while it dominated Redondo. Still, in spite of Huntington's wonder on the water, people from LA failed to flock to the shore. A greater percentage liked to ride out to the San Fernando Valley on weekends and shoot jackrabbits from Huntington's streetcars. Not that the coast was unpopular—people just had no concept of swimming in waves. "Beach culture" was still alien to the United States.

The saltwater plunge was one answer. Huntington would build the world's largest in Redondo by 1909. But he'd also been to Waikiki. Whether he met Freeth there isn't clear, but soon after the young surfer landed in California, Huntington recognized an opportunity. In his first days on the mainland Freeth went surfing near the half-built nightmare of Kinney's Folly, attracting crowds and the notice of a local paper: SURF RIDERS HAVE DRAWN ATTENTION. By the end of the year Freeth was on Huntington's Pacific Electric Railway payroll, surfing twice a day near a section of Redondo known as Moonstone Beach, where semiprecious stones lay in a natural mound along the waterline. "In those days moonstones were sought after," said an elderly C. M. Pierce in 1955, recollecting his job as a sightseeing manager on the Red Line just after 1900. "Many of our guests turned up excellent specimens after only a short search. These they could later sell, for stores [on Moonstone Beach] bought them by size, or they could have them polished for a half dollar and have something very nice."

So Jack London's handsome "brown Mercury" walked up and down a heavy plank in sloppy Redondo whitewash while tourists in Edwardian suits browsed a mound of colorful surf cobble for "excellent specimens" to offer their sweethearts, or just to have something very nice. Clanking red streetcars and an improbable Moorish Pavilion gave the once-industrial coastline a carny atmosphere that must have seemed as ridiculous in 1907 as it does a century on wherever old boardwalks or pleasure piers compete with the roar of the sea. But surfing had arrived in California, never to vanish again, and George Freeth would be remembered as more than just a sideshow freak.

Every picture I had ever seen of Mike Purpus showed an insolently aging blond punk with an unfashionable '70s mustache and a floppy leather hat. He was born in Hermosa Beach and retired to Redondo, about a mile away. "Almost alone among his contemporaries," reads Purpus's entry in *The Encyclopedia of Surfing*, "he kept his sense of humor. In a 1970 magazine poll in which top surfers were asked 'What other experiences parallel surfing?' answers ranged from 'ballet dancing' to 'love' to 'being filled with the Holy Spirit.' Purpus said, 'Riding my Makaha skateboard after getting sauced on a gallon of Red Mountain.'"

He'd been a young champion surfer when sleek, pointed short-boards replaced longboards in the late '60s. Now he wrote a column for the local paper. When I tried to track him down, his editor could only say where they sent his checks. "Purpus doesn't have e-mail, a phone, or a car," he told me. "He shows up in the office here about once a month."

The address in question was a blocky, white complex near the so-called Hollywood Riviera, a stretch of Redondo Beach with a nickname that always struck me as sarcastic. Parts of the neighborhood were pretty, but Purpus's building had dying ivy in the yard and a tall, unwell banana tree. I knocked on a faded apartment door plastered with surf stickers (OLD GUYS RULE; THE OLDER I GET, THE BETTER I WAS). A muffled yell came from inside. The bare-chested man who finally answered had sagging eyelids, a trimmed white mustache, and cartoonishly flowing white hair. He leaned on a crutch.

"Mike Purpus?" I said.

"What do you want?"

I said I wanted an interview.

"Well, I just got outta the hospital. They took a bone spur off my hip that was this long."

He spread his fingers about six inches. That explained the yelling.

"I got you out of bed, didn't I?"

"Yeah," said Purpus.

"I'm sorry."

But he let me into a living room cluttered with surfboards, ten-speed bikes, stacks of chairs, old ashtrays, posters of himself as a young surfer in Mexico and Japan, and literally mounds of surf trophies, including five dusty Oscar-style figurines from the Duke Kahanamoku Classic, a big-wave invitational. Hanging from the ceiling near the kitchen bar was also a colorful board airbrushed with a naked, blonde teenage girl.

"That's my ex-girlfriend, No-Pants Nance," he said. "She posed for a Polaroid when she was sixteen." The Polaroid had been the model for the board. "Except when I tried to get that board into South Africa, I had to cover up her beaver with a sticker, 'cause they said it was pornography."

"No kidding."

"Yeah. Anyways, that's about half my trophies," he said. "The rest of 'em are in my bedroom."

Purpus sat painfully in an armchair near the window. The sill bore a few more trophies. He was a squat guy, with a crackling high voice that must have been reedy in the 1960s and '70s, when he was busy winning contests in Hawaii, California, Mexico, and Japan, helping to change surfing from the ancient longboard tradition as practiced by Freeth to the quick-footed sport you see now in surf videos.

Purpus went to Mira Costa High, my alma mater. He started the interview with a little hometown pride.

"I got all pissed off when Huntington Beach and Santa Cruz were fighting over the rights to call themselves Surf City," a designation related to the origins of American surfing that would give a city bragging rights. "They don't have a fuckin' thing to do with Surf City. The first guy that ever waxed his board, used paraffin on his surfboard, was from Palos Verdes [just south of Redondo]. The guy who invented the wetsuit was Bev Morgan,"[2] who founded an equipment shop called

_____

[2] This claim is controversial.

Dive 'n' Surf in Redondo. "The first commercialized surfboard manu-
facturer was Dale Velzy. He was from Manhattan Beach. George Freeth
caught the first wave—well, almost the first wave in the continental
United States—right here. Everything started in the South Bay."

Southern California was the center of innovation because Los
Angeles had a glut of tinkerers and engineers with access to not just
boating materials like resin and wood, but also new chemical by-
products of World War II. Oh, and the water was warm. Surfing caught
hold in California for anyone strong enough to haul a redwood board.
It wasn't a problem of buying equipment, even in the Depression; most
surfers built their own. "There *was* no Depression for surfers," said
Dorian Paskowitz, who learned to surf in the '30s and brought the
sport to Israel. "They were an elite group of aristocrats, with or without
money."

Tom Blake, a California transplant, changed the sport for good in
1935 by fixing a foot-long speedboat keel—the world's first surf fin—to
the underside of his board. His highly turnable kayaklike designs
became all the rage for those surfers who could afford to buy boards in
the '30s. Joe Quigg, a former navy man, built a board with a polyurethane core in 1947. Using foam as the buoyant core made boards both
lighter and easier to shape than those made entirely of redwood or
balsa. Quigg also made a thin, "potato chip" board for his girlfriend,
which turned so well with its fiberglass fins that surfers in Malibu
started handing it around. This board became the prototype for the
famous "Malibu chip" that Greg Noll and three other Americans
brought to Australia in 1956, when they competed in a paddling competition with Australian lifeguards on the sidelines of the Melbourne
Olympics. "Me and Mike Bright and I think Bobby Moore had brought
down our regular surfboards," Noll told me. "We were at the airport,
and the Australians got up on the flatbed. This guy sees the boards, and
he looks down the rail of one of 'em, then he spits on the ground and
he goes, 'Two bob for the works.' Well, this was the first Australian

reaction to what they still refer to down there as the Mal," or Malibu longboard.

Noll was a board shaper from Manhattan Beach as well as a brilliant young rider of giant Hawaiian waves. A film of the Melbourne paddling contests that also had footage of their Malibu-style surf session—angling on the wave, trotting up and down the lightweight wooden boards—made the rounds of Australian lifeguarding clubs. "That was what really kicked it into gear," Noll said. "But Australians don't like to admit that Yanks were involved." In a memoir, Noll said he spent the next two years answering requests from Australian surfers for "pictures, templates, design information." But he admitted that Australia now produces some of the best surfers in the world. And, he wrote, "the Australians deserve the credit for designing the true shortboard, and for causing the shortboard revolution."

Most of the early California innovators were as brilliant as they were disreputable. Quigg and another shaper named Matt Kivlin were protégés of one of surfing's few design geniuses, a man named Bob Simmons who had never graduated from high school. Simmons had taken up surfing as physical therapy after a bicycling accident shattered his elbow, then started fiddling with balsa instead of redwood, Styrofoam instead of wood, and so on. The sum of his innovations is now considered to be the modern foam-core board. He'd earned a degree from Caltech and had some understanding of fluid dynamics; in the '50s he was known in surf circles as a notorious pain in the ass, "driving along the coast alone in his rusted-out 1937 Ford Tudor sedan," according to *The Encyclopedia of Surfing,* "in which he kept hydrographic charts and abstruse hand-drawn graphs and computations, along with cans of baked beans, a bag of oranges, weather maps, unpaid speeding tickets, a quiver of homemade boomerangs, and a sleeping bag." He died at the age of thiry-five while paddling out in heavy surf at Windansea, near San Diego, in 1954. He drowned after his board thunked him in the head.

"The foam board," wrote Corky Carroll in an essay called "The Totally Unofficial History of the Modern Surfboard," "was the biggest and most important breakthrough in the history of surfing. These new [longboards] weighed only thirty to forty pounds. This opened the door to anybody that wanted to take up surfing, including women, children and geeks from inland. Previously it had taken a beach version of Hercules to carry one of those hundred-plus-pound monsters from your car to the water and back."

Purpus is right that a large fraction of the tinkerers who developed the modern board lived and worked in the South Bay. But surfers from fancier towns like Malibu still treat the beach cities as poor country relations. The waves just aren't very big. A surfer from Malibu named Rabbi Nachum "Shifty" Shifren put it like this: "By any standards the waves are less than desirable. Yet we see that the greatest surfers of the world, let alone watermen and lifeguards, come from the South Bay. Mike Purpus said, 'If you can surf the South Bay, you can surf anywhere.' Mike proved his point [by] blowing minds in the early seventies, surfing twenty-foot Pipeline as well as any of the locals." For Shifty it's a lesson in mystic Judaism. "The Kabbalah tells us that the heart is a place of 'fire,' enthusiasm. As Mike Purpus proved to us, if you put your heart into something, not even the two-foot mush of the South Bay can cool your stoke."

Purpus went to Mira Costa High between 1962 and 1966, when surfers were dropout jocks but not hippies. They were broke and mistrusted, which made them natural allies of Mexican gangsters. "They were our best friends," said Purpus. "Jocks would come up and threaten me—I was only four foot ten—and Conrad Rubio and his gang at Costa would come up and say, 'Drop Purpus right now.' I was the second-smallest guy at Costa. Rubio would go, 'If you're gonna pick on Purpus, you gotta pick on me.' All the low-riders had switchblades.

"Anyways, we had this one dance called the Coronation Ball. Everyone voted for the most popular guy at the whole school, and two years in a row we voted for Conrad Rubio as the Coronation King. The guy was an F student, and here he was in the yearbook picture, crown falling off the side of his head, all whacked on 'ludes, with his hand on the Coronation Queen's tit. Just because we'd voted for him."

Later Purpus was friends with Jack O'Neill, now a rich man who wears old jeans, a black eye patch, and a beard like Jerry Garcia's. O'Neill shares credit with a number of South Bay businessmen for inventing a surfer's wetsuit in about 1952. Bev Morgan, Bob Meistrell, and Meistrell's twin brother, Bill—who were all involved in Morgan's Dive 'n' Surf shop—worked from plans the military released in a public report around that time.[3] O'Neill says he just experimented with rubber and neoprene. He opened his first shop in San Francisco and later moved his show to Santa Cruz. Bursts of wetsuit innovation during the '60s and again in the '90s would help the sport migrate to the coldest, most peculiar corners of the world.

But O'Neill and his son also invented the surf leash. Purpus told me about that.

"The first ones they made, they went out in Santa Cruz on a six-foot day." They were using simple elastic surgical tubing attached to the deck of the board with a suction cup. "Jack O'Neill eats it on this wave, and his board stretches all the way to the beach like a rubber band. He comes out of the water and his board goes *boink,* right in his eye. That's how he lost his eye. So after that day—after Jack O'Neill got his patch—they put a catch line in the middle of the surgical tubing, so it wouldn't stretch out. But then sometimes the catch line would break anyway. I used one of those in Hawaii, and on a ten-foot day I fell off. All of a sudden I feel my board tug me from the bottom

<hr>

[3] Bev Morgan told the *Los Angeles Times,* "Jack O'Neill didn't invent the wetsuit, the Meistrells didn't invent the wetsuit and I didn't invent the wetsuit. Hugh Bradner invented the wetsuit. [He] was the first to use neoprene, and came up with the whole concept." Bradner, a physicist and professor at Scripps Institute of Oceanography in San Diego, wrote the report on neoprene suits for navy divers in 1951.

all the way up to the surface. It was kinda neat. But then I get up to the surface, and I look, and my leash, first of all, is just like a thin rubber band. And I see the tailblock of my board all the way practically in the beach break. But it's going *fffww, fffww, fffww*"—he made a skating motion with his hand—"straight back at me. So I go, 'Oh, *fuck!*' and dive straight to the bottom. And above me I feel my board whippin' around on the surface. I had to wait before I came back up out of the water."

Purpus also knew Lance Carson, a longboarder who helped define the Malibu era of the late '50s. Carson was a young hellion who later cofounded the Surfrider Foundation, a conservation group. Purpus likes to tell the story of "No-Pants Lance" and a glazed donut. It started during a crowded showing of a surf movie in Hermosa Beach. Carson sat next to Purpus in the theater with a bottle of tequila. When the movie ended, Carson stood on the seats with his pants down, let out a yell, and left the hall with six hundred surfers trailing him down Pier Avenue in Hermosa Beach to Fifteenth Street, where a Fosters Old Fashion Freeze stood near a Winchell's Donuts.

"Back then Hermosa Beach was just like *American Graffiti*," said Purpus, "and Fosters Freeze was where everyone hung out with their cars. So Lance hops up on a woody. He's got no pants on, he takes a long drink of tequila, and one of these groupies reaches up and gives him a hand job. Then another girl starts doing it. Suddenly he's got a hard-on and he yells, 'Lookit this, guys, whaddya think of *that*?'" And so some guy goes into Winchell's and buys a glazed donut and slides it onto Lance's pecker. Then he leans back with his bottle of tequila and this donut on his hard-on, standing on the car like some kind of hood ornament."

"I thought it was beautiful," wrote Mike Doyle, who was also present, "a kind of performance art that made a mockery of people's fear of nudity."

Winchell's Donuts was a police hangout, naturally, and four cops watched the incident, then came over and asked about the car. "It belonged to some of Lance's friends," said Purpus. "The cops said, 'Where are you from?' and they said, 'Malibu.' The cops said, 'We want you to take this guy home right now and get him sobered up. If you don't get out of town right now we'll arrest all three of you.'"

"Out of town before sunset," I said.

"That's right."

Purpus estimated the year at 1964, the middle of his time in high school. "Now Lance is all Christian, and every time I publish that story I get a letter from him or his mother saying, 'Lance would never have done that.' And he can't stand it when I call him No-Pants Lance. But I was there, man, I saw it."

When he was a young beach rat collecting bottles on the sand in Hermosa, Purpus looked up to Carson's group of longboarders in Malibu—guys like Miki "da Cat" Dora, Terry "Tubesteak" Tracy, and Noll. You could call them the Gidget crowd of surfers, accurately, but they would resent you, rightfully. "Everything was eight to five in those days, you had to have an eight-to-five," said Purpus. "And they knew if you were workin' eight to five, you weren't getting better in the surf."

For a few days in 1956, Miki Dora and Tubesteak Tracy tried to work regular jobs. They were hired by the Home Insurance Company in downtown LA. But "Miki and I got shit-canned," Tubesteak said later to *Vanity Fair*, "him for drawing surf cartoons of Shmoos riding waves, me for having my desk drawers stuffed with Hollywood Park racing forms." This shit-canning took Tubesteak by surprise. He had no money, so he spent a night on the beach. When that seemed to go well, he hiked up Malibu Creek to collect palm fronds and driftwood. He piled them on his surfboard, floated everything downstream to a depression in the sand called The Pit, and with a number of friends built a smallish, square-walled shack draped in palm fronds. He lived there for the rest of the summer.

The longboarders at Malibu turned surfing into something dark and hip, a California subdivision of American cool. In the 1950s a glut of Hollywood and aerospace money turned Los Angeles into a glittering, suburban-industrial Moloch, and its malcontents would need a new way to live. "We listened to the Olympics, the Coasters, and Hank Ballard and the Midnighters," Tubesteak told *Vanity Fair*. "We'd burn tires on the beach for warmth, and no one cared," added his friend Bill Jensen.

By now the notion of "cool" has been turned to garbage by the entertainment industry, and any value it used to have is not just dead but in danger of being forgotten. But surfing is still a universal expression of freedom, so, for the record, I'll try to define what radiated out from California after 1959.

When industrial America was young enough to be shocked by urban high-rises and corporate conformism, a breed of romantic individualist grew up in resistance. Woody Guthrie was one early example. So was Tennessee Williams. So were Williams's characters, in particular Val, the wandering guitarist in a snakeskin coat from *Orpheus Descending* (played by Marlon Brando in the film version). Williams wrote about wandering loners years before James Dean or Jack Kerouac made causeless rebellion fashionable to mainstream American kids. He became an architect of hip culture in the '50s, not just by writing about the romance of the streets, but also—this is not quite an exaggeration—by creating great roles that called for Marlon Brando to strip half-naked. "In the age of Calvin Klein's steaming hunks," wrote Gore Vidal in 1985, "it must be hard for those under forty to realize that there was ever a time when a man was nothing but a suit of clothes. . . . Brando's appearance on stage, as Stanley [Kowalski, in the 1947 Broadway staging of *A Streetcar Named Desire*], in a torn sweaty T-shirt, was an earthquake."

Surfers understood all this. You couldn't surf in a full suit of clothes. The Polynesian freedom to frolic half-naked in the waves was a deep challenge to the hat-wearing straights. "Malibu was a counterculture before the counterculture," an early Malibu surfer named Larry Shaw told *Vanity Fair*. He called Miki a "Beatnik athlete" and "this Fagin-like character, who was ten years older than us but was just as adolescent as we were."

Miklos Dora was the son of a Hungarian wine merchant. Born in Budapest but raised in LA, he became an honorary local at Malibu because of his stepfather, Gard Chapin. "My own father taught me a gracious manner of living," he said, "while my stepfather showed me how to survive when confronted with adversity." Chapin was a tall, blond, unpleasant alcoholic and veteran of the Depression-era San Onofre surf scene who had not only invented a new longboard maneuver (the drop-knee turn) but also introduced Bob Simmons to the sport. "Gard Chapin," Miki told an interviewer, "was a relentless individualist with whom no holds were barred and all the moves were unconventional. Once, in the middle of the night, he came into my bedroom and woke me up." He drove Miki to Hollywood, where parking meters had appeared on the streets for the first time.

He said, "Look around . . . What do you see that's wrong here?"

Then he opened the trunk on his car and took out a sledge-hammer and walked me over to the curb.

"Miki, these bastards want to control everything. Now they want to make us pay money to park on the street."

Chapin then smashed the head off every brand new parking meter that the city had just installed. It was the first day they had been put out, and he creamed every one of them for several blocks. His anger and the point of it were something that you could never forget seeing. When he was finished he suddenly became very calm, and he climbed up the sign pole on the corner.

"Here's a souvenir."

He handed me the street sign from Hollywood and Vine.

This outlaw individualism could be splendid and hard or just plain mean. Chapin was a drunkard, but he also had an instinct for liberty that seems to be missing now in LA, where not just parking meters but also closed-circuit TV cameras, "private" squares and sidewalks, pristine private toll roads, officious rent-a-cops, and velvet-rope doormen have polluted old notions of free public space.

Miki learned a number of attitudes from Chapin and became a hip older-brother figure to other surfers, the kind of guy who would hang around his own high school even after graduation. One day, according to legend, he laid a trap for a group of "hillbilly hair hoppers" who didn't like him. He parked his convertible across the street from Hollywood High on a wet afternoon, after a heavy rain, and draped a "strap of woven metal" from his distributor box to a puddle under the car. Then he chatted up a number of the enemy's girlfriends. "The lunkheads see me charming their goo-goo girls and they are out for blood," he said. "The entire school is watching because they know I'm going to get it. The head thugs run up to my car door and bingo, I've got them right where I want them. I hit the switch and an electrical jolt travels down the strap and across the puddle and right into these dolts. Zap bap a lop a dop a bop bam boom. These retards were so stupid that they couldn't comprehend what was happening to them. The car was grounded because of its rubber tires. Victory was mine."

It should be evident from this tale that Miki was a hustler. He cut an elegant figure at Malibu, dancing up and down his longboard with the grace of a cat (hence his nickname), but he also turned his stepfather's toughness toward making a dishonest living. He was the sort of lunkhead who would scour Malibu Canyon for surfers' wallets while they sat in the water. He would also pull money and jewelry from the bedrooms of Hollywood parties where the guests had left their coats. He stole from the boys who admired him—surf wax, money, food from their freezers at home—to the point where Larry Shaw and the others bragged about what they'd lost. "He did it all for a simple reason: freedom," another Malibu surfer named Duane King said. "Every guy on that beach wanted to do nothing but surf all day, but only Miki had found a way to do it."

This freedom was in the grand old American tradition. Beaches constituted the last few yards of the frontier. After George Freeth imported the sport, it was discovered that America still had a number of corners where pioneer hobbyists could test their mettle against the wilderness. Malibu had never been a crass public beach like Redondo or Hermosa; Huntington's streetcars didn't run that far. But by 1950 its status as a wild preserve was threatened. The last owners of the Spaniards' original Rancho Malibu grant had been selling off beachfront parcels since the '20s, and Miki wanted to defend Malibu against "the subdividers, concessionaires, lifeguards . . . before exploiters polluted the beaches like they do everything else."

The irony in Miki's case is that he helped the destruction along. One excellent way to scrounge for money in the late '50s, if you surfed, was to surf in a *Gidget* film. Miki did this as often as he could. His real father had connections in Hollywood, which gave him both a way in and a dropout's snobbery about moguls and financiers. "The soul-sucking Hollywood harlots were bigger thieves than any of us," he said. Not that he kept his distance. He hung around long enough to get paid.

But he also belonged to the ur-Gidget myth. The novel *Gidget* came out in 1957, written by a screenwriter who had fled the Nazis. Frederick Kohner was a Czech Jew who had worked in Germany's Babelsberg studio system until 1933. At a premiere of one of his films in Berlin that year, he noticed Joseph Goebbels had erased every Jewish name, including his, from the credits. He moved to California as soon as he could. He and his wife raised two daughters in Hollywood and at an actors' retreat called the Malibu Colony. One daughter, Kathy, learned to surf. "My father and I would walk down [to the beach], and I would tell him about all of the surfers," she said many years later. "I told him I wanted to write a book. He said, 'Why don't you tell me your stories and I'll write it?' I said, 'OK.'"

Kathy Kohner hung around in The Pit, drinking and smoking with Miki and Tubesteak, Bill Jensen and Duane King. They really did call her Gidget, short for "girl midget." As a female surfer, she was odd but not unique: Mary Ann Hawkins had been a known face on Southern California beaches since the Depression. Hawkins was one of those first-wave feminists of the '30s who saw no reason why women shouldn't ride horses, fly stunt planes, or wear slacks. The recent surge of female surfers in Western countries has more to do with shifting social ideas—in Mary Ann Hawkins's direction—than with anything natural or even traditional to the sport. Women surf through ancient Hawaiian legends and songs as readily as they wrestle sharks.

Anyway, the kids' slang at Malibu fascinated Kohner *père,* whose first language was German. He drafted *Gidget* from Kathy's anecdotes with a plain ambition to write a female *Catcher in the Rye.* "I'm writing this down because I once heard that when you're getting older you're liable to forget things and I'd sure be the most miserable woman in the world if I ever forgot what happened this summer," is the first sentence. Kohner's brother Paul, a Hollywood agent, couldn't stand the book. Frederick found another agent who sold the manuscript as well as a lucrative movie deal. New York literary critics proved more indulgent than his brother; they compared Kohner's novel to *Lolita.* Apparently a formula for success in the '50s was for Old World émigrés to write in a second language about chirpy American girls.

It's possible that no other American subculture has moved from wildness and authenticity to Technicolor cheese as quickly as the scene at Malibu. When the first *Gidget* film appeared in 1959, the surfers in America numbered about five thousand. By 1963 there were two or three million. Mike Purpus said the aftermath "was like discovering gold, or oil—everyone went into the surfboard business, and they started makin' money. Like crazy. It was so weird. People in Kentucky and Kansas and Tennessee, they were buying surfboards just to put 'em on top of their cars and drive around so they could pick up chicks. Because the movie *Gidget* was so big. It was unbelievable."

So Miki was in at the birth of surfing's twentieth-century image as well as its hopeless corruption. He mounted a violent resistance to the Hollywood nonsense even while he surfed in the films. He was "incapable of diplomacy," according to a woman who knew him, and when the surfing craze brought kooks to Malibu in the '60s he tended to lose his temper. He was used to controlling who came and went; he and his friends "ran" the beach in the absence of lifeguards. They would shove people off waves or launch their longboards at strangers' heads. Once—according to *Vanity Fair*—Miki sliced open the bare back of an intruder with the sharp edge of a board fin, making the stranger bleed in the water and "sending him screaming to Malibu General." He was a local. He all but invented localism. "My only regret," he said near the end of his life, referring to the cinematized version of Tubesteak's hut, "is that I did not torch Gidget's palm-frond love shack with that phony Fafoonie and Tubesteak and Minnie the Mongoose and Jerk Off Johnnie and all of the rest of the cast and crew inside. What a glorious imu oven it would have made. We could have had a kamaaina luau with Hollywood long pig as the main course. The Hawaiians ate Captain Cook; it is unfortunate that the rest of us at Malibu learned so little from these gallant combatants."

&&&&&&&&&&&&&&&&&&&&&

Did George Freeth know what he was starting when he sailed to California in 1907? He did want more people to surf. But he must have seen the sport as his "main chance," a meal ticket for himself rather than a potential marketing phenomenon from France to Indonesia. He would have been surprised by its transformation. But he would have recognized it, just as a singer from Mali who brought songs to Charleston in the hold of a ship would have been startled two centuries on to hear the same rhythms and melodies in the electric blues of John Lee Hooker and the Rolling Stones. Duke Kahanamoku lived to see the foam-core revolution and the advent of shortboards. He accepted it all with Hawaiian equanimity. His primary advice in old age to the nervous modern sport and the crowds who tried to learn it was "Be patient, wave come. Wave always come."

In 1917 the simple arc of Freeth's life struck a dissonant chord. The Prometheus of American surfing lost his job as a lifeguard in San Diego and wound up behind the register at a sporting-goods store called the Cycle and Arms Company. "As a salesperson, he lost much of the status he had enjoyed while working along the beaches of Venice and Redondo," wrote his biographer, Arthur Verge. Freeth liked to be in charge of a beach or a saltwater plunge, he liked to teach swimming, and he liked to invent. He'd invented those bullet-shaped "rescue cans" that most American lifeguards now carry, including David Hasselhoff in *Baywatch*. In 1908, he'd saved the lives of seven Japanese fishermen when a winter storm caught their small fleet of boats in high surf off the Venice Pier. Instead of waiting for his lifeguard crew to launch a boat from the beach, he dove into the rough water alone. "For the next two-and-a-half hours," wrote Verge, "Freeth braved gale force winds, pounding surf, and a frigid ocean temperature to save single-handedly the lives of seven men. In the process he nearly lost his own life to hypothermia."

The rescue became national news. Abbot Kinney put Freeth up for a Congressional Gold Medal, which he won in 1910. Freeth marched with his crew in the 1909 Rose Parade, and the Japanese fishermen renamed Maikura, their fishing village near Malibu, Port Freeth. The village burned to the ground in 1913. But the *Herald Examiner* reported in 1911 that local Japanese "performed a nightly shinto ritual," according to Verge, "during which they burned incense and made offerings of rice and poi to honor the young Hawaiian responsible for saving seven of their own."

Freeth was twenty-five at the time of the rescue. He would live another eleven years. During World War I, wounded veterans returning from the trenches of Europe were laid up in barracks around the port of San Diego. Disease flourished under the balmy sun. The Spanish flu pandemic that killed more people in the world than the war itself swept this corner of California so ferociously that in 1918 a San Diego law compelled people to wear gauze face masks in the street. There was even a government rhyme:

> *Obey the laws*
> *And wear the gauze*
> *Protect your jaws*
> *From Septic Paws*

Freeth fell ill while he was out of work. A local rowing club set up a collection, and people up and down California sent money. He was destitute but well known. He'd arrived in California with a suitcase, writes Verge, and "when he passed on"—quietly, in the spring of 1919—"what he had in the way of worldly goods could be placed in the same suitcase. Freeth was never a man of money; instead he was a man of deeds."

In this sense both Freeth and Kahanamoku led quintessentially American lives. Duke died broke, too. But they were enthusiasts. Their wandering careers were guided by abiding curiosity and a passion for the sea. They would have been "American" even if a law had not naturalized all Hawaiian citizens in 1900, long before statehood. "Enthusiasm is the leaping lightning," wrote Emerson, "not to be measured by the horse-power of the understanding." Freeth belonged to the great American force that battles every day against America's mass-market cheapness, its relentless stupidity, the mindless opposition force that people have connected with surfing itself since *Gidget*. "The cheap idealism of the Americans . . . the ubiquitous bathtub, the five-and-ten-cent store bric-a-brac, the bustle, the efficiency, the machinery, the high wages, the free libraries, etc., etc." is how Henry Miller's narrator puts it in *Tropic of Cancer*, ranting—presciently, for 1934—about an Indian man who loves everything practical and cheap about America.

"His ideal would be to Americanize India. He is not at all pleased with Gandhi's retrogressive mania. As I listen to his tales of America I see how absurd it is to expect of Gandhi that miracle which will reroute the trend of destiny. India's enemy is not England, but America. India's enemy is the time spirit, the hand which cannot be turned back. Nothing will avail to offset this virus which is poisoning the whole world. America is the very incarnation of doom. She will drag the whole world down to the bottomless pit."

Well, maybe not. It can be dangerous to take Miller too seriously. But the spread of surfing, like the heart of America, hasn't all been sweetness and light.

2

INDONESIA:

BULÉ BULÉ

··*Kuta, Bali, 2002*

LOMBOK IS ONE of the poorest islands of
Indonesia, and Kuta, on the southern tip, is
a weird assemblage of thatched huts, surf
bungalows, and luxury hotels. It suffers from semi-
overdevelopment. You can sleep in a plush bed behind
high stone walls for over a hundred dollars a night, if that's
your style, but there's no bank machine. The village is a slum-
bering cousin to the electric-lit surf capital of Bali, also called Kuta,
where Islamic fundamentalists set off bombs in 2002 and again in
2005. Lombok's Kuta has no sushi restaurants, sports bars, or
gleaming flagship stores for surf brands, but it faces south, and its
beaches receive the same Indian Ocean swells.

I found a $4 surf bungalow near the beach, an orange-painted rattan
hut with a stinking pit toilet and a jaundiced lightbulb so weak it had
trouble penetrating my mosquito net. I couldn't read. Loitering in the
room for any reason besides sleep was unbearable because of the toilet.
So I spent the evening on a wide breakfast terrace where young Indonesians served beer from a bar and surfers played cards under the fluorescent light.

Among the guests was a Frenchman, Maxim, with wild blond-
touched curls, who seemed to be touring Indonesia with four surfboards and a change of shorts. There was another Frenchman,

middle-aged, with no hair at all. Also a tidy Swiss girl who had taken surf lessons in Bali and an Australian hippie with long brown hair who wore no shirt because the night was so warm. His chest had a fluffy carpet of graying thatch.

"Ekas?" he was saying in a thick down-under drawl. "Yeah, mate, I been to Ekas. Bloody beautiful surf. You gotta leave early, though. A fisherman at Awang can ferry you across the bay. First time I went we started late, an' our captain didn't know his arse from his outboard. Landed in the wrong spot. On that side of the bay you can't be too careful of the Muslims, right, they're not like on this side, most of them here are so bloody nice to Westerners. On that side you've got a cleric in Sungkun incitin' the locals.

"Anyway, we landed on the beach an' we're pullin' our boards outta the boat, wonderin' where the feck we are, and here comes three guys with machetes. Robes and beards, too—the whole enchilada, mate—ready to hack us to pieces if we're Australian. And then they ask us: 'Are you Australian?' I say, 'No, mate, we're from New Zealand.'"

He worked on his fried rice as he spoke.

"So what happened?" asked the Frenchman.

"They just melted away, mate."

"Why?"

"Didn't wanna kill a New Zealander." The hippie shrugged.

The terrace backed onto a dusty road that was just visible in the fluorescent light. Beyond it, in the dark, I heard crashing surf.

"So anyway," the hippie went on, "there we are on the wrong beach on the far side of Ekas Bay, and we know there's Islamic militants in the fecking trees with machetes. And our captain won't take us out again. Says he's got to go home. But he runs after these militant guys to ask directions. Tells us it's easy—there's a road to Ekas that starts a couple hundred meters away. He takes us there, right, we're loaded down with our boards, the sun's goin' down and the mozzies've started ta hit"—he slapped his bare arms to illustrate—"and it's a fecking *buffalo trail*. We pay the fecker off and start tramping. The mozzies're everwhere, no keepin' 'em off. The mud in the trail's the kind you leave your sandals in. Soon it's blood, buffalo shit, and mud to your knees, mate. By the time we hit Ekas it's fecking black as shit, we can't even see the trees. We knew about a hotel in Ekas, like a bed 'n' breakfast—turns out it's been closed for eight months. Now it's just one family rentin' out old fishing cottages. So we stayed there, thinking this is fecking miserable, right. It even started to rain in the night. But when we woke up in the morning it was like bougainvillea, papaya, and six-foot crankin'."

The Frenchmen wondered why the militants would spare a New Zealander. The hippie had an answer for that, too. "I figure they hate Australia for supporting Timorese independence. I don't really know. But the Timor militia has a base in Sungkun."

Which brought the conversation around to politics.

"You are from America?" the middle-aged Frenchman asked me.

He was a windsurfer, not quite one of the tribe. He was also the sort of European who engages stray Americans about US policy. In the spring of 2004 the torture scandal from Abu Ghraib was a fresh nightmare.

"Yes," I said, and the Frenchman was off. Why did Americans hate the French? he wanted to know. Had Congress really changed the name of french fries to freedom fries in government cafeterias? He talked on and on about the sort of nation America had become. Had I heard of Michael Moore? Had I seen *Bowling for Columbine*? That was the most astute film about America he had seen in a very long time. Was Michael Moore known in America?

"He's a celebrity," I said.

"Yes, but do people see his films? I think they can learn a lot about their culture from him."

He talked about Israel, the Palestinian cause, the free market, and terrorism, always coming back to his theme that America was no longer a force for freedom in the world. Some of his babble I agreed with, some I didn't—but all of it was regurgitated secondhand opinion, as unoriginal as it was passionate.

At last I said, "Have you ever been to America?"

"Once, yes. I was in Maui for two weeks."

"Aha."

٭٭٭٭٭٭٭٭٭٭٭٭٭٭٭٭٭٭٭

The next morning I rented a board from a shack across the road and paid some kids for a ride to Grupuk, a beach with black mud roads and a pervading odor of fish. The arrival of a car with a surfboard caused a fuss. Thatched wooden houses gave up naked staring children and idle teenagers. A local boy took my board from the rack and waxed it. My driver knocked at one shack to hire a "captain" to pilot me out to a break. Soon a short, skinny boy in surf trunks whose name was Hajak told me to follow him. Someone else carried my board and we walked between the houses to the edge of the bay, where long, engine-powered outriggers floated in the water.

Grupuk Bay is one of those tropical inlets that look like paradise from a distance, with palm-carpeted hills rising from an expanse of blue water. The sun was direct and diamond-bright in the waves. Hajak had to steer between weathered wooden frames, marked with ragged flags, that were floating on the surface. Here and there along the shore we could see red-and-white Indonesian flags flying, emblems of national feeling on a traditionally independent-minded island.

The naturalist Alfred Russel Wallace thought the undersea trench between Lombok and Bali marked part of a natural boundary between Asia and Australia. To the west—on Bali, Java, Sumatra, Borneo—he noticed macaques and tigers, magpies and woodpeckers, the sorts of animals that characterize an Indian jungle. To the east, from Lombok and Komodo to New Guinea, he found marsupials, parrots, monitor lizards, and people descended from Australian aborigines. About fifteen miles of ocean separate Lombok and Bali, he wrote, "yet these islands differ far more from each other in their birds and quadrupeds than do England and Japan." What Wallace had noticed was the boundary between two ancient supercontinents, Laurasia and Gondwanaland. Most biologists no longer recognize a hard "Wallace Line," but biologically, the central islands of Indonesia are still considered a transition zone between the Asian jungles and the arid Australian plain.

The odd part of this "Wallacea" transition zone is that Lombok's native race, the Sasaks, probably migrated from southern India and Burma. So even if the plants and animals had drifted in from the east, the people on the island came from the west. For centuries they were animists and rice farmers. Then, in the 1700s, Balinese Hindus invaded. For protection Lombok aligned itself with a Javanese sultanate, and in spite of long and fitful colonization by the Balinese, the Sasaks have mostly remained Muslim. Like other Indonesian races— the archipelago has almost as many citizens as the United States, but they are scattered across thousands of islands and splintered by 730 different languages—the Sasaks have learned to deal with invasions by absorbing them.

Hajak was a Sasak. He was stoic, serious, and maybe eleven years old. He dressed like a California surf kid. He sat in front of his Evinrude, navigating between the wooden frames.

"What are those?" I said, in a mixture of poor Indonesian and sign language.

"*Rumput laut,*" he said.

Seaweed. Deep columns of it were cultivated under the frames. Those are the industries in Grupuk: fishing, farming seaweed, and ferrying surfers.

The first person to surf Indonesia was Bob Koke, in 1936, when the islands were still called the Dutch East Indies. Bob had a career as an art photographer when he moved from Los Angeles to Bali with his wife, Louise, on the same wave of Western exiles as the German artist Walter Spies and the American anthropologist Margaret Mead. At the time Bali was almost naked of Western development. The Kokes painted, sketched, and photographed until they began to run out of money. Then they thought of building a hotel on Kuta Beach, Bali. What's now a mini-Tokyo for surfers and tourists on the southern isthmus of Bali appeared in 1936 to Louise as a "broad, white beach [that] curved away for miles, huge breakers spreading on the clean sand. Behind were endless coconut groves. . . . This was what we had been looking for, not the sun-baked streets of Denpasar and its rows of shacks and shops tended by men in shapeless pyjamas."

Bob Koke was a dashing Californian with a Clark Gable mustache and well-pressed slacks who had brought his "Honolulu board" to Bali. He rode it on empty waves while the small complex of rattan cottages went up at Kuta. Later he gave lessons to guests. Locals learned to surf, and so did Louise. But the Balinese were farmers more than watermen. It had never occurred to them to conquer the waves. In Bali, she wrote, "danger from evil spirits is greatest nearest the sea—that is, furthest from the mountains above which the gods dwell. Leyaks [demons] may appear as blue lights or hideous monsters and the sea is the dwelling place of unknown dangers. This is partly why the Balinese, unlike most island peoples, know little about swimming and are reluctant to fish more than a few miles from shore."

The Kuta Beach Hotel became the prototype for a surf camp. Bob Koke acquired a collection of longboards from Hawaii, which his guests and staff could ride. Soon boards "leapt and bucked" in the water. One afternoon, when the surf was breaking above head-high—no good for a beginner—an English guest named Lady Hartelby came down the beach. Louise said she wore "a severe black bathing suit, her stern English features lit with determination." Lady Hartelby was keen to surf. "My heart sank. Only a few days before she would have drowned in a deep and turbulent spot had not Bob been there to grab her. She could not swim, she was nearing seventy. . . . I tried to dissuade her, but the undaunted spirit of the great British Empire won."

Louise followed Lady Hartelby into the water and pushed her bobbing bulk into the smaller shorebreak, hoping the board would float. She tried to explain how to stand. One wave carried the Englishwoman all the way in on her belly. Louise hoped that would be enough for one day, but the old woman soldiered on, struggling in the whitewash and trying to catch another wave until the nose of her board dipped under the surface and pitched Lady Hartelby into the sand.

The rest of her board, naturally, swung around to clobber her.

For a week, her meals were served in her room. Patient about being bedridden, she never complained about the ugly green and purple bruises along her thighs where the board had hit her.

Bing [another guest] called on her each day.

"Awfully tough luck, Toots," he commiserated. He always got away with calling dignified dowagers 'Toots.' . . .

"Oh, I don't mind," she said. "I had one jolly good ride. It was worth it. My only regret is I won't have time to try it again. How did you catch on so quickly? You're really topping."

It would be nice to trace a direct line from Lady Hartelby and the long-suffering Kokes to modern Indonesian surfing, especially since Bali and Java receive some of the best surf in the world. But the Kuta Beach Hotel closed in 1941, just before Japan invaded the East Indies. The thunder of Pacific war would end Bali's bohemian paradise. The same shock would (eventually) break Dutch colonialism. The Republic of Indonesia would be declared in 1949, and then it would be twenty or thirty years before hippies from Australia and California rediscovered the islands as a surfer's mecca.

Hajak let the outrigger glide to a halt near a clean blue break just off a sandy beach. He dropped anchor next to a pair of other canoes, and we hopped out. A number of people were paddling for waves. All the young Sasak captains rode new tri-fins while a handful of white guys (bulés) struggled with waterlogged rental boards. Hajak and his friends wore baggy Quiksilver shorts. It made me think of a group of students I'd met on Java who wore leather jackets, earrings, and dreadlocks. Their mode of rebellion was Western. Kids who dressed like them in America might have been suspected of a lack of patriotism, a certain sympathy for strange ideas. In Indonesia the ideas, but not the styles, were different. Artists and students and surfers were the left wing of a nation where part of the far right commited Islamist terrorism. One reason Indonesian kids wore leather jackets or surfed was to distinguish themselves from the robed conservatives or from the green-uniformed *militeri*. Not that any of the Grupuk captains would have spared a word of praise for America. But a world style of rebellion seems to exist where disaffected kids from almost any nation can converge in a hazy middle, bound by pop notions of freedom and cool still descended from the American '60s—or, really, from the Beats.

*   *

From a distance, in the early 2000s, Indonesia looked like a breeding swamp for radicals anxious to bomb Westerners and their local collaborators to make way for an Islamic caliphate. Violent Indonesians made news after 2001. There was the gleefully shouting terrorist Amrozi ("Death to *Amérika!*"), proud of his guilty verdict in the 2002 Bali bombings; there were bombs at the Jakarta Marriott in 2003 and the Australian embassy in 2004, and more bombs in Bali in 2005. There was the bent figure of Abu Bakar Bashir, in his lacy white beard and pristine *peci* cap, declaring that Jemaah Islamiyah and al-Qaeda were just figments of the government's paranoid imagination.

But these radicals were new to Indonesia. Or, newly returned. General Suharto, toppled in 1998, had thrown them out. Bashir had spent decades in Malaysian exile. The new wave of democracy gave the terrorists freedom to move, so they were back in the archipelago to fight for Dar Islam, the House of Islam. Most Indonesians didn't like them. Indonesians, in fact, are tolerant. Someone had told me Indonesia is "the California of Islam," meaning a loose, freethinking, Pacific culture, where peculiar ideas flourish in the balmy weather, far from capitals of orthodoxy like Tehran or Mecca.

So fanaticism and mayhem were no truer, as a national image, than breeze-stirred palms and placid rice paddies. You had to keep both images in mind. The languid tropical islands bred a sweet, hospitable people who erupted now and then in spasms of blood. "In the minds of Western tourists and armchair travelers," wrote Theodore Friend in *Indonesian Destinies*, "there still exists an image of Bali . . . as an enchanted land of aesthetes at peace with themselves and with nature." Friend pointed out that about 5 percent of Bali's population was hacked to death with machetes by self-appointed executioners in the 1965 anti-Communist purges that brought Suharto to power. The killers may have been instigated by the CIA and its allies, but they weren't government goons. They were neighbors and sometimes friends of the victims. They were groups of men from a given village who were given a list of people in the next village and ran over at night to slaughter godless "Communists" in their beds. The same hysteria swept through Java and other parts of Indonesia, and in some places the surviving victims and executioners still lived side by side, uneasily, in the same villages where tourists came to photograph ducks.

In 2004, Indonesians were electing a president by direct vote for the first time in history. I was curious to see the process at work. It was another example of Western influence—direct democracy in the world's most populous Muslim nation. General Suharto had stepped aside as dictator after mass protests in 1998, and those hot spring afternoons were still fresh in people's minds. During the intervening six years, the parliament in Jakarta had selected the country's presidents. This time it was up to the people. Not even America chooses presidents so directly; we have the Electoral College.

I met Amat, my guide on Lombok, by accident. Someone had said the nearest bank machine was twelve miles away, in a town called Praya, and I wandered the main road puzzling over how to get there when a man on a motorcycle said, "Hello! Where do you come from? Where are you going?"

I said, "Praya."

"Yes? Round trip? How much?"

Praya was halfway across the island. I decided to halve the amount of a taxi ride across Lombok the previous day.

"Fifty thousand?"

The driver double-checked. Did I mean fifteen, or five-zero?

5-0, I said. Five bucks.

He tried for sixty thousand, but I knew the offer was good. It was the making of my afternoon. Amat was a somewhat fierce-looking Sasak with a potbelly, dressed in white pants and a red polo shirt and hailing from a village called Sengkol. We stopped there on the way to Praya to unload a bucket he was carrying and ask for a helmet. Amat went into his house to talk to his wife. A white-capped Muslim with a thin fringe beard brought out my helmet.

Then we sped along the highway, past fields of rice and watermelon. Outside Praya we passed a procession of men in formal costumes with bright sarongs and black shirts, walking behind women in head scarves and Balinese *kebaya* blouses, carrying fringed parasols. I had to ask if it was a Hindu or Muslim wedding.

"Muslim, Muslim."

"Where are they going?"

"To the groom's house. They will have a party for two days."

A few men wore soiled plaid shirts and old thongs, as if they'd only joined the parade after a hard morning's work. Smiling kids in street clothes ran along, too. Everyone kept in tight formation on one side of the road to let cars pass.

On Lombok, said Amat, the groom doesn't ask for the parents' permission to marry a girl. He just takes her. Or, actually, they elope. Friends or brothers of the groom then inform the parents of the bride, who may or may not be outraged. It's a ritual. Assuming no one has sent men with cleavers after the groom, the families organize a celebration, and soon a wedding parade with parasols and silks processes down a country road.

We stopped for a while to watch. "Did you get married like this?" I asked. "You stole your wife from her parents?"

"Yeah."

"Where'd you elope to?"

"We were hiding, just in my neighborhood. I was living in Grupuk, that's where I grew up. But Johar lived in Sengkol. She was, I don't remember, fifteen. At first her father was very angry. He had a long knife, and I worried he would kill me."

"Did he come after you?"

"Nah. He looked for me, but he could not find me."

"How'd you sneak her away?"

"Her parents saw me arrive, they saw me talk with her and everything. They sent us coffee or tea and food, things like that. It was around seven o'clock at night. I arrived with the motorbike, and I do a negotiation. We agreed that we love each other—she liked me and I liked her—and then I took her away. I went first, and she went next."

"You didn't ride away on the same motorbike."

"No, no."

"And then you hid for a week?"

"No, for one day only. After that I lived with my parents. Before the wedding I had to see the Muslim leader, we had to do the promising as a couple, a wife and husband. Next night, we can live together and we can do anything. Then we do the marriage ceremony a week later. Her parents asked me for about three hundred thousand rupiah, plus food, rice, and like that."

"For a dowry."

"Yes."

"And by then everything was okay with her father?"

"Was okay, yes."

"Because of the dowry?"

"No, because of getting used to it."

I had the impression that the show of temper, for Johar's father, was a way to save face. Her family owned a shop in Sengkol, which meant they had money and position. Amat was a poor fishing-boat captain from Grupuk.

"You were a beach kid?"

"A beach kid, yes! Very black from the sun."

"You fished and took surfers out to the waves?"

"Just like that, yes."

After we went to Praya, a dirty, traffic-choked town in the middle of Lombok, and did battle with vans and horse carts and *becaks,* Indonesian rickshaws, Amat took me back to Sengkol, which was a cluster of buildings roofed with corrugated tin. Food stalls, odds-and-ends stores, and shacks for bottles of gasoline hung out signs to draw business from the highway. Trees overhung the pavement, and kids riding on top of rice trucks would crouch to avoid getting knocked by branches.

Johar, slender and beautiful and quick-tongued, was about twenty-nine years old, with long black hair and a smile she preferred not to show. She spoke no English. She did laundry while we talked. Amat was earning his money from me, so he could relax. We drank coffee on the dirt porch of the family shop and watched a sudden spate of rain.

"Good coffee," I said.

"Yes? You want some?" he said.

"—I have some."

"No, you must take some home. A kilo of Lombok coffee! To remember your trip!"

"No, really—"

Amat told Johar I wanted coffee. Soon they rode off on a motorbike to buy—to my horror—some unroasted beans from a dealer down the road. For the rest of the afternoon Johar worked at winnowing husks from beans in a bamboo pan, roasting the coffee in a nearby oven, and grinding the beans by hand. "Seriously," I told them. "I don't need the coffee." But Johar smiled. Her hands worked while Amat and I chatted. To me she was sweet, but she seemed to make pungent, sharp-tongued comments about anything her husband said.

"Anyway, we met in a party. Her uncle has circumcision party because he had a son. About eight o'clock I come there, to the party, and she was waiting for me. I had long hair, I was very skinny, and very black, and she was scared of me. After that, she said if you come to my house, please cut your hair, and no earring, please be polite."

"And you had a big parade, like we saw on the road?"

"Bigger than that, yes."

"In Grupuk?"

"Yes."

There was a series of cloudbursts that afternoon. Amat looked out at the rain. "Sometimes people are too young to get married," he said. "They do not understand each other. That is one reason there are so many divorces here. And also—you know that pregnancy problem, pregnant-before-marriage? When you do not love the girl, but you fuck her just for fun?"

"Yes."

"Well, after that you have to marry her. After that, you're finished."

He wasn't talking about his own marriage, but there was strain or regret in his voice, an obscure fear.

"Also, the interfering of the parent-in-law," he said. "For example, my father-in-law always interferes with my problems. That makes the problem more so."

"This causes a lot of divorce?"

"Yeah. And also, having an affair. There's many people having an affair now, in Lombok. It's a big problem. There are many divorces, many widows here."

"Widows?"

"Yes, young. Thirteen or even twelve years old, and they've already been married."

"What happens to their husbands?"

"The husband is just—divorced, that's all. And the girls go back to their parents."

"Oh. But a widow is when a husband dies."

"Is when a husband dies, okay, but widow can also be when something happens in the family. Like divorce."

I decided to change the subject.

"Who do you want for president?" I said.

"Not Megawati," he answered, shaking his head. "And not Gus Dur."

Gus Dur was a blind, moderate Muslim who served as the country's first president after Suharto fell. He was famous and well liked, but old. Through backroom machinations he had been replaced by Megawati Sukarnoputri. In the 1950s and '60s Megawati had lived like a princess in the home of her father, Sukarno, Indonesia's first president and independence hero. She was close to royalty, so Indonesians tolerated her. But they weren't sure a woman should be president. She'd never stood the test of an election.

"Gus Dur is a crazy man," Amat said. "It's not good. Also, he's blind. How will a blind man govern the state? Uh. No. Stupid." He shook his head. "I think Susilo will win the election."

Indonesia needed peace, he said. The Bali bombings had ruined Lombok's economy. The island depended on tourist overflow from Bali, and for this reason Amat would vote for Susilo Bambang Yudhoyono—a military man who could keep the nation stable and who, in the end, would win not once, but twice.

I asked, "What's wrong with Megawati?"

"Woman president, no good. Must be a man."

"For Islamic reasons?"

"Yes."

"What does Johar think?"

Amat translated. Johar shook her head. Politics wasn't her thing. Strange question from a tourist, anyway.

"You want to see a traditional Sasak village?" said Amat.

A tourist attraction. "No thanks."

"You want to do anything now?"

"Actually, you know what? I'm a journalist. I'd like to interview Johar." I pulled out a recorder I'd been carrying all day.

"Interview about what?"

"The elections."

This excited Amat. A journalist! He went to find neighbors who could give me their opinions. A mother with a child in a sling, a young athlete with a pink volleyball, and the devout-looking Muslim in loose clothing and a white pillbox cap who had handed me the helmet all came in for a chat. Johar went first. She said Susilo was her man. She wanted to throw something at the TV every time Amien Rais came on; he was too pompous. Megawati was unacceptable.

"For the same reason?" I asked Amat, who translated.

"Yes," Amat said. "Woman no good as president. Not strong. She needs to stay in the kitchen!"

"Johar said that?"

"Yes."

Sengkol was a conservative place. Everyone had roughly the same opinion. Only the devout-looking Muslim disagreed about Susilo. I could tell he loathed the United States. He had dark almond eyes and that quiet manner of a radical—a limp, resigned, watchful silence—that reminded me of a line by V. S. Naipual: "The Islam that makes people withdraw, the more violently to leap forward." He wore a thin curtain fringe of beard and hid his laughing mouth behind the collar of his shirt, as if embarrassed to show his teeth. Amat called him Haji.

"Who would you vote for?"

"I don't like any of the candidates."

Did he feel the Iraq invasion was a war on Islam? I decided to ask.

He was slow with his answer. He had an Indonesian politeness, but also religious scruples of honesty. "All Muslims are brothers," he said carefully. "When anyone attacks a part of Islam, all Muslims feel a pain in their hearts."

"That's how I feel, too," Amat blurted, pointing to his chest. "It hurts to hear about Muslims dying."

Haji stared with his eerie quietude. He'd made clear that we were enemies. Now that I was a journalist a shadow of politics fell between me and everyone on the porch. Washington had enough trouble explaining its rationale to Americans; I wondered how the war could begin to make sense to Muslim villagers in Sengkol. Speeches, rationalizations, good intentions meant nothing. I asked one other neighbor, who had mixed opinions on the war, if he saw it as a result of September 11, and his answer was the surprise of that rainy afternoon. When Amat described the world's most recent defining disaster, this tall, secular-minded man, reticent behind squarish glasses and the brim of a driving cap—by no means unintelligent—had no idea what I was getting at.

"He's never heard of September 11?"

"He doesn't watch much television," said Amat.

Bali and Lombok are like mismatched twins—Hindu and Muslim, rich and poor—and Lombok relies, as Amat had said, on Balinese tourism. I figured most Muslims on the island would follow the antics of their terrorist-minded spiritual kin, which is why his neighbor's answer about September 11 was so startling. But then many rural Muslims get their news from Friday prayers or local scuttlebutt, and it was no one's business here to make excuses for Washington.

Bali is unique among Indonesia's thousands of islands because it has clung to Hinduism, the religion of Indian traders who first colonized the archipelago almost two thousand years ago. Compared to other islands it feels cheerful and bright. Devotional flowers litter the side-walks, gaudy white Hindu statues fountain up from odd street corners, and some towns have overgrown temple ruins of stepped orange brick, in the Javanese style. The bricks are centuries old. The ruins are leftover from Indonesia's first great period, when Hindu trade empires spread outward from Java in radiating districts actually called "mandalas."

The Indonesian military has tried to link itself with the mightiest old trade empire, Majapahit. In other words: Generals in the world's largest Islamic nation refer back to a glorious Hindu past. "It is nation-alism," a guide on Java told me. "Patriotism." A way of holding the islands together. General Suharto had promoted something called Pancasila, a code of loyalty and patriotism for the stitched-together republic. It gave most Indonesians a headache. As a rule, people felt more loyal to their local customs than to "Indonesia." And under Suharto, the military had become a hideously corrupt parallel government, a dark administrative machine with its own laws of disappearances, kickbacks, killings, and bribes. So an Islamic purist could present himself as a religious rebel against the corruptions of leftover Hinduism as well as Jakarta's military machine.

That, very briefly, was the domestic background to the bombings in 2002. The foreign background is easier to understand: Kuta's a surf town. Huge gleaming restaurants, throbbing nightclubs, and flagship stores for international surf brands compete on the main strip with souvenir shops and Western fashion outlets. Other parts of Bali might be ruined by tourism, but Kuta's been swallowed whole. It looks like a neighborhood airlifted from Hong Kong or Tokyo. Lights flash, CD stores blare oversweet pop. The main street, Jalan Legian, is notorious. People on the sidewalk make indecent offers.

"Marijuana, boss?"

"Hashish."

"Woman, woman."

"Traspor? Taksi?" is also normal, and once I heard "Helikopter?" No idea what that was about.

The Kuta sprawl started when surfers made it a stop on the hippie trail. By the late '70s the Kokes' hotel was long gone. "The only traces Bob could see [in 1946], as he walked over the ground," wrote Louise, "were the vague outlines of the foundations and daffodils growing wild. Even the bricks which lined the sumps underneath each bathroom had been scavenged, because bricks were worth one or two cents each." Jalan Legian was a muddy footpath between tall coconut palms.

A legend says a Qantas aircrew on layover in Denpasar surfed Kuta Beach in the 1960s, and they may have been the first Westerners to ride Balinese waves after Bob Koke. In any case, a filmmaker named Alby Falzon heard about the surf and brought a handful of Australians to

Indonesia for a segment of his 1972 movie *Morning of the Earth,* which turned a generation of Australians into surf bums.

"Kuta was a peaceful little village with miles of coconut groves fringing the beach," said Peter Neely, who now publishes a guide called *Indo Surf and Lingo.* "I'd been working in Sydney city as a disillusioned advertising writer when I first read about all these incredible new waves that had been discovered in Bali. All we knew about Java and Sumatra from schoolbooks was that there were jungles and tigers. A couple of hippie friends tripped over to Bali in the early seventies and returned with bright eyes and wonderful tales of an exotic Asian 'surfer's paradise,' with hippies surfing naked and smoking chillums on the beaches. Then I saw *Morning of the Earth,* projected onto a sheet in a smokey Sydney backyard. The fuse was lit. Soon after, I quit work and headed over to Bali for two months in April 1975.

"Electricity had only just arrived, with TV not arriving in Bali until around five years later. . . . Spicy meals in small cafés lit by kerosene lamps were around one dollar. There was only one neon sign in Kuta, a Peter's Ice Cream sign sitting on the ground on Jalan Legian, at the end of Poppies Lane One. Follow the electric lead two hundred meters down the dimly lit lane and you'd end up at Poppies restaurant, one of the first places with electric refrigeration, cold beer, and ice cream. Surfers on a strict budget couldn't afford the imported ice creams (for one dollar), so we'd wait at 'Bemo Corner' for the coconut ice cream vendor to push his cart along at seven p.m. and scoop out his tiny one-hundred-rupiah cones [twenty cents]." Bemo Corner, named for the beat-up Datsun pickups that served as taxis in the '70s, is now a busy urban roundabout served by rattling, beat-up minivans.

"I would surf the beach breaks at Halfway each day with maybe twenty other Western surfers and ten or so local kids. One day I walked to Legian Beach and found perfect three-to-five-foot peaks without another soul in the water. On my way back I walked through the shade of the palm groves, not having seen anyone for an hour, until I was almost back at Kuta. An old barefooted grandmother, wearing an old brown batik sarong around her hips, totally topless, without a care in the world, walked past me leading a six-foot-long pig on a rope. Talk about culture shock. She smiled at me, exposing her few remaining teeth, stained bloodred with the betel nut and tobacco she was chewing. I said the only words I knew in Indonesian—'Selamat Pagi,' good morning—but she just giggled and shook her head at the strange-looking tourist with the 'ski' under his arm. I now realize she probably didn't even speak Indonesian, as the older locals mostly only spoke Balinese back then."

The island wasn't innocent of tourism. Resorts in the '60s went up on the other side of Bali, in Sanur, where misguided Westerners looking for James Michener's Bali Hai—a fictional South Seas island based loosely on Fiji, about four thousand miles away—could get drunk and sleep with each other's wives in the horrific, chalky-white Bali Beach Hotel. But Kuta overtook Sanur as a tourist trap in the '80s. Australian surfing boomed, and there was a big push for tourism by Suharto. Money from Jakarta and international investors turned the bucolic village into the Cabo San Lucas of Southeast Asia. Now, instead of grandmothers walking their pigs, Jalan Legian has big, dumb sports bars and drunken yobs spilling into the street yelling obscene suggestions at blonde-dyed women on coke.

So much for background.

On a warm Saturday night in October 2002, a white Mitsubishi van parked outside the Sari Club, a dance joint on Jalan Legian with an open patio and thatched roofs over the bars. "It was chockers," said an Australian who was there. "No room to move. There was probably, you know, at least three hundred people plus, I reckon." At the same time a man wearing a vest walked into Paddy's Pub, an Irish-themed bar across the street. Daniel Whiston had just settled down with his friends to rest from the noise and crush of the Sari Club. He was a surfer and paramedic from New Zealand. "I was sitting there drinking and having a pretty good time when 'boom,' and then a second one," he told the London *Times*. "After the first one, I stood up, and the second one just picked me up and threw me over a wall."

The first blast came from the vest-wearing bomber inside Paddy's. The second blast was the Mitsubishi van across the street. It had been packed with potassium chlorate, aluminum powder, and sulfur, organized in twelve plastic filing cabinets. That was enough explosive material—whether the bombers knew it or not—to create a thermobaric explosion, which ignites and burns off surrounding oxygen. "Terrified dancers, many bleeding profusely, struggled to escape the flames, trying to get out of the club's single narrow entrance," wrote the *Times*. Whiston ran out of Paddy's and found another New Zealander, Mark Parker, lying in the street with his legs blown off. He talked to Parker, who was conscious. "He was a real fighter, that guy," Whiston said. Parker turned out to be a cricket player, third in a line of famous cricket players in New Zealand. He'd just pulled up in a taxi when the van detonated. Whiston tried to stop the bleeding, and an ambulance took Parker to Sanglah Hospital in Denpasar, where he later died. "Craziness, pure madness—people everywhere, shock, body parts, just fear, fear," Whiston said. "People running, screaming, just madness, dark except for the fires burning around the place, pure madness."

Amrozi, the man who bought the explosives and became a poster boy for the bombings, was a slight, smiling Muslim from eastern Java. His friend Ali Imron had planned the operation and placed a smaller bomb outside the US consulate in Kuta, which exploded without doing much damage. Their friend Idris had set the two suicide bombers in motion on Jalan Legian and buzzed away on his motorcycle. They targeted the Sari Club as a "place of adultery." They were only a little disappointed that more Americans had not been killed. "Australians, Americans, whatever—they are all white people," said Ali Imron. The idea was to hurt America for the Afghanistan invasion and Australia for backing East Timor's independence. An interviewer for the *Times* asked another plotter, Imam Samudra, if he regretted that Muslims had also been killed. "I don't know if they are Muslims," he answered. "Because they are also customers. Muslims in jilbab [Muslim clothing] in Bali?" he said skeptically. Kuta and the Sari Club made good targets because of their reputations. He'd simply read up on Indonesian tourism and made his choice.

A year later, from his prison cell, Amrozi sang for the benefit of journalists: "Continue the holy struggle, get rid of Zionists, get rid of the Christian filth. God is great, this is my song." If professional clowns had been hired to play the role of Islamist radicals, the show could not have been better. (There are almost no "Zionists" in Bali, and only a handful of Jews in all of Indonesia.) "You will be killed just as you kill," said Osama bin Laden's voice in a recording one week after the explosions, taking ultimate credit on behalf of al-Qaeda, "and will be bombed just as you bomb."

Bali used to be known in Europe as a paradise where both men and women bathed topless in the heat, like Peter Neely's betel-chewing old woman. But the echo from Iran's revolution in 1979 has revived fundamentalism in many parts of the Muslim world, including Indonesia, and the nation as a whole has grown conservative, both under Suharto and after his fall. Now the local women wear more clothes than the tourists. On some islands it's dangerous for white women to lie topless on the beach. It is as if *bulés*, Westerners, had rediscovered the islands as a tropical Eden and stripped off their clothes to join the locals—who then recoiled and said, "That isn't what we meant."

After September 11 it was fashionable to write about terrorist attacks as flashpoints in a new war of civilizations. But in Kuta, civilization itself seemed to be missing. The naked hippies smoking chillums on the beach had been succeeded by well-adjusted kids paying top dollar for easy obliteration. Car bombs on Jalan Legian were not some dramatic form of philosophical discussion; they weren't "totalitarianism versus freedom," or spirit versus flesh, or the Sages of Islam versus the Paragons of Western Thought. They were acts of unreason against another kind of unreason. The original dropout surfers had no intention of pioneering the island for tourism—they wanted to surf and learn a thing or two from an apparently placid Asian culture—but the antimaterialism of the '60s was as easy to make material, to cheapen and destroy, as Miki Dora's Malibu.

Not that Indonesian surfing is just a foreign phenomenon. Bali has a generation gap, like any other part of the world. There are parents who stand for tradition and kids who want to know about anything else. I met a bright-eyed university student from Bali named Termana who had long hair and an earring and looked like a cheerful pirate. He played in a punk band, and said some traditionalists wanted to wipe out punk on Bali and force everyone to play gamelan. But gamelan bores Balinese kids. So do most aspects of Bali that Westerners come to absorb. Shadow puppets are tedious because no one can relate to the language. "It's too stiff," he said. The puppeteers use an old, formal Balinese, but regular people speak a low vernacular.

What about the placid Hinduism, the old Vedantic balance of human thought with effusive nature? The daily offerings of incense in little palm-leaf boxes on the street? The women in silk dresses, the statues of gods in the gardens, the stone figures of frogs adorned with saris and fresh blossoms? Eh, said Termana. The old harmonious way of life, where everyone had a place in the village and the family compound, where the stages of life from birth to death were fixed by Hindu belief, where first- and second- and third-born children received certain traditional names, whether they were boys or girls—all that is confining. The latest trend on the Island of the Gods is "prayer contests," he said, competitions for correctness and speed in executing ancient rituals. "It's too much ritual. Too much religion."

In this sense the throb of city life in Kuta is an escape from the torpid village. You can be a liberated individual in Kuta, self-sufficient and cool. The famous lanes near the beach, Poppies One and Two, bustle with backpackers and motorbikes and Balinese surfers wearing mirrored sunglasses and baggy shorts. This is their home. Poppies is urban but laid-back, just a few yards from the beach, and the surf shops—different from the blazing flagship stores on Jalan Legian—are mixed in with souvenir stores, cheap hotels, smoking food stalls, and banana-shaded restaurants and bars.

Surfing, in other words, isn't a foreign sport. It's a way to prove yourself as a local. Rizal Tanjung is a mixed ethnic Chinese from Sulawesi who grew up in Bali and became one of Indonesia's most famous and accomplished pro surfers. The beauty of the waves at his local spots, Ulu Watu and Padang Padang, are matched in high season by the size of the visiting crowds, and Rizal has no shame about asserting himself. These spots need "policing," he told an Australian writer named Alex Leonard. He and his friends sit far out in the water at Padang Padang and dominate the waves. "We decide which waves we take and which waves other people are allowed to take," he said. "We have to control the lineup. Nobody else is allowed to control it. After all, we were subjugated before, so why should we allow ourselves to be subjugated again now? Now we have to prove that our country has changed, that we're moving forward. We have to be the ones to show them how, not they the ones to show us how."

Rizal is a youthful, modern guy, with floppy black hair and lean, semi-Chinese features. When I talked to him by phone, he was the boss of Electrohell, a surf shop on Poppies Two. He'd been surfing since 1983, when the sport had started to explode. "People back then thought we were a bunch of weirdos," he said. "We were super-tanned, and our hair was bleached out from the beach and the salt. We were like out-siders." Their parents didn't approve of Australian hippies. "But it's a different story now, because surfing has become one of the biggest life-styles. All over the world, people wanna be a surfer. They wanna have a surfer body and they wanna have the clothes."

When the Australians arrived, some fishermen's sons on Bali were already riding scraps of wood in the sea. "We called it *serup*," an old-timer at Kuta told Leonard. "Or another way of saying it was *nyosor umbak*. We lay on pieces of wood and rode already-broken waves to shore. We also used parts from the fishing boats that lined Kuta Beach then—the lengths of bamboo attached to the sides of the boats, the *pangantang*. So we understood the foreigners' surfing."

This habit of bodyboarding on scraps of canoe recurs around the world. Rizal told me it started in Bali only after the hippies arrived; but I doubt Leonard's sources are lying. What may be true is that bodyboarding never became a pervasive part of Balinese life, and the kids never ventured beyond the whitewash, until the '70s. "In imitation of the foreigners," wrote Leonard, "the Kuta boys began to paddle farther out in order to catch waves before they broke, and, once they could do this smoothly, then they stood up, fell off, stood up and fell off. . . . "

Surfing was still slow to catch on. Most Balinese kids couldn't swim. Even now, some talented and well-traveled professionals from Bali—including Rizal—have never learned that particular skill. They rely on their boards as life preservers.

"Isn't that scary?" I said.

"Aw no, we just be sure we got lots of people around us." If the leash snaps, Rizal said, "we swim like a dog."

By the '80s Kuta had two local hives of surf activity, the Bali Surf Club and a shop called Bali Barrel. Another now-famous surfer named Ketut Menda ran Bali Barrel. Kids worked for him to earn the privilege of borrowing a board. He saw it as a form of character building. "You had to work hard first," one surfer told Alex Leonard, "clean the displays, sweep the floor, mop, hose down the pavement in front of the shop—and only then would Ketut Menda allow you to go surfing or take you surfing himself. In my opinion, Ketut Menda was the best at encouraging kids to develop and become strong and independent without spoiling them."

So along with foreign corruption and money, surfing brought Indonesian kids a form of self-reliance. Now, according to Rizal, surfers across the archipelago have a distinct Indonesian style, with flourishes informed by traditional dance or a martial art called *pencak*. "All the people in Indonesia grow up learning either martial art or traditional dancing," he told me. "When I was at school you had no choice, you had to take these classes. But now that I'm older I realize this stuff helped me, it even helped with my surfing . . . how to hold your hand up, spread wide, or how you throw your elbow or your shoulder, you know. Learning how to make it unique. The Balinese people, they've turned surfing into like an art.

"It's kinda like drawing. First you learn how to draw, and then you relax and have your own style. It's the same thing in surfing. First you learn how to do it, and then you become who you are. So people surf from their personalities. You cannot fake style. Style, you either have it or you don't."

eeeeeeeeeeeeeeeeeeeee

Pramoedya Ananta Toer, Indonesia's most prominent novelist, was a folk-hero survivor of the massacres in 1965 and '66 who wrote well about mass thought and Western individualism. He spent fourteen years in jail as a political prisoner, and by the end of his life in 2006, he was a moral figure for Indonesians equivalent to Mandela in South Africa or Solzhenitsyn in Russia.

I managed to talk with him in Java just before he died. He belonged to an older generation of Indonesians, different from the surfers, who had imbibed deep lessons from the United States and Europe. He was a lifelong anticolonialist who had translated Steinbeck, loved Mark Twain and gospel music, and studied the French Revolution.

Pramoedya was forty-one when the anti-Communist hysteria in Bali and Java reached his doorstep. He lived in Jakarta and had a literary career and a personal friendship with President Sukarno, who was about to lose his job. Sukarno and most of the nation's intellectual left would be purged by a combination of palace coup, led by Suharto, and mass murder.

In October 1965 a mob of masked vigilantes surrounded Pramoedya's house and smashed the windows with rocks, then threatened to burn the place down. Pramoedya picked up two weapons—a mop handle and a Japanese sword—and came to the gate. "Take off your masks," he said. "Then I'll talk to you."

The men jeered and threw stones. There was a burst of gunfire, then a group of soldiers and police shoved through the crowd to lead Pramoedya away. He brought a typewriter, a bag of clothes, and some manuscripts. On the way out his escorts tied his hands behind his back and looped the rope around his neck. "In the early days of the Indonesian revolution," he wrote, "that kind of knot was a sure sign that the captive was to be killed."

Instead he went to prison, where he wrote his Buru Quartet of novels about independence from the Dutch. The new Suharto government had thrown more than a million dissidents in jail and building a legal case against each prisoner would take years, so about twelve thousand of them were shipped to the island of Buru. Pramoedya spent ten years hacking elephant grass, clearing rattan and bamboo for fields of rice and sweet potato, constructing barracks to live in, and catching rats or geckos to bulk out sparse meals of rice.

Buru was a tropical gulag. Like Solzhenitsyn, Pramoedya had to memorize what he composed. So he told the other prisoners stories. He told them about a journalist and independence agitator who'd established the first native-run newspaper on Java in the 1920s. Pramoedya used him as a model for a hero named Minke. In the made-up stories, and in the novels that became the Buru Quartet, Minke grows up by agitating for independence. His coming-of-age mirrors the awakening of a vast new nation in what had been a scattered colonial plantation with a variety of names—the Malay Archipelago, the Dutch East Indies.

"Usually, during a break in forced labor," Pramoedya told me, "the inmates and I were gathered and they would listen to my stories. When they worked somewhere else, they retold the stories to their friends. One day there was an inmate who escaped. A week later the guards found him in the forest. The guard asked him why did he run away? He said, 'I want to be Minke!'"

Sometimes his jailers let Pramoedya use paper and pen. He stole time to write, but the labor and near-starvation had weakened his mind. At last other prisoners arranged for him to be excused from hard labor for a few hours every day so he could sit at a desk. "Eventually," he wrote, "I rediscovered myself as a man in all his nakedness, free from pretensions and ambitions, a creature not powerless but, in fact, equipped with the will to define his own course in history. I found, in the end, that the man is far more important than his pretensions and ambitions. The man himself determines who he becomes."

From his books I had expected a stern and serious old writer, but Pramoedya was impish. He smiled a lot. He was short and sinewy, with sparse gray hair and heavy fingers, squarish bifocals, and a light batik shirt. He chain-smoked a strong brand of *kretek*, clove cigarettes. Since mass violence was one of his themes, I asked why Indonesians flared up sometimes in spasms of blood. His answer was simple: no habits of debate. Indonesians are polite until they disagree so furiously that they need to kill each other. To Pramoedya it expressed a lack of character.

"Violence emerges because Indonesians have no individual courage, except for the Acehnese," he said. "What they have instead is group courage, and the consequences are gang fights. When I was sixteen or seventeen years old, I had an argument with a classmate and we ended up in a duel. One-to-one. After that the loser shook hands with the winner, admitted his mistake, and everything went back to normal. It's different now. People fight in groups. In fact we can say that rioting in Indonesia happens because the people rarely use their brains. If they were to use their brains, they would have discussions or debates instead of fighting."

So Indonesians are subject to mass thought, mass movements, and riots because they have no tradition of individualism. That brought me up short. Pramoedya thought democracy, as a Western idea, needed even more Western ideas to make it work. "Political parties in Indonesia are like a sack to be filled with as many members as they can stuff in it. And when it's full, the leader decides what to do with it. That's my opinion," he said, "as an individualist." He smiled and pulled on his cigarette.

Not that Western countries are immune from hysteria; not that Pramoedya romanticized Europe or the United States. He was convinced the CIA, in fact, had instigated the coup to overthrow Sukarno. But he was an iconoclast who had learned a lot from the West, and he was brutal with his opinions.

"The nation isn't mature enough for democracy yet, anyway," he added. "It's a Western idea."

"Is it still a good one?"

"Yes, of course. That's the idea that has been pumped into my mind since my childhood—freedom, democracy, modernity."

"Some people think Indonesia just needs practice."

"That's right. The entire concept comes from abroad. No concepts come from us, you know. Except to be loyal and obedient to superiors."

Aji, my translator, sat next to Pramoedya on the couch and spoke into his ear. He was half deaf. She was pretty and young and they struck up an instant conspiratorial friendship. She called him *bapak*, an honorific that happens to mean, and sound like, "papa."

He said none of the presidential candidates had real charisma, and he was pessimistic about the rise of anyone new. "Every major step forward in Indonesian history has grown out of a student movement," he said. "The problem now is that the students aren't organized. In fact, they don't seem to care."

Soon Aji went to the kitchen for another cup of tea and left us alone in the living room. We smoked *kretek* and smiled. I made some bland comment, but he cupped his ear and uttered a single sentence in English. "I'm sorry, I don't understand foreign languages." This was an outrageous modesty. A glass case next to the couch had a few novellas translated by Pramoedya decades before, not just Steinbeck but also Tolstoy and Gorki. But he was deaf and detached. He hadn't written a word in years. He couldn't even type. The writer's work was over. Even his opinions had an automatic quality, like pinballs clanking out of an old machine. But he still had an immediate, good-humored humanity. On my way out the door, he slapped me on the shoulder with a heavy hand.

"Oh, that man is so stubborn!" Aji said in the car. "I could never be married to him. He won't even wear his hearing aid!"

"He's an individualist."

"Well, if I were his wife, I would never tolerate so much individualism. I don't know how she does it."

<hr />

"I'll tell you why democracy's failin' here, mate," said an Australian to me on the terrace of the surf bungalows on Lombok. "Most Indonesians equate democracy with wealth. Six years ago, when Suharto came down, they'd noticed that the rich white tourists they saw were all from democratic nations. They figured the economy under democracy would automatically get better. But it didn't. In fact their country's fallin' apart. Everyone feels insecure, so they want a general to come back into power. So they're votin' for Golkar again." Suharto's party.

The Australian was a bent, sinewy, humorous old surfer with weathered skin and keen blue eyes. He wore a Quiksilver T-shirt and shorts. His friends at the table were just as old—about sixty, with white thinning hair—but Dave, as I think he was called, had the hardbitten authority of an alpha wolfhound.

"Remember when we were in Bali six years ago?" he said to one of his friends. "People marched in the streets against Golkar. It was so tense you risked your life admitting you'd voted for them. They hated Suharto with a passion. They all thought Megawati was Balinese because she had some relative from Bali"—he pronounced Bali as *bally*—"and then she added Sukarnoputri to her name to remind everyone of Papa Sukarno. But that's not working now. She's not like her father. People can tell. So they're voting for Golkar again. And that bloody Wiranto might win."

Fear of a Wiranto presidency was on everyone's mind in the spring of 2004, like fear of bird flu.

"They don't know what democracy is, mate," said Dave's friend.

"That's right. They're not used to it."

I mistrusted Dave's speech. It seemed to me that most of Amat's neighbors had a clear idea of what it meant to vote for president, even if their grasp of current events was weak. The simpleminded Indonesians who equated suffrage with money were like the simpleminded Christians who prayed to God for an Oldsmobile. Of course they existed—people like that exist all over the world—but they weren't the basic problem.

But we got no further on presidential politics over breakfast because most people at the table had come to surf. Breakfast on the terrace of the Kuta surf bungalows was quiet, sleepy, sullen, and tense.

"Mawi Bay should be workin' now," said Dave.

"Grupuk might be okay this afternoon," ventured his friend, "with that swell comin' up."

"I think I'll give Are Goleng a look," said the Canadian.

The Swiss girl, Inga, was picking up surf lingo. She sat chirpily over breakfast in white shorts and a small bikini top and said, in English, "I shall surf today at Grupuk," in a crisp fastidious accent. "If it's working."

Maxim and the other Frenchman were on their way to Ekas. I said I'd look at another fishing village, Selong Blanak, but Dave thought the angle of that bay was wrong; it might not catch a south swell.

By our choice of breaks, and the way we tackled our food, we announced our prowess as surfers. Later we would compete for waves according to talent and skill, but the jostling for position started over fried rice and pancakes. Fresh advice was welcome; new friends were always interesting. But most of us had dreamed for months of crowd-free surf on a remote equatorial island. No one wanted to hang with a kook, and no one wanted to tag along. This winnowing and sifting had to occur without uttering an impolite word. It was a poker game. Breakfast was civil, thoughtful, boastful, and gruff.

Afterward, we split up. Amat came over on his motorbike to buzz me to Selong Blanak. We climbed along winding roads through faded green hills of palm trees and half-dried grass. But along the way we turned off to check Mawi. Dave had suggested dropping by, just in case. We followed a muddy goat trail, and the motorbike skidded and slipped. ("It'll be rough, you'll think you can't make it, but you can," Dave had said.) On the path we startled a meter-long monitor lizard warming itself in the sun—glistening, muscular, almost black. It slithered heavily into the brush.

The goat trail was a private road maintained by farmers. Their sons showed up at the beach to enforce a kind of toll. If you paid, nothing got stolen. The price was fair, so the arrangement satisfied everyone. "You don't grudge the locals a little money," Dave had said. "Sometimes you buy things from 'em, like cigarettes, even if you don't smoke. It's not a matter of handouts, 'cause they don't want that. They just want to make a living like everybody else."

A stout sectioning wave broke from a rocky outcropping on the left and moved evenly across the bay. Amat spoke to the kids in Sasak. Soon Dave and his two friends showed up. Then the Canadian arrived on his motorbike. Everyone from breakfast, in the end, convened on Mawi Bay, and the coincidence caused some embarrassment. There was a lot of squinting and careful discussion.

"Bit sloppy now, mate."

"Swell might give it some shape, though."

"If the wind turns offshore, it'll be bloody nice."

"That's workable . . . What does Billy think? Hey? Oh, he doesn't think anything, that's good. Easier to get through life that way."

In the end we all wound up in the water. All of us hard-bitten individualists had become a thronging crowd. Now the real hierarchy established itself. Instead of poker-faced bravado you started to hear excuses. I'm a bit sick today. My board has a new ding. This rental piece of shit isn't long enough for this swell. But a mist hung over the green hills, and the landscape itself seemed to absorb the complaints. The largest waves shattered on the black volcanic outcropping at one end of the bay, with whitewater streaming between sharp crags. There was a sense of danger as well as a deep sense of peace.

Dave and his older Australian friends went out on "skis," kayaks with bulbous tails designed for larger surf. They raced ahead with double-bladed paddles and trimmed the waves like old men on fiberglass UFOs. The rest of us crawled along on our boards. The swell increased while we sat there. Soon deep blue water mounded into a wave that pitched up in angry steps. I slide to my belly and paddles. There was a sound like rain from the feathering peak as I leaned the tip of my board through and floated for a few seconds in a muted netherworld.

The next wave was bigger. We stroked up the surface as it rose; I turned and took off. My feet lost contact with the board. For a second I was like a man on a free-falling elevator until I landed again, leaned into a turn, settled into the face, and sailed along. The curtain of water slopped over my head and for a second or two I heard the rushing echo of a tube. A moment later the wave shot me forward along the face and I ran out ahead and let the wave collapse and push me with a mound of whitewater toward the beach.

We did that for two hours. Spare boards were offered around, and two of the beach boys paddled out. (Amat didn't surf.) When I came ashore, a group of women had collected near our cars. They also belonged to the sprouting surf industry at Mawi. One woman ran up to hand me a skinned pineapple on a stick, ready to eat. An ancient woman with no teeth and a tongue stained red from betel nut also cried "Hello!" and sold me bananas.

When Alby Falzon and his crew first discovered waves at Ulu Watu, south of Kuta, local Balinese, according to Alex Leonard,

lined the cliff top when the surfers paddled out and shouted and cheered when they rode waves. After that first encounter between Ulu Watu villagers and foreign surfers, relations between the two groups developed rapidly. Increasing numbers of visitors enabled local people to transform their economies by selling food and drinks to surfers and by carrying boards and camera gear from the end of the road near the temple down to the beach. Local people also constructed *warung* [food shacks] on the cliffs overlooking the surf spot, so surfers could rest in shade and be served drinks and food before and after surfing.

Mawi, as a surf spot, wasn't that far along. But the surfers stood around with their fruit, talking like parrots and looking very pleased. There were no more excuses, no more jostling for position. All the boastful bitching had fallen away. Surf smashed against the craggy rock in the water, the raw beauty of the bay was overwhelming, and—as usual in Indonesia—*bulés* and locals got along just fine.

"This is the sweetest part, mate," said one of Dave's friends, wiping pineapple juice from his chin. "After the surfing's over."

3

GERMANY:

THE FUN-GESELLSCHAFT

·····················*Uwe Drath and friends, Westerland Beach, Sylt, c. 1954*

STEFFEN DITTRICH IS a short, rough, happy guy with bad teeth and thinning red hair. He looks a bit like a madman on the wave—coarse beard growth, bulging eyes—but he has grace as well as aggression. He kicks and carves, bashes the churning whitewater, pulls a 360, slides a bit, carves, and cuts back again. He stays on the wave for five minutes at a time, longer than anyone else, while tourists and other surfers watch from the bank and a bridge over the canal. Then he falls, and a current carries him downstream.

Dittrich has surfed the Munich river system for more than half his life. He prefers the Eisbach, a waterway under drooping trees in the English Garden. He hops with his duct-taped board onto a standing wave that forms where water emerges from under Prinzregentenstrasse. He faces a nineteenth-century stone bridge and dances in place on the curl of the wave, like a bird in a wind tunnel. Surfers stand in line on each bank, waiting their turn.

Dittrich, in his forties, is an elder statesman here, an early Eisbach surfer. In 1983, he spent a surf-bum summer in the English Garden, living in a VW bus. "I was a student at the Ludwig-Maximilians-Universität," he told me, "and my girlfriend at the time dumped me, and I had no place to live. But I did have a VW bus, so I just parked it under the red birches over there." Dittrich, dripping wet from his session in the water, pointed across the canal at a leaf-spangled clearing behind the Haus der Kunst, a museum built by Hitler. "It was easy to walk to the university. I just had breakfast every morning in the cafeteria."

City officials will flat-out refuse to talk about surfing in the Isar system because it's still (technically) against the law. Signs warn that surfing and swimming the canals is dangerous, and it's true that the Eisbach is a fast and shallow wave. Surfers here have been known to dislocate shoulders, break bones, bleed, and even die. But after the number of outlaw surfers in Munich swelled in the 1980s and '90s to three or four hundred (the current number), the police quit handing out fines.

The scene in Munich is small but not laughable. It takes a special talent to surf the Isar canals. But it still causes consternation. Germans who know nothing about surfing—or who confuse it with *Surfen,* which in their language means "windsurfing"—view the sport as trash culture from the United States. Or, if not trash, frivolity. "*Es gehört zu du dieser Fun-Gesellschaft, die wir überall sehen,*" a sweet-tempered schoolteacher called Hildegard said to me in a town outside Munich, implying without wanting to cause offense that the influence of pop culture, and my home state, had changed her nation perhaps for the worse. "It belongs to this new fun-society, which we see everywhere now."

Eisbach surfing is a tourist attraction. People sit on the Prinz-regentenstrasse bridge or stand under the trees on the canal bank, watching surfers. On the bank you hear the thrilling rush of white-water and smell neoprene wetsuits and surf wax, mixed (oddly) with cool river air instead of sand and salt. You wait in line and place your board on the crest of the rapid. You can push off from your butt, or jump in feetfirst. But the wave is tricky. Perpetual motion reverses the usual rules. The wave moves more than the surfer. I wasn't used to that. Instead of building speed and running forward ahead of a moving swell, with the wave's energy at your back, you have to balance and steer into a powerful, oncoming current. The idea is not to move forward, but to resist going backward, if possible with lots of fancy tricks. You feel like a bird in a wind tunnel. I fell more than once and floated down to a meadow in the English Garden, where German women in bikinis giggled when I climbed out with my board.

Next to the Eisbach, between waves, I watched a kid with blond, spiked hair and an elaborately pierced face dump his surfboard under a chestnut tree. He pulled his suit on. He asked for advice from another surfer in the line. "It's shallow," the other kid said. "And there's concrete under there, so if you fall, fall flat."

The pierced kid, a German named Emi, rode it three times but gave up after a nasty wipeout. Later he showed me a gouge on his hip that oozed fresh blood. "I've gone surfing in Portugal for seven years," he told me, "but this is different. The water comes fast, and there are rocks underneath."

A regular at the Eisbach was a twenty-year-old named Sebastian, or Basti. He took a few turns, trimmed expertly, but decided the wave was no good. He got out, clambered across the wet stone arch of the bridge, and balanced on one of the piers. Water rushed around his feet.

The Eisbach wave is an accident of civil engineering. Water boils up from under the city through two stone arches next to the Haus der Kunst, below street level. It curls into a sudden wave formed by a concrete weir on the canal bottom. Makeshift wooden planks jammed upright into the water—anchored by colorful maritime ropes—give the curl a steeper shape.

Basti pulled on these ropes to adjust the wave. A sign behind him warned against standing where he was. Climbing on the bridge was illegal and could be "fatal." Rules in Germany often announce the risk of death, but Basti had no fear.

"Who put those slabs in the water?" I asked before he went out to adjust them.

"We did," he said. "We surfers."

He meant a loose affiliation of locals who guard the Eisbach and other Isar waves. They're misfits, delinquents, like Dora in Malibu, or the pump-house kids in La Jolla. They have Attitude. It's almost funny. Munich is a clean, rich European city packed with baroque churches and a famous Bavarian glockenspiel. But four decades after Tom Wolfe published a magazine piece called "The Pump House Gang," fresh-faced versions of his California toughs could be found in a Munich park.

"The Pump House Gang" is only eighteen pages long, but it may stand as the best-known piece of American surf literature. That's a shame. The number of facts Wolfe managed to flub is astonishing. He liked to pose as a wise but hip writer who could saunter into any subculture and give the lowdown to the squares. He was right that surfing delinquents who hung out at the Windansea pump house in La Jolla, lived "as though age segregation were a permanent state, as if it were inconceivable that any of them would ever grow old," and he was eminently right that even antisocial beach rats had a rigid social pecking order. But Wolfe didn't bother to get his lore straight. "Simmons," he wrote with sarcasm, "was a fantastic surfer. He was fantastic even though he had a bad leg. He rode the really big waves. One day he got wiped out at Windansea. When a big wave overtakes a surfer, it drives him right to the bottom. The board came in but he never came up and they never found his body. Very mysterioso."

Bob Simmons, as any pump-house rat would have known, was the man who first finished a board in fiberglass in the late '40s. He was not just a "fantastic surfer"—Wolfe treats the preeminent shaper of modern boards as just another lost member of the gang. He'd been dead for more than ten years by the time Wolfe heard of him; his body was found after just a few days; and his defining debility was a bad elbow, not a bad leg (some cancer in his foot had healed years before). "Wolfe's real error comes in reading the gang's wonderment as vanity," wrote Daniel Duane in his book *Caught Inside,* but the irony runs deeper: If not for Simmons's innovations there might have *been* no Pump House Gang, no crowd of surf brats on the steps for Wolfe to interview. Surfing might have remained a coastal curiosity instead of a pop phenomenon. And it might never have reached the municipal canals of Europe.

Anyway, Basti tinkered with the Eisbach rapid, and two green-uniformed Munich policemen ambled down the slope. They were pot-bellied, fatherly, and slow. One crooked a finger at Basti. They had a little chat. Then Basti came back to his board, a beat-up red fiberglass thing fixed with duct tape lying under an oak. He quivered with rage.

"They just ordered me to keep out of the English Garden," he said. Now he *really* couldn't surf in the Eisbach. (Technically.)

He spat and said, "What were they doing, anyway, walking by right at that moment? Normally the cops just stop and watch us surf."

Basti's friend, a tall kid with no shirt who refused to mention his name, shook his head. He had wiry muscles and as much of a tan as surfers get in Germany. "Munich cops are *assholes,*" he said.

The first surfers in Munich are considered to be Arthur and Alexander Pauli, brothers from the Bavarian town of Trostberg, who in the mid-'70s tied ropes to the banks of a canal in another part of Munich and surfed in place like water-skiers behind a boat. The Paulis surfed in the Flosslände, a green district of branching canals beside the river where people ride kayaks and swim, and where Quiksilver now sponsors a contest.

Surfing the canals in those days was a sport for outlaws, and early stories always involve the cops. Dittrich also used a rope when he started surfing the Eisbach; he said two police cruisers at a time would approach the canal from either end on Prinzregentenstrasse to block off potential escape routes. "So I'd keep one eye out, and when they came I just let go of my rope and floated away," he said. "The canal down there splits three ways, so it was hard for them to find you."

The Isar itself is a mighty river, shallow and brown in the places where Munich has tamed it, squared in by concrete embankments or overgrown with green surges of oak and linden. It's too wide to surf, but biking beside it through downtown Munich will take you from one canal wave to the other, from the Eisbach to the Flosslände. You pass damp, cold stands of trees and Isar bridges built like summer palaces. These bridges are the heart of Munich in the sense that the city grew up around its river crossings. Munich started in the Middle Ages, officially in 1158, but bridging the Isar here into the wild barbarian north was a project even before that, for the Romans. Most of the city's main bridges now are dynastic edifices dating from the eighteenth and nineteenth centuries but rebuilt after World War II, larded with pompous, mossy statues and named after Bavarian electors and princes. Luitpoldbrücke, Maximiliansbrücke, Ludwigsbrücke. Riding past them with a surfboard feels weird.

Flosslände means "raft landing." Huck Finn–style rafts were used to carry supplies like bricks and wood for the city; in fact, a good portion of Munich was built with the help of rafts floated down the canals. Now replicas of the old rafts are rented by tourists and corporations for uproarious, six-hour trips provisioned with sausage and beer.

The placid water and trees in the Flosslände have a heavy damp that seems native to Germany, or anyway isn't native to southern California. It's a freshwater forest damp, an environment for frogs and swans. It makes me think of old churches and cryptlike European cellars, Schiller-*Lieder,* and riverine strains of Wagner. But it's not ponderous enough to keep Germans from playing with modern toys. On my way to the Flosslände wave I watched a woman launch a bright yellow plastic kayak down a slick chute of mud.

The smallish Flosslände wave forms under a small concrete bridge at the bottleneck of a meadow-edged canal. The water rushes down a sloping run of concrete and lifts into a rideable curl of two-foot mush. It is another accident of civil engineering: This canal feeds a number of power stations, and most surfers understand that city engineers can regulate the water volume and therefore the speed and size of the wave.

"There are a thousand theories," one surfer called Marion explained to me. "But basically when the water level in the lake is lower, they can let more water through, and the wave is faster."

About six surfers waited for the wave, men and women. We lined up beside a damp oak and took turns. One guy was disappointed by the size. He was a broad-shouldered young husband with dark hair and a slightly hunched, anxious manner. "I've been coming here all week, sometimes at five thirty in the morning, which irritates my wife. But I won't come out tomorrow if it stays like this." He was like any surfer complaining about conditions at his local beach. "There's always somebody here," he went on. "Any time of day. Sometimes they come at night. They set up lights, with a generator. Those are the real crazy ones."

The Flosslände is a beginner's spot compared to the Eisbach. The oak was duct-taped with paper notes protected in plastic sleeves. "Beginner board wanted," they said. "Wetsuit for sale." "Lost wedding ring."

Sometimes a branch washed down the canal and the surfer in the water had to head for the bank to avoid injury. Sometimes a kayaker approached, or a crowd of kayakers. They stalled in the slower water and waited for the surfer to sit on the bank, then fed themselves down the fast concrete race.

"It's busy here," a surfer called Fabian said. He had brown, curly hair, a square jaw, and direct brown eyes.

"It's a whole scene," I said.

"*Total*,"[1] he said in German. "I was in Morocco earlier this year and

---

[1] "Totally."

I met some people from Germany who told me about the Eisbach. It's famous. People know about it everywhere."

We watched a massive bough from one of the lush overhanging trees upriver come unstuck and amble toward us, like a woolly mammoth or a great, dead shaggy dog. On its way down the slope of water it picked up speed. Marion was on the wave and before the branch came too close she laid flat on her board and allowed the whitewater to wash her downstream.

"Isn't there river surfing in California?" Fabian asked.

Interesting question. "Not that I know of."

"Have you been to Sylt?"

"Not yet," I said.

"That's for longboarding."

Sylt is an island, a windswept finger of German sand near the Danish border. It is also the heartland of German surfing. The history of the sport here goes back to the '50s, when Uwe Drath, a lifeguard on Sylt, first stood up on his rescue board. Drath was possibly the first person to surf on his feet in continental Europe, not that he realized it at the time.

To ride the Flosslände wave you face away from the concrete bridge, up the long green pane of water streaming under your board. At first I kept washing back into a lake where you had to paddle out of the rushing canal water into an eddy and climb a slick muddy trail through the trees. But it was easier to master than the Eisbach. The glassy insistent current flowed like a treadmill. You had to lean into it, push and turn, to keep from being swept downstream. "I think it's harder to learn than ocean surfing," a local named Karsten Mohr told me later. "But it goes faster because you can climb back in every time you fall. You don't have to wait around for a wave."

A freckled blonde woman standing by the oak said she'd learned to surf in California when she'd worked as an au pair. Her name was Eliza. East German by birth, from Dresden. Her family had moved to Munich after the wall fell in 1989, when Eliza was ten. This raised an interesting question. East German families used to travel behind the Iron Curtain for the holidays, so I ran through the likely Eastern bloc coastlines—Russia, Estonia, southern Yugoslavia—and asked an obvious question.

"If the wall hadn't come down," I said, "you wouldn't have been a surfer."

She made a face.

"*Maybe*," she said. "But maybe somewhere else. In any case not here in Munich."

Russia, Poland, most of the Baltic states, even East Germany had surf-exposed shores. China and Vietnam and Cuba would have had good surf, but no equipment. Planned economies rarely bothered with surfboards, at least during the Cold War.

Norbert Süss was born in East Germany and learned to windsurf on its shorelines and lakes. He used to organize contests as a *Klassenobmann* (local chairman) for the Communist party in Cottbus, which isn't far from Berlin. "I don't know of any [wave] surfers in East Germany," he told me later, though some good waves roll up against the Baltic Sea coast. "I don't want to say there were no surfers, because we did all sorts of things. But in East Germany it was illegal to use a sailboard on the Baltic Sea coast because of the risk of escape, even if that sounds absurd. The biggest thing you could use in the water was an air mattress.

"Once I tried to go diving in a wetsuit [in the Baltic]. A boat came and intercepted me.

"There was one place on the Baltic where we could windsurf—Thiessow, on Rügen Island. A good wave broke there through the Bay of Greifswald." These are dark, northern maritime names. "But we were all windsurfers. . . . Our sailboards were too heavy to ride waves. After the wall fell I did try to surf with a smaller board, once, but not with much success. In any case, when we packed our Trabants full of gear and set out from Lausitz we only had wind in mind."

In November 1986, an electrician named Karsten Klünder set out from East Berlin with his buddy Dirk Deckert in a two-stroke Trabant with homemade sailboards strapped to the roof. They drove to Rügen Island, where in the summer the beaches would have thronged with naked Communists. From a frigid beach campground they set sail. "We just hoped the radar wouldn't see us," said Klünder. They lost sight of each other in the gray murk and choppy surf; Klünder saw only the bobbing shine of a flashlight behind him. At one point, he said to a German newspaper, "A Soviet freighter came very close to me" so he lay flat in the water and hoped the sailors wouldn't try to rescue him.

After four and a half hours he arrived on the coast of Denmark. Two fishermen brought him to Klintholm, a small harbor town on Møn Island that had seen a number of damp East German defectors but never anyone crazy enough to sail across on a board. The next day his friend Dirk arrived; he'd turned back temporarily because of a problem with his wetsuit. They met again in Giessen, where the West Germans processed them for citizenship. Klünder remembered the sign off the coast of Møn that welcomed him to the free world: NO WINDSURFING.

Gregor Kollmar was an acid-tongued friend of mine who wore wire-rimmed glasses and almost never smiled. He was an artist with a finely tuned aesthetic sense and an ashen sense of humor. He had the subversive grit of a Brecht narrator, a sarcastic son of a bitch raised on beer and kraut. I thought of him as a typical Berliner, but his home was Munich, and he liked to surf.

Gregor introduced me to surfing in Europe simply by loaning me his board. He made a big production of bringing it to the Spiegel Online office in Berlin, where I worked, and where the sight of a surfboard attracted the joking attention of the newsroom.

"I think Munich is a long way to go to surf," one reporter said. "Why don't you surf in the Spree?"

"Very funny."

"They have a wave pool in Bad Tölz," someone else recommended. But wave pools are creepy to me.

"You're too tall for this board," Gregor chided me. "You should have brought a board from California."

"I didn't know there was surf in Germany!"

"Well, the waves in Munich aren't very big. Don't come back and say, 'Gregor, why was that wave so small?' I promise you will be unimpressed."

I have relatives in Germany and Holland, deep roots on my mother's side, but no one had ever mentioned the existence of surfing in either Munich or Sylt. (They claim they didn't know.) Even worse, from my point of view, two surfers I met in Indonesia never mentioned it. One morning in the water on Grupuk Bay, waiting for a wave, I heard two strangers speaking German. Until that moment I had assumed that a surf break on the far side of an inlet near the southern tip of a remote, impoverished Muslim island might be counted on to be free of central Europeans.

"Where are you from?" I asked in English.

"We are from Munich."

Amazing, I thought. What were two guys from Munich doing in the water?

I switched to German. "And where did you learn to surf?" I asked, thinking I was about to learn that the North Sea coast had a number of unsung breaks (which it does).

"On Bali."

"Oh."

They looked at me quizzically. "Where are you from?"

"California."

Still with the quizzical looks.

"—and where did you learn to speak German?" they said.

Anyway, surfing was difficult for Gregor because he had diabetes. Poor circulation made his feet numb; his eyesight was bad. But he loved to be in the water, and he maintained a deliberate distance from even his best friends because of the disease, a distance that surfing would have lessened. It's a terrific sport for loners. After he died, his friend Charlie, a colleague at Spiegel Online, showed me a picture of Gregor standing alone on a rock, holding his board, looking out at the ocean in front of some high New Zealand cliffs. "He really liked that picture," Charlie's wife Jutka said. "He was really attached to water, that's for sure. Water was his element."

The contest in Munich started under a high, hot July sun, with people sunbathing or barbecuing in the meadow beside the Flosslände canal. Several hundred spectators—shirtless men in sunglasses, women in bikinis—stood on the banks to watch about fifty surfers, men and women and teenagers, take turns trying to impress a panel of judges. The best surfers were flashy, hotdog amateurs who tore up the glassy wave with the impatience of pros. Judges sat under a tent, rating them on tricks and style. A Humvee beside them blasted music (reggae, Red Hot Chili Peppers), and a TV broadcaster from Eurosport gave glib patter in German.

"Philipp, from Düsseldorf, one of the style masters here today."

Or another surfer, whose name I didn't catch: "Thirty-three years young, he's a regular-foot and the only Austrian here today."

At least one contestant rode a longboard, a tall man called Matthias with a mischievous smile and an elegant, light-footed style. He trotted up and down on the board to keep it in place on the wave. He could even hang five (drop the toes of one foot over the nose)—a showoff maneuver from the '50s.

"Okay, now the boys are done," said the announcer, "and the girls are about to start."

Laura Mohr was a slim, long-haired teenager with a sure but tentative style. She surfed well and wound up in most photographs from that afternoon. She was also Karsten Mohr's daughter—Karsten Mohr the contest organizer, a fifty-odd-year-old guy with thin, black hair and an athletic build. He stood next to me for a while on the bank. He had stories similar to Steffen Dittrich's about Munich police in the '70s. "We'd surf at the Eisbach with ropes," he said, "and we'd dig holes behind the shrubs for our equipment. When our lookout guy whistled, we'd climb out of the water and hide all our gear behind the bushes, then lie down on our boards and pretend to sunbathe."

Laura finished and went to sit on the grass. She was self-critical about her performance. "I don't think I'll win. At least two of the girls were better than me. I wish I'd gotten a few more tricks in." She had a slight Bavarian accent.

Why did she like surfing?

"You just forget everything," she said. "You have this feeling of freedom."

A few days earlier an Australian tourist trying to swim in the Eisbach had knocked his head on the concrete bottom and drowned. A swirling current had held him under. The surfers all discussed it because the city had drained the canal to find his body; for several days there had been no wave at the Haus der Kunst. Karsten was worried. If these accidents kept happening, Munich might stop tolerating surfers. But there was only so much a government could do, he said. "They can fence off the Alps, they can fence off all our public pools . . . " He shook his head. "I mean, people drown in public pools every year."

The paradox of surfing in Munich is that it's a grassroots movement of the *Volk,* against Bavarian officialdom, to make room for something decidedly un-German. Which doesn't mean the surfers want to be American, Australian, or Polynesian. On the contrary. They've seen enough outsiders get drunk in their beer tents. ("It gets bad around Oktoberfest," said another woman who surfed in the contest, Eliza Weber. "All these Americans and Australians stay in the campground over there, 'cause it's cheap. Then they see the wave here and want to try it out.") At first glance the contest in Munich did look like a bunch of Germans trying to pretend they were in Hawaii or California, and except for the landlocked heat and freshwater smells, the Munich Riversurf Open was not so different from a small-surf contest in Malibu or Huntington Beach. But every now and then the contest had to stop for a massive, sodden raft loaded with bratwurst grills and an oompah band. The rafts drifted lazily down the flat canal and then plunged through the rapid, with tourists aboard hollering. The surfers jeered back. More than once the deejay switched the blaring contest music to a goofy song called "Käsebrot" ("Cheese Sandwich"):

> *Käsebrot*
> *Ist ein gutes Brot*
> *Super sexy Käsebrot*

One raft had an oompah band playing—God help me—"Volare," on French horns and accordions. It splashed through the wave, and minutes later I found a young surfer on the bank with a soaked pretzel in one hand and a sodden hank of schnitzel in the other.

"One thing about those rafts," he said. "They have good food."

I blinked. "Did you swim out there to cop that schnitzel?"

"Of course," he said. And it was hard to deny that the Bavarians were on to something new.

~~~~~~~~~~~~~~~~~

The Sylt Shuttle is a freight train built to move cars, with their drivers, from the mainland of northern Germany to the remote strip of marram grass and sand called Sylt. The train rolls first through a rural Frisian landscape of glowering skies and horses spooked by the wind. Then the land narrows, and tidal flats the color of nickel stretch away like deserts of salt mud. At high tide this is the North Sea. Sylt has the shape of a spindly mushroom cut sideways, with the top of the mushroom facing the ocean. The stalk is linked to the rest of Schleswig-Holstein by a causeway called the Hindenburgdamm, built in 1927 and just wide enough for a railroad.

It's a Nordic Martha's Vineyard, expensive and chic, but also raw and beautiful. Sylt was a fancy resort island even before the railroad crossed the sea, and long before the Nazi government promoted it as a spot for jaunty young Germans to refresh themselves. "Beach games and athletic activities of all kinds—in particular the old Teutonic art of archery," reads one Nazi-era pamphlet for Sylt, "will reawaken your joy of living."

Germany's first nude beach opened here in 1920. Some people still strip naked and swim in the freezing water all year long, but famously on Christmas Day, some of the nudists wear Santa hats. Uwe Drath was a young lifeguard here in the '50s, when British troops occupied the island and houses were still heated with coal. Lifeguards watched swimmers from little booths equipped with wagon wheels, which they rolled over wooden planks to the waterline every morning. One summer the lifeguard service supplemented the standard rowboats with massive rescue boards more than twelve feet long, painted yellow and green.

"They were *very* heavy," Drath told me. "No fins, no curve in the nose, nothing. They were built to just lie on. We got these boards, and I immediately thought of pictures I had seen from Hawaii. We had seen these pictures of how they rode their big boards in the water. And I thought, 'I can try that.' And that's how it started. As soon as we got those boards, I tried it."

Like other early surfers, he had no wax. Without a fin he couldn't angle on the wave. But he learned to stand on the board and ride white-wash into the beach. "Ach, it was a sublime feeling, when you slid down a wave like that," he said. "A sublime feeling. We didn't call it 'surfing,' you know. We called it 'wave riding.'"

The difference between *Surfen* and *Wellenreiten* still confuses Germans. Windsurfing was such a popular German sport in the 1970s and '80s—spreading down from the windy beaches of Sylt to lakes across both East and West Germany—that "Surfen" became the everyday word for riding a wind-propelled board. Now wave riding has seen a German renaissance, so the meaning of "Surfen" has blurred.

On my first visit to Sylt I went out in wild pre-storm surf between two *Buhnen*, or remnants of wooden jetties, north of Westerland, the main town. The sky was iron gray, and the wind was so stiff it kept sea foam from returning with the water. The froth would slide up at the end of every wave and remain on the beach while the rest of the wave slid back. This foam piled up in yellowish banks along the tide line. Sometimes little frothy chunks would break off and scurry like tumble-weeds over the beach.

I paddled into the storm chop and tried to sit still in the rocking waves. The bobbing whitecaps had faces as tall as the true waves, and their crests broke over my head, one after another, like eggs in a comedy routine. Then the wind half froze my hair and blew through my ears until I had an ice cream headache. Sometimes as I paddled over a wave I had my board nearly blown out from under my chest. People stopped on the beach to watch. A seagull hovered over me for a while, like the albatross attending the ship in *The Rime of the Ancient Mariner*. The small, junky surf peaked in different places along the sand, but now and then a clean face opened up, a burnished curving section of metallic water that gave my board a thrilling burst of speed.

***

That was off-season. When I returned to Berlin, I offered to give Gregor back his surfboard. He said I should keep it. I mentioned this to Charlie one day over lunch.

"I never expected a gift," I complained.

Charlie chewed his food and seemed to think.

"Well," he said, "Gregor's been unloading things on people because he's decided not to live with kidney dialysis. His kidneys are failing. The doctors give him about six more months."

"Jesus," I said.

"Don't tell him I told you."

"I had no idea."

"He's known for a while."

Gregor was thirty-seven. The kidney problem had snuck up on him slowly, but another long illness in his twenties had kept him in and out of hospitals for two or three years. He'd resolved never to live again with regular mechanical intervention, and dialysis requires about five hours on the machine every two days. "He's basically spent so much time in hospitals that he doesn't want his life to depend on that anymore," Charlie said.

Wariness about his health was one reason for the distances in Gregor's character. But when the kidney problem started to wear him down, he seemed to second-guess his strategy. "He kind of boxed himself in with his own logic," Charlie said. The stream of visitors to his bedside may have depressed him. After my trip to Morocco I called Gregor to show him pictures of his board on a beach with a camel. He sounded weak and short of breath.

"They've put me on some new drugs," he said hazily. "Why don't you just call tomorrow morning or on Friday and we'll see how I feel?"

I called the next morning and left my number with a messaging service. The next day, a Friday, I called Charlie. How was Gregor doing; did he think I could visit him in Spandau (which is just outside Berlin)?

"Spandau? He's not there anymore," Charlie said. "He's at a *Palliativklinik* in Munich. That's where I am now."

"You're kidding."

"He's not doing so hot. He's not responding to his drugs."

"How long has he been there?"

"Since Wednesday morning."

When your kidneys fail, there can be two major consequences for the body. One is a buildup of cadmium, which makes your muscles twitch. Gregor had that. The other is a buildup of water in the lungs. Gregor had that, too. The drugs in the *Palliativklinik* were meant to stem this horrible tide. But on Saturday after I talked to Charlie, the nurses noticed Gregor was having more trouble breathing. To comfort him they put him on morphine. He lasted into the night, according to Charlie. They put him on an increasing dose and Gregor died in his sleep, peacefully, having drowned in his own lungs.

♪♪♪♪♪♪♪♪♪♪♪♪♪♪♪

When I returned to Sylt for the high season, I had not just Gregor's board but also a seven-foot board covered in epoxy that had wide rails and a generous scoop in the nose. It was lightweight and all-purpose, a good board to travel with. I'd felt lucky to find it. Berlin has a handful of "board shops" with surf and snowboard equipment, but the selection of real surfboards is as small as you'd expect from a metropolis near Poland.

I was back in Sylt for its annual Longboard Festival. The organizer, Sven Behrens, had invited me to compete. The weather was windy but clear, a brilliant Indian summer, but since it was tourist season I had to buy a "beach pass." This was new to me; I'd never in my life paid an admission fee just to surf. A long dune separated the beaches on Sylt from the rest of the island, and little guard shacks were posted at each dune crossing. I suppose it would have been possible to charge through the thick marram grass at some wild point between the shacks, but I decided to observe the law. I presented ID, proof of a local vacation rental, and a fistful of euros to a lady in the shack. When everything was registered, stamped, and signed I received a green pass that was valid at any entrance along the defensive dune and had to be kept in my wallet.

The *Kurtax*, as the beach fee was called, paid for maintenance. And the Sylt beaches were swept and clean. A neat wooden boardwalk clung to the long dune and you could stroll there and watch Germans relaxing in *Strandkörbe*, covered wicker beach baskets that dot the sand all along the northern European coast. The sun in these latitudes is never fierce—it's pale and milky white—but Germans have a horror of sunburns, so they sit in these baskets with legs up on footstools and white cream slathered on their bellies and thighs. They let the breeze blow through their toes and sleep while the sun gently fries unprotected patches of skin. Then they wake up, complain about sunburn, and spend the rest of their vacation behind a glass wind-break in a clifftop seafood restaurant, feasting on lobster and wine.

On the morning of the contest I got up early, drove to the relevant parking lot, and started a long hike through grassy dunes to the Behrens' family restaurant, Buhne 16. I hiked for twenty minutes, showed my beach pass at the guard shack, and crested the final hill, expecting to see surfers in the water for the early heats—judges in bleachers, boards in the sand. But it was flat as a pond. The only waves in the deep blue water were, literally, ankle-high ripples. Wind blew through the marram grass, and the beach reminded me that one source of the name "Sylt" was an ancient German word, *Silendi,* which means "forsaken country."

The Behrens family ran a beachside café with tables and plexiglass windows around the wooden terrace. No other buildings existed here; it was an outpost. A man setting up tables said the contest had ended. "They finished the heats yesterday because the swell died. But people will show up today for the award ceremony, so we might play soccer."

He gestured out at the sand at a pair of goalposts.

So much for the contest. I decided to order breakfast.

The day wouldn't be a total wash, since the Behrens family went back a long way on Sylt. Sven had wire-framed glasses, light mutton chops, and blond-brown hair. He was about forty years old and seemed to be in charge of the café; his aging father and uncles constituted Germany's first generation of surf brats, the boys who got excited in the '50s at the sight of Uwe Drath walking in the surf.

Drath lived down in Westerland and rarely bothered with the teeming enthusiasts up here at Buhne 16. But Uwe Behrens, Sven's father, was a man of the people. He hung around the café in a sweatshirt, jeans, and a frayed baseball cap, walking with his shoulders hunched and his hands in his pockets. I talked to him in the café's rear office, where a broad window overlooked the water. It was a gray, Spartan, lived-in space with the feel of a bridge on a ship. An older man with fleshy lips and glasses—Uwe's brother—sat silently at one end of the table.

"When we were young, ten or twelve years old," said Uwe, "we would steal the rescue boards whenever the lifeguards got off work. They were big boards, four meters long and very dangerous. But we didn't know about real surfing; we didn't know it existed. We may have seen pictures of old Hawaiians standing on their boards, but we knew nothing about the modern sport."

The transformation came in the early '60s, when Uwe and his brothers found a *Reader's Digest* photo of a surfer on a large Hawaiian wave. "We thought, 'Hui! They do it like professionals there.' In 1962 I ordered a board from Michel Barland," a shaper in France, "and that was the first true surfboard on Sylt. A couple of years later we started a surf club and ordered about ten more boards."

The club consisted of Uwe, his brothers, and a few other boys who used a small house in a town called Tinnum as a private theater for Super 8 surf movies, a storeroom for equipment, or a place for parties. The house had once been a cow stall.

"That was a great club," said his brother.

"It was only surfers," said Uwe. "About twenty of us."

"But with everyone else around, it was maybe fifty," his brother said.

"For two years we tried to surf without wax," Uwe went on. "It didn't work very well. We had one member who covered his board in fresh paint and then threw sand on it [for traction]. Then we took a road trip to Biarritz in '64 and saw that surfers put wax on their boards."

But surfing remained a fringe sport because of the frigid water. In the 1960s and '70s the Behrens brothers and their friends used thick, heavy dive suits and crude rubber leashes. "In about 1972 I ordered twelve O'Neill wetsuits from California," said Uwe, "and those were our first real wetsuits. A year later Jack O'Neill came to visit. He wanted to know who was buying his suits in this part of the world. It was October '72 or '73. We had an amazing swell. I didn't want to go out, it was too cold. But he took my board, and he was very excited. He said the water was warm. Northern California must have cold water."

Uwe lit a pipe and inspected boats in the distance with a pair of binoculars. He had a guarded, unsmiling, laconic manner. It was cold but not unfriendly.

"Is that the Greenpeace ship?" said Uwe's brother.

Greenpeace had been dropping boulders in the water to create an artificial reef and keep dragnet fishermen from decimating the local fish population.

"No," Uwe said after a while. "But I think it's good, what Greenpeace is doing."

There was a comfortable silence. I asked his brother for his name. With old-fashioned reticence and a faint smile, he said, "Behrens."

"We're all called Behrens here," Uwe said.

The surf community on Sylt was now just a larger version of that early club in Tinnum. Many of its members would show up at the award ceremony that day to watch the contest winners get larded with trophies and prizes. The same people would assemble later in the weekend to watch a film about German surfing in one of the main cinemas in the center of Westerland. The venue had moved to an upmarket location compared to the cow stall, and the group consisted of several hundred surfers rather than fifty, but the essence of wave riding on this odd little island was still a matter of stoked individuals forming a familylike club.

Later I talked to Dieter Behrens, a mild-voiced old man with a curling white mustache. He'd founded the Buhne 16 café as a lunch kiosk; he'd also worked as a stonemason and a windsurfing instructor. "I'm the one who first saw that picture in *Reader's Digest*," he boasted. "And then I drove with my friends to surf in Biarritz. We'd heard the waves were good in France, so we packed up tents and sleeping bags in my Mercedes and just left. It took three days to get there. In those days, flying was like going to the moon. We spent six weeks surfing."

He had a remarkably gentle voice, with no hint of swagger or slang.

"We didn't get to know many French surfers, except for Michel Barland, because they tended to get along with English-speaking surfers who came over from Jersey [in the English Channel] or from California. We were a little isolated." The war had been over for only twenty years, and Germans were mistrusted—Dieter implied this rather than said it. "But it was a beautiful, carefree time—*eine unbelastene Zeit*," he said. "You could have a liter of milk, a baguette, some fresh cheese, and the day was fine. Everything was that simple."

Surfing, like Sylt itself, represented an eccentric and carefree lifestyle for some Germans after the war. Jens Körner fell in love with Sylt as a young soldier from Hamburg in 1964. When he became a lifeguard the following year, he started to surf with the Behrens brothers. Körner told me this on the deck of the café that night, after the award ceremony. People and dogs milled around; his large face flamed with wine. He was expansive and generous with his stories, and he spoke with the energy of a man who had made a bundle of money and felt no shame about the glamour of Sylt. "Back then it was a kind of *Gründerzeit*," he explained, a foundational time for postwar Germany, "when people who are powerful now were here as young people. I learned to surf in 1965 and here you could have drinks afterwards with Günter Sachs or Rudolf Augstein." Sachs was the millionaire playboy and mathematician who married Brigitte Bardot in the '60s; Augstein had founded *Der Spiegel*. Germany's Economic Miracle was in full swing, and Sylt was like the Hamptons. "For me in my twenties they were perhaps older men, but we could play soccer on the beach and address one another as *Du*. It was glamour, yes— but only glamour for Germany. As surfers we had no stars, no Miki Doras. We didn't even have wetsuits! So when we went to France, we thought the water was warm! Hahahahah. We didn't have surf shorts, we just wore bathing suits—Speedos!—so the French and Californians looked at us and said, 'Where are *you* from?'" He lapsed into English, with an exaggerated accent. "'Oh, ve are from Chermany.' Hahahahah."

Körner talked about Uwe Drath as a godfather figure for surfers, remote and feared. "He was known as a good waterman. I never worked with him, but I think it wasn't all that nice for people who worked under him in Westerland. I never saw him surf, that was before my time. But boys always tried to steal our rescue boards when I was a lifeguard, too. Including Jürgen Hönscheid. He was ten years younger."

Hönscheid became a hot young surfer on Sylt as well as a famous sailboarder. His career took him far from home, to the Canary Islands, where he now shapes boards at his own shop on Fuerteventura and raises a family, a whole crowd of sun-bleached blond Germans living the perennial northern dream of life on a breezy tropical island, washing waves, and endless days of sun.

It's conventional surf wisdom that the first pioneers in continental Europe[2] climbed to their feet in 1956, starting with Peter Viertel, a German-born novelist and screenwriter from southern California who paddled out in France. Viertel was a friend of Hemingway's. Darryl F. Zanuck, the producer, had hired him to write the script for *The Sun Also Rises*. Viertel didn't surf—yet—but he knew a good wave when he saw it, and on location in Biarritz he wrote to Zanuck's son Dickie in Hollywood that the surf looked promising. Dickie answered that he would smuggle a board into crates of film equipment bound for France. "He promised that on our way back from the location he would introduce me to a sport that 'would keep me away from the typewriter' for much of my spare time," writes Viertel in his

---

[2] The United Kingdom, as usual in Europe, is an exception.

memoir of the '50s, "a prophecy that turned out to be alarmingly accurate."

In the end, Dickie couldn't stay in Europe long enough to surf, but the longboard wound up in Viertel's Biarritz hotel. He paddled out alone.

> I soon discovered that surfing was a sport that would require some expert instruction, and after losing my board on my first few attempts to catch a wave, I was ordered out of the water by the lifeguards who said I was a danger to the other bathers. Somewhat discouraged, I retired to the side of the hotel pool, where a number of my acquaintances had been watching what they considered to be my attempts to drown myself in the Bay of Biscay.

This unpromising start let Viertel go down in history as the first man to ride a true surfboard in France, though he wasn't the first to stand. That honor belongs to George Hennebutte, a local who patched up Viertel's damaged board and paddled out the next day.

The French had been closing in on true surfing for years, and their early attempts remind me of those jerky films of stumbling, albatross-like flying machines built before the Wright Brothers. By the 1950s, bodyboards called *plankys* were normal equipment on the French seaside. In '52 a planky shaper called Jacky Rott had tried to shape a board based on a few seconds of surf footage in a documentary on Pearl Harbor. The film failed to clue Rott in to the exigencies of surf wax or a stabilizing fin. He built a slick, heavy *planky long,* which he failed to master. When he tried to stand up, according to Antony Colas, author of *The World Stormrider Guide,* "the board knocked out one of his friends and split when it was dashed upon the rocks."

Hennebutte, Viertel, another Frenchman called Joël de Rosnay, and eventually Jacky Rott and Michel Barland formed the hard core of the early surfers in France. They've entered the pantheon, and France is now the epicenter of European surfing, with the continent's longest Atlantic-facing shore. Talking about the sport there is like talking about the sport in northern California. Of course it exists! *Bien sûr.* Slightly out of the way, perhaps, but the surfers are serious and the origin myths are sacred.

But I had a hunch that Uwe Drath had beaten Viertel and Hennebutte and de Rosnay by a couple of years. Drath was easy to find on Sylt. He lived in a brick house near the center of Westerland. He had a strong jaw lengthened by slack jowls and gray hair that had once been blond and full. At eighty years old, he was still broad-shouldered. One finger, when you shook his right hand, was a stump.

He talked to me in a sunny enclosed patio with his son Sven, a surfer who worked as a paramedic. Sven mentioned a controversy on a French Web site. "My friend wrote on this site that my father was one of the first people to stand up on a rescue board in the early '50s, that he was a lifeguard on Sylt, and there was a giant outcry—the French surfers stirred up a tremendous commotion because they assumed it was a joke. They even kicked him off the message board. They insisted it was the French who first rode a surfboard in Europe, which of course is total nonsense."

"When did you first ride a rescue board?" I asked his father.

"It was 1952 or '53," he said. "No later than '54. When they first introduced the boards on the beaches here. I don't say I was the first surfer on the continent, because I don't know about that, but I was the first surfer on Sylt."

"The first in Germany?" I said.

"I'm not sure, but the question is where else would it have happened? When you go further south, there are almost no waves."

Waves roll against Sylt from the north, past Denmark and across Europe's broad northern continental shelf. By the time they reach the other Frisian Islands, to the south, they lose force. In that sense Sylt isn't a German surf spot so much as a far-southern Danish break. But surfing didn't start in Denmark until the '80s, and no one has claimed to surf German waves before Drath.

Uwe Behrens insisted the year was 1952. He remembers being twelve. The German Lifeguard Association (DLRG) says it introduced rescue boards in 1953. Either way it seems Uwe Drath unwittingly became the first modern surfer in continental Europe when he stood up on his board.

Talking to Drath was bracing because you had to meet his tremendous flow of energy with a force of your own. There was no easy, quiet, casual talking with Uwe Drath. He had no time for nonsense. I've noticed the same relentless energy in a lot of Germans from his generation, who had seen part of the war. It was an energy required for what at least one Thomas Mann character calls *Selbstüberwindung,* self-conquest. (Germany's war generation had a lot to overcome.) Sylt had been a military stronghold, and everyone on the island had fought in the war. As Germany's northernmost crop of land it was both a naval station and a line of defense against Allied bombers from Britain. "It was like a fort," said Drath. "Outsiders weren't allowed on the island. Almost every dune had an antiaircraft gun. I was in the service as a gunner. I was drafted at sixteen," in 1943. "The British troops, afterward, were kind," he said. "We helped them rebuild, and lay sandbags and so on."

He was frank about it, but not detailed. Even if he'd gone to war with patriotic feelings as a teenager, his character had been shaped by the defeat. He had a Sylt postcard from the 1960s bearing a photo of himself as a young surfer, balancing on a wave, a black-and-white image kitschily framed in the shape of an early TV screen. *Germany's modern too!* the card seemed to say. *Germany can keep up!* Even in the '60s Drath belonged to Sylt's image of itself, and surfing on a German beach was a small expression of *die neue Zeit,* the shift from Hitler's nightmare and the long shadow of the nineteenth century to an outlook that was more spontaneous, easygoing, modern, and rich. The *Fun-Gesellschaft* had begun.

"Remember, we had no wetsuits!" Drath said. "My God, we froze! We surfed in the fall, not in the winter, but my *God,* we froze." Yet in those days, more people on Sylt went swimming. "You see that on television, the difference between then and now. Bathing, I mean the number of people who go into the water now—that has fallen off."

"Why?" I said.

Father and son, in unison, said,

"Central heating."

"Central heating."

"People were *much* tougher back then," explained Uwe Drath.

4

MOROCCO:
KILROY WAS HERE

·············Pierre Chalaud and Abboud "Mamoune" Kabbour, Morocco, 1967

TAGHAZOUT WAS ONCE a fishing village, like the other shambling villages along the coast, but now it rises in a sudden busy pile of smart orange buildings on the road between Essaouira and Agadir in organized tours, the southernmost resort city in Morocco. French ladies go to Agadir in organized tours; hippies and surf cowboys go to Taghazout. When I was there it felt like an Islamic frontier town. Watchful men waited on the sidewalks wearing djellabas, hooded like druids. Dogs curled up in the dust under cars. Garish signs advertised surf shops and Coca-Cola, and even the mosque had a green neon moon. Parking "attendants" in bright vests made sure you parked your car well, then charged you for a worn paper ticket. The tickets were worthless; the money was just an organized tip. But the attendants watched your car at night.

Djellabas are heavy woolen robes with peaked hoods meant to keep out cold as well as the desert sun. Roman soldiers learned to wear them when they occupied North Africa after the fall of Carthage. The Romans brought some back to Europe, where they (supposedly) metamorphosed into monks' robes. But the local Berber tribesmen as well as Roman legionnaires wore them as coarse field garments that doubled as sleeping bags. "Whenever you see someone in a djellaba," a Moroccan restaurant owner told me later in the trip, "you see a lazy person. He's like walking around in a sleeping bag."

I had no place to stay in Taghazout. Asking at the surf shop brought me to Salem (Sah-LEM), a toothy, rangy guy who showed me a cheap eagle's nest at the top of a run-down home. The price was 150 dirhams, just over fifteen dollars. Expensive for this part of Morocco. When I haggled he sat me down at a table on his boxlike balcony and poured two glasses of tea. Soon a small wrinkled man in a brown robe and a white pillbox peci cap shook hands with me delicately and sat down to discuss the price. He was Salem's grandfather. He might accept one hundred dirhams if I stayed a week, he said, but for only a couple of nights, you understand . . .

He left after some polite conversation. Salem gave me the keys, and offered to sell me hash.

Morocco, like Indonesia, has been called the California of Islam. But Morocco felt instantly more varied and tense. It's an Arab society, on the surface; it's a kingdom with a weak democracy. The teeming human crush on the streets of Marrakech could populate almost any city in the Middle East. Indonesians vote for president and speak no word of Dutch; Moroccans have a monarch, still speak French, and find themselves regulated by absurd gendarmes in jaunty caps.

One gendarme had pulled me over. I'd been in the country for half an hour, making good time along the outskirts of Agadir, when a man in uniform stepped off the center divider and pointed at my car. I had a sudden choice: I could run the gendarme down, or pull to the side of the road.

He was a fleshy, smarmy man with a trimmed mustache. He had a blue uniform straight from *Babar*—stiff smart cap, white leather cuffs. His mustache bristled.

"*Vos papiers!*" he said.

With great confidence he insisted I had been driving seventy kilometers per hour. Did I realize this was a sixty-kilometer zone?

"How do you know how fast I was going?"

He ignored the question and flipped through a notebook to show me a page with an intimidating figure in bold print: 400 DIRHAM. That was my fine for driving ten kilometers over the speed limit. Forty bucks cash.

"Where's your radar gun?" I said.

He smiled.

"I don't think I was doing seventy," I pursued.

"What is your profession?" he said.

I wasn't in Morocco as a journalist, officially. You need a pass for that. If I said "journalist," I would have to be accounted for. So I said, "I'm a writer," and he laughed. He told his partner, who had wandered over, "*Il est écrivain,*" and they both had a good chuckle.

They discussed my case. Finally the gendarme handed back my German passport. "You're okay," he said. "You're German? You look like Michael Ballack."

Michael Ballack is a German soccer star with tousled black hair who can be found on posters in the bedrooms of teenagers around the world. He's so famous in Europe that his mother's midwife had once been interviewed on German TV for her opinion about a World Cup match. It was a silly thing to say. I look nothing like Michael Ballack, and never hope to. But I accepted the gendarme's logic and kept moving.

<hr />

"You like your room?" Salem said. "Sit down, my friend. Have some tea."

My room had a mattress and blankets damp with the ocean air, a lightbulb, and a magnificent view of the water. The door was flimsy. At first I wondered if my things would be safe. The run-down building seemed to be an unofficial center of town; Salem knew everyone in Taghazout by name. His friends came and went through the house while he sat on the balcony drinking tea, listening to reggae, and watching life unfold in the street.

The view from the house made up for the damp room. The dusty main street through Taghazout was also the coastal highway, and on the other side, the smart apricot-colored apartments piled up for an ocean view. But even their satellite dishes couldn't obscure the solid blue slab of the sea.

I drank tea with Salem and watched the town. Opposite his balcony a pizza place called Le Spot was outfitted for Westerners, with a sign on the upstairs terrace offering SNACK and PETIT-DEJ. A neon phone clung to the side of the building. The sun was yellow and warm. Now and then Salem yelled to people in the street.

"Some people have TV," he said with a crooked smile. "I have this."

The waves were big right now, he said. It was December, surf season. Business was brisk. I asked if tourists also came through Taghazout in the summer, but he waved dismissively.

"French," he said. Bourgeois tourists being marginal to his specific line of work.

Salem had moved to Taghazout from the Atlas Mountains years ago. For a while he'd worked as a fisherman. It was a job for footloose men, like driving a taxi. Now most of his family lived here, which explained why he knew so much of the town. He was set up with a good, steady job now.

"What job?" I said, since he didn't seem to be busy.

"This hotel."

"Ah."

"Allahu Akbar!" somebody shouted at us, and Salem stood up and laughed. An American with a scraggly beard and a floppy fishing hat walked up with a camera tripod on his shoulder. Salem, who identified his hotel guests by where they lived, said he was "Swedish." (I was "German.") He came to sit at our table, full of enthusiasm. He produced a cell phone and pretended to call Osama bin Laden. "Osama?" he said in a loud, harsh voice. "Yeah, it's Gary. Listen, Salem says don't come out today. Nah, the surf's flat."

Salem bared his crooked teeth. "Swedish, he crazy," he said.

Gary was an amateur photographer who had lived in Los Angeles but emigrated years ago to build boats in Sweden. Now he ran a garden store. He called himself "a bit of an old hippie" and said his nineteen-year-old son had learned to surf, too. Between them they had five or six boards and a number of wetsuits. In Sweden. So there was a Swedish surf scene? Oh sure, Gary said. It was small and populated with hard-core (or just plain weird) surfers who didn't mind paddling through frozen water for a decent wave. But the surf was there.

"Where else do you go?"

"Norway's good," said Gary. "Belgium. But I come down here when I need sun."

We drank tea and went on watching the street. Taghazout is the surfing capital of southern Morocco. Boards from surf shops rested in racks next to stores piled with crates of oranges and dates, or near butcher shops hung with black buffalo hooves and red marbled flanks of goat. Surfing has become a main economic event. It's a caravan of foreigners with money and curious ways that local kids like to chase. Later, when I dropped into a cell-phone shop, teenagers piled around the glass counter to watch the owner swap out my SIM card. There was lots of phone dismantling and reading the French on the screens. Not very interesting; but then you could learn a lot about a stranger if you saw his phone, heard his French (or lack of it), and understood his complaints. Many kids in Morocco followed surfing for the same reasons.

"Salem, do you surf?" I said.

No, he was too busy running this hotel. Also, boards were expensive. But he wore surf T-shirts, listened to reggae and Ben Harper, and kept track of the waves and swells.

Down in the street a pack of dogs chased a car by running ahead of the front wheels, barking like mad. A few local women appeared in hijab and vanished quickly. Westerners—men and women—wore alien-looking wetsuits and left trails of water drops in the dust. The men in djellabas and pillbox caps didn't care. Surfing had invaded Taghazout, and changed it, but daily life moved on as before.

eeeeeeeeeeeeeeeeeee

When Paul Bowles wrote about Morocco in the 1950s and '60s he mentioned performers like Art Blakey and Josephine Baker. They were popular in Morocco then, and they turn up in Bowles's journalism rather than his fiction. Now jazz is almost nonexistent in Morocco. Roadside CD shops are full of rap. Bowles wouldn't have been surprised. "All over North Africa you are confronted with a mélange of the very old and the most recent," he wrote, "with no hint of anything from the intervening centuries. It is one of the great charms of the place, the fact that your today carries with it no memories of yesterday or the day before; everything that is not medieval is completely new."

Australian hippies pioneered a break north of Taghazout in the '60s called Anchor Point. The hippie trail at first wound inland from far-northern places like the Atlas Mountains and Tangier, where kef, tribal drumming, and writers like Bowles himself could be found. But when a fringe of the hippie movement discovered surfing, hash-fogged VW buses started rattling up and down the coast. In the meantime, French surfers had imprinted everyday surf culture here, so to travel in Morocco as a surfer was to hear certain odd scraps of Gallic slang (*"les kooks," "á max"*) and feel the influence of France the way you feel the presence of California in Baja.

But the first surfer in Morocco wasn't a hippie or a Frenchman. He was a US Marine stationed at Kenitra, a city north of Casablanca then called Port Lyautey. The Allies landed in northern Morocco in 1942 while the country languished under the confusing command of Vichy France. This invasion seemed monumental at the time, and the worst battles were fought by Americans who landed under the stone, cliff-built casbah at Mehdiya Plage, which happens to have a number of excellent breaks.

The name of the serviceman was lost to history, as far as I could tell. I'd started to think of him as an anonymous presence like Kilroy, the cartoon scribbled around the world by GIs. Everyone knew about him; no one knew his identity. But I wandered up the coast with the hope of learning something, and my last stop in the north would be Mehdiya Plage.

Moroccans in the '50s found Americans friendlier, overall, than their French colonial masters. GIs carried a number of exotic consumer goods, not just flour and matches and medicine to ease a period of starvation, but "perfumes, chewing-gum, cigarettes and cigars," according to a history by C. R. Pennell called *Morocco Since 1830: A History*. "Most excitingly, they brought Coca-Cola, bottles of which became prized possessions of Moroccan boys."

World War II would shift power in the world from colonial-minded Europe to the irreverent, wisecracking, business-minded United States. For a thumbnail sketch of this transformation I like the story about General Eisenhower and Britain's General Montgomery, sitting on a plane and planning the Allies' final drive to Berlin. World War II was almost over, and Montgomery thought a rush across Germany in the weeks after D-Day could capture Berlin for the West. He wanted to squeeze out Russia. (He was probably right; the cold war could have been avoided.) But Eisenhower was in charge of the Allies, and Montgomery was full of the old British style, overweening, better-knowing, superior:

> Montgomery pushed his way into the cramped cabin of the American aeroplane and began to lecture the Supreme Commander as if he was an "errant staff college pupil." Eisenhower listened for a few minutes and then leant over and patted the Englishman on the knee. "Steady Monty," he said. "You cannot talk to me like this. I am your boss."[1]

---

[1] *Faust's Metropolis: A History of Berlin*, by Alexandra Richie

The new style of world leadership would be looser, more easy-going. In a lot of cases there would *be* no boss. No one ordered people to collect Coke bottles or smoke American cigarettes. For old-school Moroccans after World War II this was the whole insidious problem. A woman called Fatima quoted in Pennell's book says her "pragmatic" Muslim father believed "our deadliest threat came not from the Western soldiers, but from their suave salesmen peddling innocent-looking products. He therefore organized a crusade against chewing-gum and Kool cigarettes. As far as he was concerned, smoking a tall, thin, white Kool cigarette was equivalent to erasing centuries of Arab culture. 'The Christians want to transform our decent Muslim households into a market place,' he would say. 'They want us to buy these poisonous products they make that have no real purpose, so that we turn into a whole nation of ruminating cattle.'"

⌇⌇⌇⌇⌇⌇⌇⌇⌇⌇⌇⌇⌇⌇⌇⌇⌇

Gary the Swede and I ate a handful of oranges for breakfast in the morning and set out for Killer Point. The waves weren't big, but the point was crowded, so we surfed at a nearby reef break called La Source. The cliffs looked like red sandstone, with layers worn into mesalike crags. The underwater reef must have been no different. When I tumbled under a wave too near the rocks, my leash looped under a long crag and for a minute I was stuck. I had to kneel on the rock and let a few waves crash on my head. The first person I thought of in this position was Mark Foo, the Hawaiian big-wave surfer who disappeared under a wave at Maverick's in 1994. Maverick's is a sometimes-massive break near Santa Cruz, and Foo died one of the most famous deaths in surfing. The story is that a wave pushed him deep underwater after a wipeout, and his leash looped around a boulder or a crag near the ocean floor. It failed to snap, and Foo was caught halfway between the rocks and the California sunshine while eighteen-foot breakers washed overhead.

I unlooped my leash and paddled out. Then Gary took a wave and spent a few minutes of his own on the reef.

"You okay?" I said when he returned.

"I got caught on the rocks over there. I started thinking about Mark Foo."

"The exact same thing happened to me," I said. "The same thoughts went through my head."

Surfers everywhere are bound by a common mythology.

"Yeah, except Foo went out in style," he said. "I didn't wanna drown in like a meter of water."

That night we had dinner on the open terrace of Le Spot. The restaurant felt casual and cheap, like a bar in Baja, with plastic patio chairs and a color TV playing endless surf videos. Taghazout's neon phone blinked on and off beside our table. But for all its easygoing style, no one could drink beer with their pizza at Le Spot, because Taghazout—like most Moroccan towns—is dry.

We sat with a group of European surfers. Everyone spoke English, but sometimes at cross-purposes, like deaf people. One of them mentioned Morocco's king, Mohammed VI, who appeared on billboards along the highway.

"He's a surfer, isn't he?" someone said.

"He rides Jet Skis."

"A friend of mine saw his entourage," said Gary. "This line of black SUVs with tinted windows hauling up the highway between Agadir and Rabat. It passes right through Taghazout, man. The cars are all identical so assassins don't know which one to bomb."

For a king, Mohammed VI was young, in his forties. His father, Hassan II, had been a remote and venerable authoritarian by the time he died in 1999, but the stout and sensitive son—with close-cut black hair, round cheeks, and natty suits—looked almost hip. He was the grandson of Mohammed V, an independence hero in the '50s and a sultan from the Alaoui tribe, which had maintained a continuous dynasty in Morocco for 350 years. The family claimed direct descent from the Prophet.

"People tried to kill his father," someone said.

"Who did?"

"I don't know, but they tried to kill him twice."

"Fundamentalists don't like him."

"Didn't al-Qaeda issue a warning about a week ago?" asked someone else. "Saying tourists in Morocco are targets?"

"That means us."

Mohammed VI seemed to think of surfing as a mild way to liberalize Morocco. He'd established a community center called the Oudayas Surf Club in Rabat. The theory, or hope, was that young Moroccans who learned to surf wouldn't radicalize. But the Oudayas club was also just the fanciest and most official manifestation of Established Surfing, in the form of surf camps, which had grown up on Morocco's Atlantic shore over the past ten years. A handful of these camps orbited Taghazout. They catered to Europeans.

But a young Dutch woman at the table was traveling Morocco the old-fashioned way, in a camper van. She had straw-blonde hair, wore a knit cap, and seemed to have discovered a hippie lifestyle with fresh enthusiasm, as if no one had ever thought of it before. "Most of the people in the Netherlands are only interested in what they can buy," she said. "They want jobs that are good for money and then a house, and then kids." She wrinkled her nose. "I don't know, I just don't think it's that interesting."

A native Swede, a kid in his twenties with a light blond beard, nodded at a table of big surfers lazing around Le Spot. To me they were clichés, surf-brand poster boys. But he said: "It's a lot different here. Wherever people really surf, you see big guys who are strong and so on."

"It's different in Sweden?"

"Yes, in Sweden most of the surfers are, like, into fly-fishing."

"What?"

"They're the same as the guys in Africa who play ice hockey. You know, eccentrics."

"What's wrong with that?"

"It's just boring," said the Swede. "In Sweden we don't have our own surf magazines. We have to get them from Germany or England or France. I want to start a real surf magazine for Sweden."

Around eleven I crossed the road back to Salem's. I found him on the balcony upstairs, sitting with a contraband bottle of anis, a candle, and the ruins of a meal. He asked me to sit. He'd been watching Taghazout run out of momentum. By eleven the day simply coasted to a stop. The noise and dust subsided and shops shut off their lights. The neon phone flicked off, and the road fell silent except for the occasional sigh of brakes on a long-distance truck. Soon the night was a matter of surf-soul music from Salem's radio and a tuneless cry from the muezzin.

"How much you think they pay for electricity in one month?" he asked, nodding at Le Spot. "Two hundred fifty dirham? Is not much. Water?" he said reflectively. "Is good business."

He talked about his family in Taghazout, and I realized that his vast connections in town made the hotel safe. I'd worried at first that the stream of strangers through the house might lead to some petty theft; but the opposite was true. His friends kept an eye on the hotel. Knowing Salem— and staying on his good side—was the way to protect your things.

"Are you a Berber?" I said.

"Yes, yes."

"How many languages do you speak?"

"Arabic—Moghrebi," he said, meaning the Arabic dialect spoken in Morocco, "Berber, French, English." Salem smiled. He had a joshing, happy, servile manner and a broad mustache. "English not so good," he said. But also not so bad.

"Just now Gary said the king drives through Taghazout sometimes with all his black cars."

"Yeah, he leans out the window, shaking hands," said Salem with a broad smile. "Is no problem."

But I had a different impression from Gary. "Is he a good king?" I asked.

"Is good, yes."

He lit a cigarette and sat with one arm crooked over the balcony wall. Le Spot had been around for only three years, he said; the town had changed completely in six. Before 2000 or 2001, there had been no easy surf tourism, no multistory apartment houses stretching for ocean views.

"Just fishermen and hippie surfers," I said.

"Yeah."

"What changed?"

"Six years now we have many surf schools in Taghazout."

"Ah."

Investors had noticed the town, too. Within three years everything on the opposite side of the road, including Le Spot, would be "broken"— demolished for a resort. "Saudi money, American money," Salem said. Even his hotel was scheduled for demolition.

Later I found a press release for the project, which would cost two billion dollars. King Mohammed himself had backed it, a resort stretching "over five kilometers of stunning, pristine beach." The funk-iness of Taghazout, its uniqueness as a crossroads between European dropout culture and a simple fishing village—never mind its proximity to decent waves—had doomed it to improvement. It would grow like no other town on the coast.

"Is finished," Salem said.

In the morning the African sunlight was yellow and pure. Shop-keepers unshuttered their doors and swept the fine red dust from their sidewalks. Fishing boats left trails on their way out to sea, and the men in djellabas, who seemed to have slept on their feet, watched the dogs try to revive feuds from the day before. But a morning silence held sway until the first truck with cattle penned on the roof or the first gasping ramshackle bus barreled through Taghazout as if the main street were an open highway, or until some idiot surfer tried to make a three-point turn in the center of town, blocking scooters and cars headed for Agadir or Essaouira. Then somebody honked, another person yelled, the dogs barked, and the dusty day had begun.

The road north of Taghazout was spotted with new construction. New apricot-colored houses landscaped with bougainvillea and atmospheric stone walls seemed to shine as if someone had forgotten to remove the shrink-wrap. Investors in Britain and the Middle East had discovered Morocco as a real estate deal, so homes and hotels were going up in barren places where for most of human history nothing had existed but rock and scrub.

Clusters of men sat here and there along the highway, and when they saw my car, stuffed with a board, they would point out a trail toward the beach, leading through an upstart colony of shacks converted to apartments with for-rent signs—*à louer*. The attraction was always a stunning empty surf break. Paul Bowles died in 1999, and as far as I know he never even took note of surfers in Morocco. (He hated reminders of home.) But some of these colonies might be future towns.

A character in Bowles's 1955 novel *The Spider's House* reminisces about the old Morocco. "When I first came here it was a pure country. There was music and dancing and magic every day in the streets. Now it's finished, everything. Even the religion. In a few more years the whole country will be like all the other Muslim countries, just a huge European slum, full of poverty and hatred." The novelist and cultural critic Edmund White suggested that Bowles wanted Morocco to remain dusty and sun-shot, as it was in the '30s, instead of pursuing a modern life of its own. Bowles was an essentially conservative man who left America looking for an alien culture to lose himself in. But America came running up behind.

"My own belief," wrote Bowles, "is that the people of the alien cultures are being ravaged not so much by the by-products of our civilization, as by the irrational longing on the part of members of their own educated minorities to cease being themselves and become Westerners." Edmund White added: "Implicitly, I suppose, this is a criticism of the Marxist elite of most developing countries in the 1950s."

My impression is that Morocco's been ravaged by cars. I've met perfectly healthy human beings poised between Moroccan culture and the culture of the West—people with no time for Marx who had absorbed a modern education without losing their Moroccan selves. But cars had noticeably ruined whatever romance the country had when Bowles arrived. Eighty or one hundred years ago, in the casbah of Rabat, next to an intricately painted ceramic wall fountain and a stone tower with graven designs dating back to 1195, you might have seen a goat and a man in a caftan. Now you see three cars, a tipped-over trash can, and a satellite dish, as well as the goat. I'm not about to suggest that Moroccans should give up driving or satellite TV just so their country can look romantic to Western travelers; that would be like a Moroccan coming to southern California and having a good look at the gridlocked freeways and mirrored office parks, throwing up his hands, and yelling, "There used to be haciendas here! Where are the cowboys!" I was, moreover, driving a car myself. But it was hard to deny that cars had blighted Morocco more than any other convenience. Cars had forced generic roads and overpasses into ancient cities, cars had even homogenized pollution, and cars—in Morocco and everywhere else—had ended the silence of the night.

≈≈≈≈≈≈≈≈≈≈≈≈≈≈≈

The patio at Café Imesouane, a couple of hours up the coast, had a table of Moroccan surfers in board shorts, dreadlocks, and sandals in spite of the cold. One wore a djellaba. A car parked in the dust blared a tape of Arabic *gnâwa*. The surfers' eyes darted. Except for weak light from the café, where older men watched TV, the darkness around the fishing town of Imesouane was absolute, and the atmosphere wasn't open or warm. This was a different proposition from Le Spot, but there was no enmity, either. Things just operated on a darker level of satisfaction.

The surfers asked where I was from. They said the surf would be good tomorrow, five meters high off the jetty. They were from a village up the hill, but they surfed Imesouane every day.

I'd met Hamel by accident that afternoon. He lived in a warren of cliff-built apartments that rose over the beach like a Mediterranean hill town, with painted wooden doors, flaking steps, and a population of cats. When he saw me hide my sandals and towel in the holes of a boulder on the sand, before a surf session, he told me in French to leave everything on his "porch," a flat part of the cliff about fifteen feet above, where it would be safer from tides and thieves. He had an almost horselike face, long and heavy-jawed, with fashionable Rasta dreadlocks but ancient Berber features.

Most of Imesouane had become a construction site, all asphalt roads and half-built homes. One of the few finished houses had fresh red paint and a satellite dish. But it stood alone, with black walls built up to the sides of its lot as if it hoped, one day, to be a row house on a clean suburban street.

Soon a bearded man with hunched shoulders made his way across the patio to the amusement of the surfers. His name was Hamid. I knew him from earlier in the day, too. He'd found me an apartment. Now he was drunk and uttered nonsense. He curled his hands in front of his face when he talked, then stretched his arms to emphasize a point, which sometimes never arrived. Because of this behavior the surfers called him Jackie Chan.

"Mike," he said. "What are you eating?" He could see my greasy beef stew with carrots and peppers and slabs of potato. "Come with me tomorrow. I make you a better tagine."

The surfers laughed.

"How do you like the apartment I found for you? Is good?"

"Sure."

"Mike," said Hamid. "You know—I have the oldest restaurant in Imesouane. Is ten years old. I have lived here very long. Jimi Hendrix slept here in Imesouane. He slept in my house! Nineteen seventy-one."

Hendrix—who died in 1970—once lived or vacationed in Essaouira, the white-walled fortress town to our north. Legend had him squinting with inspiration under the cool Moroccan dusk, smoke-swirled, writing indelible songs like "Castles Made of Sand." Places where "Jimi slept" were as ordinary here as taverns in New England that had once given oats to George Washington's horse.

"Mike," said Hamid. "Tomorrow you come for dinner in my restaurant, okay? Bring your friends."

He meant my roommates. He'd found me an apartment with two other people, a Cornish surfer named Dale and his German girlfriend Katerina.

I agreed, and he grasped my hand. "Thank you, Mike," he said with real feeling, and staggered off into the dark.

Soon Dale and Katerina came up to the patio, greeted us, and sat down. Dale had a minor explosion of bleach-blond hair; Katerina had startling blue eyes and a comfortably tousled way of mixing torn flannel shirts and bikinis.

"That guy's kind of weird?" said Dale in a reedy Cornish accent.

"He's a crazy man," Hamel agreed.

"He's just a drunk," said Katerina.

"He invited us over for dinner tomorrow," I said.

"Yeah, he invited us yesterday too," Dale said. "We've been meaning to go. He did us good with that apartment."

Katerina shrugged. In a fit of mischief she imitated Hamid's hand gestures. "Jackie Chan!" she said, and the Moroccan boys laughed.

They had no idea what to do with Katerina. She was forward,

bubbly, opinionated, sweet. This violated certain ideas they had about women. Her lack of reserve, and her beauty, made them shy.

When Hamid introduced us in the afternoon, Dale and Katerina had just walked up from the water. Dale assessed me through his sunglasses. "I reckon we can share the place with you," he said. "Long as you don't have any strange habits. I don't fart very often," he said philosophically, "and she barely farts at all."

"Hardly at all." She nodded.

"I never fart," I reassured them.

"Awright then."

I moved my things upstairs to an apartment with a view of the waves. Dale had just finished a stint as a surf instructor in Portugal, where Katerina was about to start a job managing a surf camp. They had a few weeks off to surf in Morocco. Katerina had uprooted her career in Germany to live this way. She'd pleased her parents by going to vocational school and landing a well-paid corporate job, but she wasn't happy. "It was a big decision," she told me. "My mother was upset. I had to decide if I wanted to work nine to five and make good money or be able to surf and lead the life I wanted." The watershed was learning to surf in the first place, during a trip to Australia. "I was so stupid, I thought Australia was the only place in the world you could surf. But they said, 'No, you're crazy, go to France!' So a week after I returned to Paderborn," her hometown near Cologne, "I went to France." She laughed. "My mother was upset."

But the career decision still weighed on her mind. Essentially she had paid good money, now and in the future, for a sun-soaked life.

That afternoon we drove to a market town called Tamri. We browsed the stalls for vegetables to stock up the apartment, and Katerina moved between the tables of oranges and onions with a flip, frank impatience. Her baggy clothes were modest enough, but they showed flashes of hip and bikini string, and the gaze of boys on the dusty street was palpable. Moroccan teenagers sat around café tables, like their fathers, with nothing to do. They made jokes; in their eyes we had no honor. Older men in *peci* caps and caftans ignored us, but the boys weren't so detached. There was a level of sarcasm on the streets of Tamri that I never felt in Taghazout or Imesouane.

Katerina shrugged off these tensions. She sensed that local notions of honor were a trap for women; she'd also been in Morocco long enough to know when a shopkeeper was charging her tourist prices. Ninety dirhams for a pile of green peppers, tomatoes, and tangerines was too much. "That's nine euros," she said. "We would pay that in Germany." She haggled for eighty. But the impassive grocer, with a mustache and belly, resented having to argue with someone so feisty and young. She felt his resentment—his lack of respect—and pushed back.

"*C'est difficile,*" she said.

"*Oui, c'est difficile.*" The man nodded.

In the end, she paid eighty. But the joke she made—with conscious irony, stepping out of the shop in sandals and careless flannel—could have been uttered by the most bourgeois ladies in Paderborn.

"You can't overcharge a German woman," she said.

Pointe d'Imesouane broke in the morning. We woke up to soft explosions of surf and saw feathery waves peeling south off the point. Dale made instant coffee. "All you really need in life is an apartment and some decent waves, innit?" he said. We hiked down to the beach through the jumble of cliff dwellings where Hamel lived and left our things on his porch.

The point was a line of sharp black rocks where a handful of men held fishing lines angled out to sea. Beside these rocks you could ride a swift current to a fixed spot where the waves started to pitch. "It's like an elevatah," Dale pointed out. "Takes you right past the boneyard."

The boneyard was the turbulent section where all the waves churned; it made a rough paddle.

The waves had a thick, fast way of rearing up, but once you were on you could surf at least a hundred yards. A small corps of locals—not the boys from the night before—dominated the peak by sitting farther out, and closer to the rocks, than the rest of us. It was no different from Rizal Tanjung and his friends in Bali. They acted as if the discovery of Imesouane by outsiders had ruined their day. But there were plenty of waves to go around.

"We were down in Agadir last week?" Dale told me during a lull. "And the king built a launching jetty down there for his Jet Skis? Wanna guess what it was called?"

"No clue."

"The King's Groyne."

"It was not."

He turned to catch another wave and we couldn't talk for a few minutes. But he paddled back and there was another lull.

"Yeah, the King's Groyne," he said. "And the waves breaking off it have formed a sandbar. So the king's done 'is work. He's made a new surf spot."

After a few hours I paddled back to the beach, leaned my board against the sandstone boulder, and climbed up to Hamel's porch for my sandals. A white plastic chair had been set out. I sat for a minute and watched the surf, until I heard sweeping behind me. Hamel put his head out the door. "Ça va." But he didn't seem surprised; in fact he invited me in for tea. His apartment consisted of a small open stone floor covered with a blue tarp—his living room—which connected to a few dark sandstone chambers, his bedroom and shower.

While the tea stewed, he rolled some kif and set out foil-wrapped triangles of cheese and sweet biscuits. Also a stack of surf magazines in French, to keep me occupied while he swept the floor and put out fish scraps for a cat. Hamel was gentle, loping, and kind. He said he lived in the cliffs because he preferred it to life in his family village, or on a fishing boat. He used to fish on big boats out of a Saharan port near Mauritania. But he'd returned to Imesouane, near his village, to run a surf camp.

A hypnotic *gnâwa* played from his double-barreled portable radio. *Gnâwa* is a serpentine, trance-inducing, percussion-heavy form of music. He complained that the gnâwa scene around there was dead; everything was reggae now. I asked if there wasn't still gnâwa in Fés and he said yes, but it was Berber gnâwa, not Arabic gnâwa.

Paul Bowles wandered Morocco in the '50s collecting *jajouka* and *gnâwa* and other forms of Moghrebi folk music on his reel-to-reel. Even then they were dying. "Like most Africans, the Berbers developed a music of mass participation," wrote Bowles, "one whose psychological effects were aimed more often than not at causing hypnosis. When the Arabs invaded the land they brought with them music of a very different sort, addressed to the individual, seeking by sensory means to induce a state of philosophical speculativeness." But gnâwa in particular had started as neither Berber nor Arabic. It was the music of black West Africans who came north to Morocco as slaves, creating an African diaspora music, like American blues, but restricted to this continent. Centuries before Europeans discovered West Africa as a source of cheap labor, Arab slave traders were trafficking tribesmen from Mali and Ghana cross North Africa. One of these groups called themselves gnâwa, and their music became a reservoir of ancestral memory.

The rise of individual consciousness from the ancient pool of tribal life had been a centuries-long process, and Islam, like all monotheistic religions, introduced the idea of an individual relationship to God. This long-bubbling individualism had reached a fierce boil in America and Europe and moved away from religion and philosophy altogether to spill over in the form of weird pop-culture froth. Now Muslims consider their religion a bulwark against what's called "individualism."

We talked about the difference between Berber and Arabic culture. Morocco feels Arabic on the surface, but "Berber pride" is a strong undercurrent. Berbers have lived in North Africa since before Rome, Greece, and Judaism, never mind Islam or the Arab invasions after AD 700. Most Moroccans have some Berber blood. Hamel himself identified as a Berber, and most surf shops in the south bore the liberationist symbol of Berber pride:

Did Hamel think of surfing as a Western sport? No, he said, it was just fun to do. Well, why did so many surf shops have Berber pride symbols? Did Berbers surf more than Arabs? No, but each side had its own surf culture. Hamel said Berbers and Arabs were just like the French, Italians, Germans, and British, all those advanced Europeans. They were neighbors, he said, but they had no idea how to get along.

I left on the fourth day with another surfer from the café named Yassin. The road above the village wound up a dusty mountainside and gave us a magnificent view of Cape Imesouane. We passed robed women, donkeys, and Yassin's brother. "Stop, stop." We gave the brother a lift. We passed through an almost suburban cluster of cracked stucco buildings and Yassin said, "This is my village." We let the brother go.

Yassin had long, flowing hair and wore a Hawaiian-print shirt. He also had a machined metal chain around his neck with a curved steel claw, which came in handy—I saw later—for building hash cigarettes. He was a quiet, groovy, piratelike presence.

Soon the dirt road became a ribbon of asphalt and merged with the highway. "Stop, stop," Yassin said. He jumped out to pluck a hand-sized tortoise from the road and placed it on the dashboard. While I accelerated the animal scrabbled from side to side, in search of a place to jump. After a while it quit scrabbling. It raised its neck, seemed to realize how fast we were traveling, and studied us both with dusty pinhead eyes.

The small city of Essaouira, two hours north, felt positively metropolitan. Boxy white buildings rose over the medina walls, some edged in light blue, and everything that wasn't white or blue had a mellow pastel color. The sand-colored walls had fat brass cannons aimed through battlements in the vague direction of the Portuguese. The wind never let up. As soon as we entered the medina, Yassin tied back his hair and donned a baseball cap and moved down the narrow streets with an almost hip-hop swagger, which was funny, since Essaouira was sun-washed and twee.

The lanes were flooded with daily business. Djellaba-hooded men steered produce in handcarts; waddling women shopped in hijabs. There were newsstands, fruit stands, olive stands, a bird market, and obscene butcher shops. But gulls shrieked over everything and the buildings were white instead of red, which was the color of teeming Marrakech. The gift and trinket shops were the same—ceramic bowls, tagine plates, hookahs, pyramids of spice powders. Yassin had friends in these shops. We stopped in one, where behind the glass shelves of all that timeless Moroccan craftsmanship there was a group of surfers.

"Tea?" said one of them, and I nodded. He poured a small glass.

"Where have you been?" they asked Yassin in French, for my benefit, since they wanted to speak Arabic.

"Imesouane."

"Any fun?"

He shook his head. "Nothing going on."

"You like Essaouira?" someone asked me.

"Jimi Hendrix used to live here," someone else said.

"For how long?" I said.

They discussed this.

"Four or five years," said Yassin.

They started to dissect cigarettes to invest with hash. The rear of a display case had surf stickers on it (ESSAOUIRA WINDY CITY, NO WORK SURF SHOP, RIP CURL). On the ceiling hung banners of Bob Marley and Che Guevara. On the stereo, hip-hop. It occurred to me that harbor towns in any nation are cosmopolitan in a low-rent way; pop fashion, and surfing, lend themselves to the culture of a neon-lit port of call. Coastal towns are tolerant, vice-ridden, mellow, accepting, and dangerous to the moral fiber of a nation. Too much washes in on the sea for these cities to remain traditional.

Yassin and his friends lapsed into Arabic. Soon I went for a walk in the narrow alleys of Essaouira. From the waterfront I had seen a door in the medina wall and a set of Spanish-looking steps leading down to the black rocks and tidepools, just under the whitewashed parapets. Kids had been swimming off the steps. I wanted to find this door and check the surf. But—of course—I got lost.

Essaouira's back alleys had the strangest charm of any part of the city, I think because I couldn't figure out what all the doorways were for. Some were tiled, open entrances to steam rooms. Some were just ornate Moorish doorways with onion-dome tops. Others were service entrances that may have once been dungeons, where men in djellabas worked by dim lightbulbs. Some were obviously apartment doors. People lived within the hollow sea-facing wall.

The streets narrowed, tilted, and climbed. Some became tunnels. It was like an Escher painting. One covered street became a ramp, and when I emerged into the daylight again I looked up at a narrow plank and the undersides of two clucking, comfortably perched white chickens. The ramp led to a parapet. A rank of old cannons was mounted on carts.

Essaouira was commissioned in 1764 by a sultan and specially built by a French architect to regulate sea trade. So the walls are about two and a half centuries old. But pirates and colonial powers had fought for control of this spot for hundreds if not thousands of years. Romans, Phoenicians, Carthaginians, and Byzantine traders had used it. Essaouira's harbor and town were called Mogador by the Portuguese, but after 1764 it was called Essaouira ("well designed") by Sultan Sidi Mohammed ben Abdallah, who wanted to tax and regulate European trade but also contain the cancer of foreign influence to the coast. (Sidi Mohammed knew about harbor towns.) One of his courtiers wrote that the reason to build Essaouira was to defend Islam from the infidel. It became the only port in Morocco where Europeans could land.

What did people trade inside the medina? Ivory, charcoal, salt, fabrics, honey, almonds, ostrich feathers, tin teapots from Manchester, gold from sub-Saharan Africa, goat and giraffe skins, olive and argan oils, mutton. Also slaves. You could still see the stone arches and heavy wooden doors to the stalls where humans were herded. The auction market didn't close for slaves until 1912, with the arrival of the French. Auctions occurred every spring, whenever the ten-thousand-camel trans-Saharan caravan loped up to the southern gate, and Arab merchants peddled tribesmen they had bought from West African kings.

Arabs were ardent slave owners. Bounty hunters from the Muslim world even caught Europeans. Moroccan pirates used to storm up to England to grab Christian slaves from Cornwall and Devon, or cruise the Mediterranean to raid seaside towns in Italy and Spain, the soft underbelly of Europe. Moulay Ismail—Morocco's most dreaded and powerful sultan—sent his pirates from Salé, near Rabat, to kidnap Christians as a form of warfare. The pirates were called Salé corsairs in Europe, but when the Salé River silted up, they sailed from Essaouira.

Some people in the West jump on these stories as balm for residual guilt over slavery in the New World. But there is no comparison. Christians and Muslims enslaved each other the way Greeks and Romans had; they made war and took each other prisoner. But the horrors of the Middle Passage, the sheer contempt for Africans as a race, and the sickening numbers of people packed like fish into the holds of European cargo ships—which could be smelled for miles on the open sea— made the trade in black slaves a uniquely hellish business. Moulay Ismail took obscene liberties with his servants, lopping off heads with his scimitar for the sin of insolence or for failing to twirl his parasol; but even a recent and credulous biographer of Thomas Pellow, Moulay's most famous white slave, had to admit that "being bought by a Moroccan slave dealer would have been infinitely preferable to being sold into slavery in North America."

Anyway, wandering in the salty dusk in Essaouira, I found an open door leading to a chamber within the city wall. This room was used for storage, maybe by a hotel next door. I saw brooms and a sort of custodian's bed. Another door, inside, was open to the sky. A middle-aged man in a long white smock stood on an outdoor landing, watching the sea. He saw me and waved.

I went through the room. He was standing on the Spanish stairs I had seen from outside the wall.

"Is this public?" I asked in English.

"No, it belongs to the hotel," the man answered. "But I own a shop in the street here. They let me come out. I like to watch the sunset."

He had short, black salted hair and alert, melancholy eyes. He wore a short beard with gray in it. Rough surf roiled in the rocks below us.

"How do you like Essaouira?" he asked.

"It's very pretty."

"It's relaxed." He nodded. "The people are friendly. Were you looking for something?"

"I thought I could surf here when there was no wind," I said.

"No, no. No surfing here. Sometimes we swim—this is our swimming pool." He pointed at a calm patch of water shaped by the tidepools and the high, rough cliffs. "Some of the boys from the hotel, they come out and dive from the rocks."

"I think I saw them today."

His name was Moussa, short for Moises. We talked for a while as the sun went down behind Essaouira's square lookout tower, the Skala du Port, to our left. A flock of seagulls floated up to the battlements, riding the wind like an elevator, then shearing off and flapping down to ride it up again. Moises said they always did that. He also said he knew about California from the movies ("Is very big, I think"). Then he asked if I'd heard of the Living Theatre.

"From New York?" I said.

"Yes, they come to Essaouira every year. Three months."

"Where do they perform?"

"No, no, they just practice. They come every year to Essaouira to practice and then they tour in Europe."

"I didn't know that."

"I was friends with Julian Beck. You know him? He came with them to Essaouira for many years. Since the hippie time! He brought Jimi Hendrix here. People think Hendrix came here all the time, is not true. Julian Beck knew him and brought him here to see it. Only two days."

"Jimi Hendrix was here for just two days?"

"Yes."

"Hah."

We talked some more, and I asked if there was any surfing at all near Essaouira. I'd heard Safi was good; maybe Safi was nearby? He pointed far up the coast. Safi was not nearby. A beach called Sidi Kaouki, to the south, where rental camels stood around near fish-grilling stands, was the closest surf spot to Essaouira. But there was a constant wind. Better for windsurfing. Moises straightened me out on a number of things. He was nothing but helpful. He even showed me the lobby of the hotel next door, with its ornate doorways and intricate ceiling work. When we finished, the sun had gone down and the sky was a reddish darkening bruise between the high buildings of the medina. He showed me his shop—metalwork and pottery—but didn't try to sell me anything. He only said I should come back if I wanted to talk again.

"Thank you, Moises," I said.

"Good-bye, Mike."

<hr>

Yassin acted like a helpful guide in Essaouira, my knowledgeable local pal, but around him I hemorrhaged cash. He kept finding things for me to buy. He took me to his friend's apartment just outside the city walls, in what was called the new town but resembled a slum. It was a crowded grid of dusty potholed streets lined with plaster apartment blocks and dim electric-lit stores. Yassin's friend, Ahmed, threw a party in a half-renovated building. He set up a plain, comfortable room where Yassin and I could sleep. We brought the turtle in from the car and tried to feed it raisins, but it made for a corner of the room. Then we went out for alcohol. Yassin had the idea that I should pay for everything he did in Essaouira, which didn't bother me at first—he'd found me free lodging, after all—and the evening went well until he suggested going to a bar.

"What for?" I said.

We had enough to drink at Ahmed's, though everyone spoke Arabic and I was slightly bored.

"It's a good bar, man. It's fun."

"Where is it?"

"Five minutes. By the medina."

We parked in front of an expensive waterfront hotel and settled in a suspiciously dark and dingy bar in a courtyard behind its elegant lobby, where businessmen sat alone and high-heeled women circulated the room. We ordered two absurdly expensive beers. Soon I realized that Yassin wanted me to pay not just for his drinks but also for his prostitute. He said the women came to Essaouira from other parts of Morocco, ordinary women, to sit in this bar, meet men, and "have sex and earn money."

"For God's sake, Yassin."

We left (I made him pay for his beer), and he was peeved.

He'd elected me to provide him with a high weekend in Essaouira—a ride up the coast, alcohol, even sex—but in return he wasn't much of a guide. He gave unclear directions in the car, then asked for refinements from people in the street, which also turned out to be wrong. He kept waving his hand and saying *"Fffffshwt"* to show how easy it was. Turn here, make a left over there, and then *fffffshwt*—straight to the bar, or out of Essaouira, or up to Safi for surf. No problem.

"Do you even know how to surf, Yassin?"

"Yeah, sure, man."

The next day we did drive up to Safi. The reef off the industrial shoreline there can hold one of the world's legendary big waves. But for us it was flat, and when Yassin realized that I meant what I had said all morning, that I was continuing north, not back to Essaouira, and not wherever else Yassin thought we should go—and no I did not want to stay in Safi and meet some chicks in a bar—we parted ways. He left his turtle behind, and I drove to a town called Oualidia with the sluggish beast under my seat.

I aimed for Oualidia because I'd heard of a camp called Surfland. I wanted to interview the owner. The town announced itself as a dusty roadside souk, with men trading goats and scarved women shopping at the fruit stalls. A road winding down toward the beach took me, surprisingly, into a modern resort town of shuttered vacation homes and darkened hotels. Restaurants were open but empty. Stores were desolate. Even Surfland was closed. Somehow I had assumed a surf camp would operate during the winter, which is Morocco's surf season; but no. When I stopped at a store for juice and chips, the man at the counter pointed out the date on each item and said, "Okay?"

Oualidia was the first sign of domestic wealth since Agadir, where I'd rented the car. But it felt like a vacant-street episode of *The Twilight Zone*. Later I learned that Miki Dora had stayed in Oualidia for three months in the handful of years before he died. He made friends with the owner of Surfland, a Moroccan-born Frenchman called Laurent Miramon.

I found a cheap room in a deserted "tennis camp" with wilting vines in a small garden. The rooms were lined up in a bright green, motellike building around a clay tennis court, quiet and peaceful except for a vicious mutt on the roof that barked at me every time I came or went.

I had dinner at a restaurant called Les Roches. The owner was a slight, gentle man with wrinkles and a graying mustache who wore the sort of rumpled suit you see in films set in Casablanca.

"*Le surfing?*" he said, because he'd seen me park my car.

"*Oui.*"

"Is it good now?"

"I hope so." I looked at his empty restaurant. "Where are your customers?"

"It's off-season. Nobody comes in the winter."

"But in the summer it's crowded?"

"Oh yes."

His name was Mr. Rouchia. He'd operated his restaurant for ten years in Oualidia. In the summer it was always full. The painted-stucco restaurant had a strip of greenery in front; an hour earlier, while Mr. Rouchia wasn't looking, I had transferred the turtle from under the passenger seat to the shelter of an edible fern.

"I think you have a turtle in the planter there," I said when I paid my bill.

"Really?"

Mr. Rouchia followed me out the door and started combing through the bushes.

The beach at Oualidia had a fleet of wooden fishing boats drawn up on the sand, and close to the boats, hidden by dunes, sprawled a camp built of wooden planks and corrugated iron. This was a fishermen's bidonville, a shantytown. Bowles wrote in the '50s: "In Morocco the very poor live neither in the country nor in the city; they come as far as the outer walls of the town, build these desperate-looking squatters' colonies out of whatever materials they can find, and there they stay."

While I looked at all this from the boardwalk, an old man trundled up on a bike and said something urgent in French. He wore a grimy gray suit and a ragged white beard; his eyes were dark and fierce. I realized he had asked—with the prophetic energy of a man asking me to save his child from certain death—if I wanted to buy mussels. A box was tied to the rear of his bike.

"*Non, monsieur*," I said. "*Je regrette.*"

I gave him some money instead. He nodded and rode on. But the next morning he asked the same question, with the same unseeing eyes, in the same urgent gush of French.

Miki Dora came to this town in 1999 from southern France, where he'd lived off and on for years in financial and emotional exile. The angry, muscular, feline rebel-chief of early Malibu had a gray goatee and a beer gut. His prostate was swollen; he had pancreatic cancer. Since the '60s he'd roamed the earth in search of an Eden similar to pre-Gidget Malibu, disgusted by "surf culture" as well as his own celebrity. The FBI was also after him for defrauding American Express and writing a number of bad checks. But his legend had only grown, and Quiksilver paid him a subsistence wage in the '90s just to be Miki— and, ahem, to work as a greeter on golf courses and tennis courts in France. He flew to Oualidia for a week of relaxation on Quiksilver's tab, but he seems to have stayed with the idea of escaping his golf-course duties. Morocco must have been alluring to Miki, since it plays roughly the same role for the French as Mexico does for Californians. Not only is it rocky and dry and poor, and a source of illegal immigration; it's a place for outlaws to vanish.

"My first impression of Miki," said Virginie Miramon, Laurent's sister, to Miki's biographer David Rensin, "was that he was a charming, well-educated, knowledgeable person. A very complicated individual. . . . Right away he told us who he was, the first day. He said, 'OK, this is who I am, this is where I come from, this is my story. I'm here to relax. I don't want to interact with people. I like my privacy. I don't like to have my photo taken.' . . . We said, 'OK, fine.' I didn't care much who he was—this 'Miki Dora' legend. I had heard of it from my brother, seen a couple of photos. To me he was like every other person."

The reason Surfland closed in the winter was to let Laurent himself take advantage of surf season. He took Miki up and down the coast. "Quiksilver called me in late December and asked me if I could host Miki Dora for a week at the beginning of January because it was too cold in France and Miki was tired," he told Rensin. "I said yes, with pleasure. He came for one week and he stayed three months. . . . He should have been back in France but he would always say, 'No, I need one more day.'

"He was traveling very light. He had a bag and a backpack. Some stones," meaning jewels, including diamonds, probably, from a stint in South Africa. "He opened a little bag and showed them to me one night. I was scared. There were some crazy pieces inside. It was a little fortune. I said, 'Let me put it in the office.' He said, 'No no, it stays always with me. This is my bank.'

"When people arrive in Morocco," Miramon went on, "I take their passports so they're really on holiday. They don't have to think about their papers. I said to Miki, 'Give me the passport. I keep it with me. No problem.' He didn't want to. When you have a client who's had his passport stolen it's big shit. I didn't understand it. I said, 'Miki, it's no problem.' Finally, he trusted me but he said, 'Hey Laurent, please take care. This is my heart. I haven't had a passport in fifteen years.' . . . His passport had no residency. That's exceptional. It means you are not registered really any place in the world. It means you don't pay any tax, any insurance, any anything."

Miki had grown old as a rebel. He was still in love with his old image, though he would have punched anyone who said so. He believed that he alone of all his friends had lived without "selling out." He'd recently escaped a house fire in South Africa and survived the traumatic death of his dog. A project stewing to film some version of his life had also just evaporated in California. The producer Michael McDonnell had offered to make a feature film about Dora to counteract the ridiculous Moondoggie character in *Gidget*. He suggested a story on the model of *Cool Hand Luke* or *One Flew Over the Cuckoo's Nest,* a tragedy of a glamorous nonconformist. Miki objected. "My life is not tragedy," he said. "My life is for living, and going forward, and surviving all this. . . . That you can condition people to look at the worst side of life, the tragic side of life, and think it's something positive, uplifting—it's also done in Shakespeare. Very depressing. Very suicidal. That's why I can't read Shakespeare. I like to go to the stratosphere. I admire somebody who survives it, and comes out ahead, and lives a fantastic, incredible life, despite adversity. That's somebody to admire. . . . Not the one who gets his head beaten to hell, and crushed by a system."

In three years he would be dead. "We were concerned," said Virginie. "This guy isn't young. He's not old, but he's not doing well." Oualidia was a meditative way station for him, a detour near the end of the road.

Sometime after Miki returned to France, an old friend named Rick Hodgson heard from him. "He told me that the only way he could get into the surf camp in Morocco was by pack mule, that a Cuban mercenary ran the camp," said Hodgson. "There were guards with automatic weapons everywhere, and if you took off in front of anybody you'd be shot. And the waves were black and the bottom so full of rocks and poisonous things that you'd die if you didn't make the take-off. Miki always liked you to think that he went right into hell and artfully maneuvered out of hell with priceless panache or priceless booty. That was his whole quest. That was the story he wrote for himself; that was his real mythology. It was beautiful, but not what was really happening."

Mehdiya Plage, north of Rabat, lies at the end of a winding country road, where the sun yellows hedges of gorse and shepherds walk their flocks of sheep. The town of Mehdiya looks like a town in North Jersey. First you see a desolate line of cheap restaurants and kitschy beachside conveniences, including one marvelous café with two cheap concrete mermaids flanking the patio. To the north, on a cliff overlooking a river mouth, crumble the stone ruins of a casbah built by Moulay Ismail.

Omari Boumediene ran the Mehdiya Surf Camp, and he was happy to talk history. His school and club occupied a pair of small houses in a residential neighborhood uphill from the beach. The front yard was overgrown with bougainvillea and bottlebrush and had a gated entrance flanked by two surfboards. Boumediene had dark, fierce brown eyes and a quick smile. He was both laid-back and intense; as a surfer and a business owner, he had to be both. He was also a onetime hotshot surfer, now forty-two, and a restless family man with an evident lack of patience for people who refused to help (with whatever it was). Right now he needed money to clean up the beach. Why wouldn't the government help? He recruited kids to clean up Mehdiya Plage at his own expense. "It's not good for kids to have to walk across broken glass," he said. "It's not fair." He once tried to convince the Surfrider Foundation in France to give him a beach-cleaning machine. No luck. "Those machines are good," he said. "They only need to use them for ten hours a year to keep the beach at Hossegor clean." Hossegor, the French surf capital. "A *year*," he said.

I asked about the king's club in Rabat. I had just seen it the day before, and I had a hunch about Boumediene's opinion. The Oudayas Surf Club turned out to be a white building with porthole windows that was flanked by palm trees and perched on the northern edge of the capital city near the casbah, within trotting distance of excellent surf. It offered lessons to local kids and arranged tournaments. But it was strangely quiet. I dropped by with a friend from Casablanca named Hakim, and at two in the afternoon we were asked to leave; it had closed for the day. Very few people surfed. More kids were kicking a soccer ball on a clay field on the club grounds. It looked, and felt, like a sluggish teen community center, rather than a vibrant *école de surf*.

My friend Hakim, a young physicist, was deeply skeptical of Mohammed VI. He thought the cool, populist, Jet Skiing "King of the Poor" would follow the same path as his father, Hassan II. "Mohammed is liberal, but they all start out that way," Hakim said. "As soon as someone tries to assassinate him, it will change." Hassan's generals had tried to kill him twice. On the way to Rabat we passed a bend in the road, beside a stand of trees next to a field of grass leading to the surf, the site of one of the attempts.

"There are these urban legends that the king travels with so many cars to confuse assassins," Hakim said. But riding with the king is just a court favor, an expensive long-standing tradition. "Once I was with a friend and we saw the procession drive through Casablanca, and it was followed by a helicopter. We asked a policeman, 'What's the helicopter for?' and he said it was for extra security. Well, fine. But I wondered, why can't the king just take the helicopter? It would be so much cheaper."

Hakim had been educated in America, so he spoke fluent English, Arabic, and French. We passed a golf course, and he said a childhood in Morocco had taught him to loathe golf courses. "King Hassan liked to play golf. I don't hold that against him. He was a wealthy man, why shouldn't he play golf? But do you have any idea how much water it takes to keep a golf course going in a desert climate? Morocco's economy relies on agriculture. We need water. We can't afford to use it for golf."

Hassan II had cultivated an image as a relaxed, regal host of world-class tournaments on the "European" circuit. Golf was his opening to the West. Mohammed VI's reputation as a surfing king could be seen from the same angle. He'd simply updated his sport. At least good surf was natural in Morocco and didn't need elaborate sprinkler systems. Then again, Mohammed VI didn't really surf.

Boumediene's opinion was: Yes, the king plays in the water. Yes, he's built a big club in Rabat. But he Jet Skis. A dirty habit. "N'est pas bien." He frowned. "Il pollue." And the club was unimpressive, considering it had royal patronage and a descendant of Mohammed as a founding member. "It's just money paid by the government. He doesn't work with his heart."

It was clear that Boumediene worked with his heart; he just wished his chosen sport wasn't so Eurocentric. He complained about European surfers who swooped down to snap up Moroccan contest money. He complained about Western surf companies that failed to donate more than a hundred dollars' worth of equipment every year. A school like his needed wetsuits! It needed boards! "When I went to Bali, I gave out some money," he said. "They needed it there. I made a tagine and baked some bread. They live on rice there, it's not healthy. They don't know how to bake bread."

Boumediene's surf-school dining room, where we sat, had rough wooden walls and a picnic table for communal meals. When I asked about the first surfers at Mehdiya, he sprang up to show me clusters of photos on the wall. I had come the right place. "Yes, an American soldier in the '50s," he said. My heart leapt. "But I don't know his name." Oh.

He did have pictures of the first locals to surf Mehdiya in 1960. One was a Frenchman living in Morocco called Pierre Chalaud, who wound up photographed in the local paper. The surfboard came courtesy of Claude Bérard, another Frenchman, who worked as a fireman at the US naval station. Later Bérard and Chalaud and another man called Henri Coggia traded waves on Mehdiya Plage with a local lifeguard named Abboud "Mamoune" Kabbour—"the first Moroccan surfer," as Pierre Chalaud put it to me later.

I asked Boumediene about the casbah on the hill, since I knew the marines had waded ashore under its crumbling walls.

"You want to see it?" said Boumediene.

"Can we?"

"I'll take you."

Boumediene drove his surf-school van at top speed through the neighborhood, past the town's old fishing harbor and under the rocky cliffs. The harbor protects the mouth of the Sebou River, and two parallel jetties curve into the ocean like a funnel, to shelter wooden boats. Surf broke on either side of the jetties. Boumediene said a perfectly aimed swell could send lines of clean waves straight down the funnel.

The casbah has a noble face of stone arches overlooking the Sebou, with a rank of old cannons. But when we had driven around to the rear of the ruin, up a dirt road, I saw the rest had collapsed in the grass. "Typical," said Boumediene. "In Spain or Portugal, this would be restored, and someone would charge admission. In Morocco, nobody cares."

The casbah had been more than a fort; Moulay had designed a sprawling stone village, with a governor's palace, a mosque, a hammam, a market, and a prison. It went up after he drove the Spaniards out of Mehdiya in 1681. Lithograph portraits of Moulay show a wily, self-satisfied man with a mustache, earrings, and a scepter. He was a grand and terrible Alaouite sultan who first unified the other sultans in the Maghreb into something resembling a European state. Then he declared independence from the Ottoman Empire, kicked out the Europeans, and took hold of the coast. In that sense he was a founder of "Morocco," though it wouldn't have that name until later.

Boumediene thought Morocco's traditional relationship to the beach had bred mistrust of the waves. "When you go back in history, four or five centuries," he said, "you notice in any Moroccan city by the sea, what do they do? A casbah, ramparts, a wall with cannons. In Rabat and Essaouira, too. Moroccans are afraid of the beach." He shrugged. "Walls, ramparts, cannons. It's not like this in Australia."

Roman legionnaires came from the water. So did Phoenician traders, Portuguese privateers, Spanish colonists, and the French. The Americans washed up in November 1942. The Allies considered the French Maghreb an easy target because the French soldiers, the foreign legion, had questionable loyalties to the Vichy government in Paris. The goal of the invasion was to seize French colonies from Nazi control and stop General Rommel's romp through Egypt. American soldiers landed not just at Mehdiya Plage but also near Safi and Casablanca. The worst fighting, though, was here at Mehdiya. Hundreds of invading soldiers died, and history would remember the landing as a rehearsal for D-Day.

The Allies, at the time, tried to read the minds of the French legionnaires. Would they even shoot? Why fight Americans if you hated what the Nazis had done to la France? Leaders of Morocco's independence movement—including Mohammed V, the current king's grandfather—had said out loud that Moroccan regulars had no reason to fire on Americans. The first GIs to wade through the surf were wrapped in the Stars and Stripes, on the assumption that soldiers on these cliffs would hold their fire. But the French legionnaires may have reasoned that Nazis would go easy on la France only as long as her soldiers behaved; and Port Lyautey, just upriver from Mehdiya, was Morocco's most vital port. So men in artillery nests near the casbah, and in small planes overhead, began to shoot.

Boumediene and I found the casbah cannons and looked out across the harbor. The view was magnificent. Arabic graffiti had been scratched in the walls over the iron guns. The surf, however, was flat.

We went back to the truck and drove to the harbor. Boumediene showed me the remnants of an American pier built just after the war. Clusters of wooden posts rose out of the water like bundles of telephone poles. "These were the old pilings. They'll be here forever," he said. "But nobody wanted to use them. It's like the casbah—they just let it fall apart." In the meantime Spanish and Italian and Portuguese companies ran fishing operations from a newer concrete dock.

Busloads of Moroccan workers—mostly young women in hijabs—sat on the concrete eating lunch, on a break from cleaning or canning sardines.

After Moroccan independence in 1956, the new government gave Port Lyautey a more traditional Arabic name, Kenitra, and the United States maintained bases there into the '70s. The Naval Air Station was a fortified American village, like any US base in any part of the world. It had a "teen club," an American high school, a movie theater, and a pool. American pop culture had arrived by force of arms.

I asked Boumediene if there was a serious conflict between surfing and Islam. "Not with moderate Islam," he said. "In Morocco we've never had surf provocateurs, the guys who trail a bunch of bimbos, except on the beaches of the rich. Of course surfing is frowned on by representatives of radical Islam as too 'American' and too Western. They think it breaks down traditional values. But these people don't see that surfing has values of its own." Still, the boom in surfing followed a fundamental shift in Moroccan society. "There is a failure in education, a crisis of values," he said. "Young people are lost between a tradition which is very hypocritical, which no longer exists, and a modernity that makes them unhappy because they can't afford to take advantage of it as people from rich countries can. Surfing gives them a chance to live a little like young people today, to meet other people, perhaps to travel. Surfing is like a breath of fresh air."

Boumediene had the impatient energy of an athlete facing middle age. He wanted Morocco to move faster, to live more. At the same time he thought the Moroccan bourgeoisie was effete and irresponsible. The real surf champions, the Moroccan kids who grew up hungry and joined the professional tour and wound up living in California or France, were relatively poor. Boumediene came from the same stock. As a surfer he belonged to the fringe of Moroccan society, while as a businessman and an athlete he saw how it could be changed. He was full of love and criticism. The government, the economy, the traditions, the morals of the young, never mind the state of the world at large—the whole thing made him restless.

"I'm from the generation of the 1980s," he said, which was the first boom generation of surfers in Morocco. He compared the '80s to the post-Gidget '60s in California. "Back then, surfers were freaks. And most of us were well traveled. You didn't need a visa to go to Europe or the United States. There were about forty surfers here in Mehdiya, and it wasn't difficult for us to get around. There was no fundamentalism, no war and everything, no problems. Surfers could travel someplace and stay. When they came home, they came with beautiful surfboards, with new cameras, with pictures. Real surfboards." He fixed his brown eyes on me. At last he shrugged. "It wasn't bad."

The real Kilroy was a Massachusetts shipyard inspector, J. J. Kilroy, who wrote his famous phrase on the walls of ships, in chalk, wherever he left off counting rivets. The slogan later mystified maintenance crews who discovered it behind hatches or under floors, and soon it joined forces with a sketch of a bulbous-nosed face to become one of the country's best-known scraps of graffiti. Kilroy seemed to be everywhere.

No one else in Mehdiya could tell me the name of the surfing American serviceman, though. Subsequent research was tough. A Frenchman called Jean Jacques Mayssonnier who served as a midshipman in the French navy reserve was stationed at Port Lyautey from 1955 to '56. He rode waves in inflatable dinghies. "I experienced 'surfing' on rubber crafts at Mehdiya Plage only a few times," he told me. "As far as I can remember it happened only by chance the first time, when a navy helicopter was training with some people at sea. But my American friends and myself had no idea of any sport connected with riding on waves."

Jerry Zimmerman, who served on rescue ships called crash boats at Port Lyautey just after the war, remembered a guy called Smokey Teugel wake-surfing off Mehdiya Plage in 1947, on an "aquaplane" board shaped by a US Navy carpenter. He even had a photo of Smokey getting towed behind a crash boat. "Smokey broke his arm when he fell off the board," Zimmerman said. "To the best of my information, after this heroic try, no one else ever had enough courage" to surf a wake in the open Atlantic.

So the real start of surfing in Morocco, the start that mattered, came in 1960 with Pierre Chalaud and Claude Bérard. Chalaud was a young Frenchman who lived with his family near Mehdiya Plage. His brother-in-law Bérard worked as a civilian fireman at the air station. "He bought a longboard in a surf shop in France, in Biarritz or somewhere in the southwest," Chalaud told me. "This longboard came to Port Lyautey on a boat, with a cargo of wood.

"We caught the first waves at Mehdiya, but it was difficult, because we had no wax and no leash. Afterwards I wrote to a junior champion in France, Alain Weber, and he gave us help. He told us we needed wax. Later I met Weber in Hossegor, and then he came to Morocco in 1962 or '63 to train as a professor at Tiflet," which is east of Rabat. "He surfed at Mehdiya, and it's thanks to him that we learned to surf well."

In about 1964, a young Moroccan lifeguard called Mamoune Kabbour saw Chalaud and Bérard surfing at Mehdiya. "He also worked as an electrician at a factory in Port Lyautey, in the town, but he was a lifeguard on weekends," said Chalaud. "He saw us surfing, and he came with us and tried also to surf on the longboard. And that was the beginning. He was the first Moroccan surfer."

In the mid-'60s Chalaud went to France. He met not just Alain Weber in Hossegor, but also a group of Australian college students who were globe-trotting for surf spots as a way to dodge the Vietnam draft. Chalaud told them about Mehdiya and later found them a place to stay near the beach. They stayed for a couple of years, off and on, making the first excursions south for waves; and soon there was a regular trickle of hippie vans up and down the Moroccan coast. The hippies left behind boards, which helped a handful of young Moroccans, like Boumediene, pick up the sport.

But something was missing from Chalaud's story. Why did he and Bérard bother to ship a surfboard down with a cargo of wood? How did it occur to them to surf in the first place?

"We saw pictures of surfing in American magazines," Chalaud said. "Surfing had just started in France. It was the Hemingway era, you know, and they were filming his book in Biarritz, so we heard about surfing there. Also, I remember one time, I saw an American from the base, a marine. He'd made a surfboard out of balsa wood. It was very—I could tell he'd built it himself. I saw him on the waves, and I said, 'Ho!' This man is walking on the sea."

Ho! "Do you remember his name?"

"No, I never knew him. I saw him a couple of times, before 1960. In 1957 or '59, I don't know. I told my brother-in-law. Then we talked about surfing. *Et voilá.*" He chuckled.

5

UNITED KINGDOM:
ENGLISH INCOMERS

PEOPLE SAID CORNWALL was a separate country from England—Celtic end of Britain's southwest peninsula, separated in the old days from London by three hundred miles of soggy road and one deep river, which was never truly bridged until the railroad crossed it in 1847, or even until the highway in 1961. Cornwall was all but an island, a sometime-breakaway province, a tough tin-mining region, and a graveyard for ships. "All things conspired to make [shipwrecking] in Cornwall a callous and brutal business," wrote F. E. Halliday in his history of the county, "—natural greed, the poverty of the wreckers, remoteness, and the law itself, which defined 'a wreck of the sea' as anything from which no living creature reached the shore." In the age of sail this gave locals a reason to ignore shouts of help from a drowning man, "or, if his shouts and struggles could not be ignored, to shove him under the waves." Cornwall sticks out into the shipping lane between England and Ireland. Its rocky tip reaches for the open Atlantic, and its north-facing coast scoops up shipwrecks as well as deep-ocean swells.

Cornwall looks dark enough in the Sam Peckinpah movie *Straw Dogs,* about a mathematician who moves to the brooding and violent

West Country with his beautiful wife in the 1960s. But crossing the border by car couldn't be less dramatic. We drove from the damp green moorland of Devon over a bridge into the damp green moorland of Cornwall.

"There was supposed to be a river," I said.

"Yes, that was a river," said Robin, who was driving. "The Tamar."

"Where?"

"Under that bridge."

"Oh."

It had rained for most of the day. Cornwall was rural and damp, in some places misty, and the gentle green hills were crisscrossed with stone walls. The cottage we rented south of Newquay lay along a narrow lane squeezed on both sides by head-high hedges and trees.

I was here with my girlfriend, Suzy, and her parents, Robin and Rosemary. They live on the east coast, in Norfolk. We'd strapped my board to the car and driven most of the way across England. Robin had just been named emeritus professor of computer science at the University of East Anglia. He had a tough skeptical Scots expression behind his bifocals; he was quiet, observant, and thorough. Before the trip he had sent me a diagram of his car, along with a series of questions to work out how to secure the board without causing disaster on the A30.

"Will you go surfing now," said Rosemary when we had settled into the cottage, "or shall I put the kettle on?"

Tea in general seems to pass through me without making an impression, and afternoon tea is a ritual I still can't understand. I went out for a surf.

Newquay is the site of England's only massive wave, the fickle Cribbar, and it's a tourist-ridden "surf capital," the rotten core of British surfing written up in all the magazines. The town itself, detached from its reputation, is a smallish and sometimes pretty cluster of gabled houses rising on slopes around a fishing bay. A lot of the mock Victorians are faced with stucco or pebbledash; some have been converted into surf hostels. The representative specimen is the Shark Bait Lodge, with a rubber mask of a Great White gaping out from its gable. Near the waterfront, a row of arcades and nightclubs alternate with new cafés, an old Gothic four-spired church tower, and oaken, black-windowed pubs.

The river opens into an estuary to the south, near our cottage and a village called Crantock. Newquay is so full of surf shops renting boards that the townside beaches, even on a cold day in March, can be crowded with beginner surfers. But the real surf was on our side of the estuary, at Crantock Beach. There was a rocky cliff and a cauldron of cold-looking waves. I paddled out from the beach, thinking that would be easier than jumping off the sharp-looking rocks. Wrong. A riptide carried me out to sea.

British coastlines were made by God for amusement parks, chalky cliffs, deep-fried whitebait, Brighton rock, and palace hotels with a Union Jacks snapping in the wind. Or else just terrible weather. "You drive to the seaside," explained Suzy, "park by the water, and stay in your car because the weather's shit. Then you eat a packet of crisps and drive home."

I paddled out of the rip and struggled toward a peak. The tide would be low in an hour. Already the jumble of greenish chop was starting to resolve into clean, cold, steep faces. An offshore breeze was hardly noticeable until you challenged it by paddling after a swell. Then a rain of heavy spray hurried up the slope of water and numbed your face. But the waves, when you dropped in, had power. The greenish faces sometimes opened up into a tight hollow curl. The water wasn't freezing—I'd been colder in Sylt—but I needed gloves. The paddling had turned my hands into raw chunks of meat.

A few locals paddled out. One of them nodded.

"Awright, mate."

"What's going on," I said, feeling foreign.

"Good waves?" he said in a sharp Cornish accent.

"Not bad. Is there a riptide here?"

"Yeah. We're probably in it right now. But you can paddle out of it that way." He pointed away from the rocks, into the bay.

I'd noticed that.

By low tide, a gang of young Cornishmen was in the water. They were greyhound lean and hungry for surf. Some had excellent style, and later Suzy said photographers were perched on the gorse-grown hillsides with two-foot telephoto lenses.

"You American?" said one of the surfers.

I nodded. "I came to see Cornwall and surf the Severn Bore."

"Aw, right."

The Severn is Britain's largest river, and it has a tidal phenomenon. A swell gathers in the estuary at every high tide and pushes a mass of water upstream. These surges are called bores, and on very high tides, about twelve times a year, the Severn Bore is large enough to surf. Britain has a community of surfers who chase the wave in boats and cars, and some hold records for the longest surfboard rides on earth.

"You'll need a longboard," the Cornish surfer said. "And look out fer dead sheep."

He turned and caught a spitting wave. I'd been half prepared to see sharks in the water in Britain. But sheep? I never came near him again, so I never had a chance to ask.

<center>~~~~~~~~~~~~~~~~~~~~</center>

Cornwall had been a busy mining region for about four thousand years until 1999, when the last tin mine closed. Fishing, an even older line of work, was just as hopeless. Fish populations off Cornwall had collapsed for most of the twentieth century; only the demand for young men in two world wars had revived the numbers of mackerel and pilchard and lobster, and then only for a few years. "Cornish boys are miners, Cornish boys are fishermen too," reads a famous piece of graffiti in Cornwall. "But when the mines and fish are gone, what are Cornish boys to do?"

A surf renaissance took hold in Cornwall as the older economy skidded to a halt. Between the mid-'90s and 2008, the number of British surfers grew to about half a million—an astonishing rise of

900 percent—and the scene was centered, unimaginatively, around Newquay. One reason was cheap flights from London. Another was sun, sand, chicks, and surf. Newquay's surfing past had gained it a reputation as a good place for stag parties, like Vilnius or Prague. Some Cornish towns, like Saint Ives are expensive and pretty, with jumbles of houses by the seaside and at least one stone pub dating back to Chaucer, but Newquay is expensive and vulgar. A venerable store called Bilbo Surfboards is still a fixture in town, but the original owners sold out long ago, and the former rail quays near the water have been replaced by a pedestrian mall crammed with gift shops and tawdry clubs.

A feeling of local pride had risen up in resistance. A small group of self-described Cornish militants even made bomb threats against restaurants run by English celebrity chefs. One chef, Jamie Oliver, had opened a slick franchise called Fifteen Cornwall on a cliff overlooking Watergate Bay, just north of Newquay. The point of Fifteen was to buy local food and hire local kids and give them experience for future careers. But it was also what Oliver called a "top class" restaurant, and some disgruntled Cornish patriots noticed the sweating wineglasses, the ocean view, and the bourgeois brushed steel. "We have seen the effects of this arrogant English man in our Country causing property prices to swell," read a press release from the Cornish National Liberation Army (CNLA). "We also declare this man, his business and the Watergate Bay Hotel, clients and cars bona fide targets" of firebombs.

Surfing played a strange role in this crossfire. On the one hand, it attracted London posers who just wanted to get themselves wet for a weekend: It brought the worst aspects of modern trash culture to Newquay. On the other, it was considered a local sport. I saw ads for surf shorts with Cornwall's black, white-crossed flag of Saint Piran's on the pocket. The caption said LOCAL PRIDE.

"This St. Piran's flag," read the CNLA manifesto, "is a guarantee of safety whilst those flying the Flag of St. George [the red and white English flag, distinct from the Union Jack] . . . are bona fide targets of the CNLA, be such flyers English incomers, misinformed Cornish Nationals or Tourists. To fly this flag is an invitation for our devolved operatives to take action and other damage to property cannot be ruled out."

The CNLA never bombed anyone. I also have no proof that any of its members could surf. But local Cornish surfers felt the same patriotic resentment of rich weekend holidaymakers from London—"driving new German or Scandi estate cars," as one commenter put it on a blog by British surf writer Alex Wade, "ordering sea bass and chardonnay, and occasionally venturing into the sea (to 'do some surfing—yah!') with their wetsuits on back to front."

Somehow surfing lends itself to localism wherever it migrates in the world. Which, on the surface, is absurd: How can the grandchildren of Cornish tin miners or the descendants of Berber rebels—or for that matter the children of insurance adjusters and aerospace engineers in suburban California—pick up an ancient Hawaiian watercraft and sneer at outsiders for not being "real"?

One reason is that surfing needs a knowledge of both local conditions and the ocean as a whole. Surfers will understand each other even if they can't speak the same language; at the same time they have an intimate relationship with the tides, rocks, and marine life in their local breaks. Outsiders may be welcome, but the kooks who vacation with expensive wetsuits and no instinct for waves, who bring a sense of entitlement to match their general lack of clue, who clutter up the water with slick new boards but no obvious respect for the sea—not to mention for the locals next to them—can bring out any surfer's inner Miki Dora.

Still, these passions have just attached themselves to surfing. They aren't new. As early as 1898 a writer named Arthur Quiller-Couch was trying to negotiate between the Cornish soul and the "second English invasion" of holiday pleasure seekers. He saw the declining fish and tin industries and realized tourism would be hard to resist. "I merely ask it to be noted how rapidly the strain has come upon us, an ancient people," he wrote, "with its inrush of motors and descent of the ready-made-bungalow builder, the hotel-investor, the holidaymaker who thinks no cove complete without a minstrel (negro) and a gramophone, the *paterfamilias* who brings his youngster to Tintagel with spade and bucket. Cornwall is not an improvised playground; it is not a 'Riviera,' and the use of that word, whoever first applied it to Cornwall, was and has been a commercial 'inexactitude.' To any right Cornishman, Cornwall is a mother with a character, a most egregious one, definite and dear. Having that character, she has a character to lose. At least let me implore the reader beyond Tamar to help us in protecting our noble coast from defacement by the Philistine."

The next morning I went to Newquay in search of a long, cheap sponge board to ride on the Severn. The Longboard House, uphill from the beach, was crowned with the most gargantuan surfboard I'd ever seen, a thick red wooden plank running the full width of the building, with a fin the size of a wide-screen TV. A lanky clerk inside said the board was thirty-nine feet long and shaped by the shop owner, Tim Mellors, who'd surfed it in 1999 at one of Newquay's town beaches.

"Can it be turned?" I said.

"No."

"..."

He smiled. "It takes a Jet Ski to swing it round. But another time, fourteen people rode it at once."

"You're kidding."

"It spanned three waves."

He showed us a plaque from the *Guinness Book of World Records*. It was "the longest board ever ridden." He said it had been surfed not just in Newquay but also in Saint Ives, down the coast.

"How did they get it there?"

He didn't know, but a circus troupe had returned it to Newquay on a caravan of cars driven by clowns. "They drove it through the streets and honked and waved out the windows. But they said that when they hit the brakes, the wheels of the cars would go up."

The clerk was full of information. But the shop had no sponge boards. They proved ridiculously hard to find. Suzy and I tried a few more shops along the high street, mainly bright new fashion stores with crisp flannel shirts and flowered board shorts in the windows. No one had a sponge. "Most of those boards don't get sold round here," one clerk told me. "They're too good for holiday rentals."

But casual talk about the surf yielded nothing in these stores, either. It wasn't local recalcitrance; they just weren't true surf shops. I asked one expressionless, bored-looking girl if she had foam boards for sale, and she seemed almost offended.

"Well, what about a surf guide to Cornwall?"

"No."

Nothing? A magazine?

"No."

"Is surfing always like this?" asked Suzy on our way out the door.

Newquay's resident surf historian is Roger Mansfield, a lean man in his fifties who wore wire glasses, a flannel shirt, and a patch of beard under his lip. We had lunch near the water on a foggy morning in something called the Irie Café, where the reggae was incessant. He objected when I asked about the origins of "English" surfing.

"British surfing," he corrected, "if you want to be accurate. I'm a Cornishman, and the history of Cornish surfing is different from the history of Irish, Scottish, Welsh, and English surfing."

But the fact remained—I said—that the first surfer on the British mainland had paddled out in Cornwall, which was part of England at the time. Cornwall had been annexed to England in the centuries after the first English invasion, about AD 600, and at the very latest the county had not been independent since a bloody Catholic peasants' uprising in 1549.

"There are treaties that still have to be settled," said Roger stiffly. "And it would be embarrassing to Westminster to have them settled.

Basically, Cornwall is still the last colony of the British Empire. But we don't have to go into that now."

The blood had risen in his face. I relented.

The main British surf pioneers were Pip Staffieri, an Italian immigrant who operated a pony-drawn ice cream cart on Newquay beaches in the 1930s, and a dentist called Jimmy Dix. Probably inspired by a picture of surfing Hawaiians in his *Encyclopedia Britannica,* according to Mansfield, Dix had tried and failed to build a Hawaiian-style board in Nuneaton, a landlocked village in Warwickshire hundreds of miles north of Cornwall. He then wrote to a Hawaiian wave-riding club for more precise dimensions. Instead of a helpful note, the Hawaiians shipped over a fourteen-foot, hollow-bodied board shaped by Tom Blake. These old boards look almost like rowing sculls now, but in 1938 a boat like that would have been the latest thing. Jimmy Dix roped it to his car and drove to Newquay.

Whether he stood up isn't clear. "It's possible, even probable, that he stood up and rode a few Cornish waves," according to Mansfield, "but we have no definite proof." Pip Staffieri, though, came across Dix's two surfboards lying on the beach. Staffieri had read about surfing in *his* encyclopedia, so he made a mental note of the nicer-looking board, and by 1940 he'd built a Tom Blake knockoff.

Staffieri is the first man on record to stand on a surfboard in Europe. His wave-walking presence on the beaches around Newquay made him a local celebrity, like George Freeth in California. Eventually Dix drove down to Newquay again and saw him. He was as impressed by the surfing as Staffieri had been by Dix's gear. The two men, members of carefully segregated classes—the dentist and the ice cream vendor, the middle-class tinkerer and the Italian immigrant—had drinks in a pub to compare notes. But apparently they never surfed together.

"Pip only died in 2005," said Roger. "And you should have seen his funeral. Masses of people were there. He had a huge Italian family scattered all over Britain, and most of them sold ice cream."

The United Kingdom has a ridiculous number of "first surfer" stories. One reason is that Brits like to travel. Not only does every subdivision of Britain and Ireland have an interesting surf pioneer, like Mansfield said; the pioneers could be fabulously far-flung.

George Freeth, to start with, had English as well as Irish blood—"my father being a native of Cork, Ireland, and my mother, part English and part Hawaiian." But he was born in Hawaii. The first British-born surfer was "quite possibly" Nigel Oxenden, according to the Stormrider Guide, a man from Jersey who learned to surf from Duke Kahanamoku on Waikiki in 1919. Oxenden returned home and formed the Island Surf Club on Jersey in 1923. It started as a club for bodyboarders, but according to Mansfield, the first serious British surf movement flourished on Jersey about twenty-five years later.

Jersey, though, is over by France. Its first surfers never had much influence on the UK mainland. That left room for Pip Staffieri, Jimmy Dix, and their successors.

The first Welsh surfer was Viv Ganz, who rode bodyboards in the waves near Swansea until he saw stand-up surfers on newsreel footage from Biarritz in 1960. Ganz tried to build two wooden boards of his own, but never quite learned to surf until he sent away to lifeguards in Jersey for a fiberglass board in 1963. Now Swansea—Dylan Thomas's hometown—is the surf capital of Wales.

Ireland is not part of Britain, but it may receive the best surf in the cluster of what cartographers call the British Isles. The first Irish surfer was a teenager called Joe Roddy, son of a lighthouse keeper, who built his own thirteen-foot paddleboard out of "tea chests and lashings of lighthouse paint," according to a description repeated in Irish newspapers. He paddled it around off the beaches of County Louth in 1949. Eventually it occurred to him to stand. "One time I came in and there was a line of people along the beach, just gobsmacked," he told a journalist. "They must have thought it was Christ back on the water again."

But the first great Irish surfer, Kevin Cavey, made a pilgrimage to Hawaii and California and brought modern boards home with him in 1966. Now Ireland has a respectable hard core of big-wave riders on its frigid western coast. Cavey probably first read about surfing in the same issue of *Reader's Digest* that excited the Behrens brothers on Sylt.

An Edinburgh teenager named Andy Bennetts learned to surf in Newquay around 1965, but never considered surfing anywhere else until he bought his own board from the Bilbo shop in 1967. He loaded it onto a train to Aberdeen, Scotland, walked two miles from the rail station, and became the first man to ride Scottish surf, according to Mansfield. In the meantime, an annual big-wave contest has been established at Thurso, on Scotland's north-facing shore, where surfers catch frigid swells rolling down past the Orkney and Faroe islands.

Edward VIII, when he was Prince of Wales, was the first British royal to surf. Like Nigel Oxenden, he took lessons from Duke in Hawaii. He spent three days in 1920 canoeing and surfing on the big island. "His Royal Highness has enjoyed his visit to Honolulu immensely," read a cable from his royal yacht back to the British consul. "He was especially delighted with the surfing. He was frightfully keen about it."

But the first British surfer in human history was probably neither Edward VIII nor Nigel Oxenden. During Captain Cook's fatal Hawaii landing in 1779, a midshipman on the *Resolution* called George Gilbert wrote a detailed description of six-foot alaia boards, built for commoners (different from the long, royal olo boards). He added these intriguing lines:

> Several of those Indians who have not got Canoes have a method of swimming upon a piece of wood nearly in the form of a blade of an oar. . . . These pieces of wood are so nicely balanced that the most expert of our people at swimming could not keep upon them half a minuit [sic] without rolling off.

Talk about English incomers! Whether the most expert of Cook's men stood up on those oarlike boards is open to question. But it would have been fun to watch them try.

The influence of the South Pacific on Europe is hard to exaggerate. The crews of Cook's ships learned to stop worrying about scurvy, debt, and homesickness for soggy, industrializing Britain. They bathed in tropical heat. There was exotic fruit, roasted pig, rich-tasting sea turtle, sweltering sunshine in February, and the sheer beauty of the islands and the tropical skies. "Ten thousand lamps, combined and ranged in the most advantageous order, by the hands of the best artist, appear faint when compared with the brilliant stars of heaven that unite their splendor to illuminate the groves, the lawns, and streams of Oparree," wrote one officer, describing a province of Tahiti. "In these elysian fields, immortality alone is wanting to the enjoyment of all those pleasures which the poet's fancy has conferred on the shades of departed heroes, as the highest reward of heroic virtue."

Through all these descriptions, next to sublime pleasure, there's a strain of danger and death. Maybe the best-known surf passage in all the diaries comes from Tahiti in 1777. William Anderson, the Scottish surgeon on the *Resolution,* saw a man trimming surf in his canoe at Matavai Bay. The quote is normally credited to Cook and called "the first Western description of surfing." It's not. But it is a sample of what Europeans were thinking when they met Pacific tribes who frolicked in the waves.

> He went out far from the shore, till he was near the place where the swell begins to rise; and, watching its first motion very attentively, paddled before it, with great quickness, till he found that it overtook him, and had acquired sufficient force to carry his canoe before it, without passing underneath. He then sat motionless and was carried along, at the same swift rate as the wave, till it landed him upon the beach. I could not help concluding that this man felt the most supreme pleasure while he was driven on so fast and so smoothly by the sea.

That man could be killed! you can almost hear the alarm sounding in Anderson's brain. *But he's having fun.*

Just as frightening for some of Cook's men, but easier to accept, was the sexual freedom they found in Polynesia. Many strange things were taboo in the South Pacific, but not prostitution. The islanders simply put no value on it. During Cook's first landing at Atooi, Hawaiian women came out in canoes with the men to trade with the strangers and offer their bodies, for trinkets or for free. "The woman who prostitutes herself does not seem, in the popular opinion, to have committed a crime," wrote one officer who wanted to correct the notion in England that Polynesian women were whores. "It must be confessed that all the women in this part of the world are complete coquets, and that few among them fix any bounds to their conversation; therefore it is no wonder that they have obtained the character of women of pleasure: yet we should think it very unjust if the ladies of England were to be condemned in the lump from the conduct of those on board of ships in our naval ports, or of those who infest the purlieus of Covent Garden or Drury Lane."

Cook's men, of course, brought Western venereal disease from Drury Lane to the South Pacific and started a lethal epidemic. Some had such a marvelous time they tried to desert. David Samwell, the Welsh surgeon on the *Discovery,* described how Cook found one sailor "lying down between two Women with his Hair stuck full of Flowers & his Dress the same as that of the Indians, that is with some Cloth about his middle & all other parts uncovered."

This loose island life would change Europe for good. Andrew Martin, a Cambridge don who also surfs, argued in the journal *Eighteenth-Century Studies* that scientific reports by Cook, Louis Antoine de Bougainville, and other explorers in the 1700s were gobbled up like romance novels back home. They inspired French revolutionaries like the Marquis de Sade and Camille Desmoulins. "Tahiti seemed to provide hard evidence that happiness was something more than an idea," wrote Martin. "Happiness was not a concept but a place." Cook and Bougainville reported back with (apparently) anthropological evidence of Rousseau's noble savage, which gave a scientific foundation for Europe's Romantic insurgencies.

Martin argues this new vision of happiness drove forward the French Revolution. It seems to me that the discoveries of paradise in the Pacific and the pursuit of paradise in politics happened, if anything, at the same time; but it's true that Hawaii and Tahiti lit the white man's imagination. *"O ma chère Lucile!"* wrote Desmoulins, journalist and poet, to his wife in 1794. "I was born to write poetry, to stand up for the unfortunate, to make you happy, and, with your mother and my father and a few other kindred spirits, to create a Tahiti!"

> Tahiti, in 1794 [interprets Martin], operates as an antithesis to the Terror: to France, prison, blade, blood. Tahiti is all pleasure, Paris is nothing but pain.

Of course, the struggle to bring Tahiti to Paris led to rivers of blood on the Place de la Révolution, and Desmoulins died with Georges Danton on the guillotine. But history, if not fortune, was on their side, and now Paris, with its trail of broken Romantic movements and Socialist insurrections; Paris, with its political freedoms, its bikini designers, its sex clubs, and its feverish democracy; Paris, with its Quiksilver store and its warming northern climate, is closer to Tahiti than Desmoulins ever dreamed.

⌇⌇⌇⌇⌇⌇⌇⌇⌇⌇⌇⌇⌇⌇⌇

Chris Jones runs a Newquay board shop on a small street overlooked by slate-colored gables and clusters of chimney pots. A sign in the window gave instructions for finding him in the back, and his shop appeared to be closed.

Chris has white hair, a beard, and a plump neck overgrown with white bristles. He's one of Britain's best-known board shapers. I found him in front of a band saw, wearing overalls and a pair of goggles. I told him my business. He watched me explain that I wanted an interview, but if he had no time right now I could come back later in the week. His hands were dusty; he had no pen, maybe no calendar to mark up. His whole gentle, heavy presence seemed to reject the idea of a plan.

At last he said, "I'll put the kettle on."

We drank tea and instant coffee at the back of his shop, in a clutter of board scraps and books, around a wooden crate. He rolled a thin cigarette. He said he picked up surfing in Newquay in 1964. "My parents ran a hotel, and they were very busy all summer," he said. "They used to pay the deck-chair guy to look after me on the beach. So I spent the whole day on the beach. And I had a little board we called a chicken run—a plywood surfboard with a little bent-up nose. And I used to see these other guys on fiberglass longboards, and basically, a fellow named Jack Lydgate let me get on one."

The problem in those days was water temperature. Wetsuits didn't exist. "When we started surfing, we had to make our own," Chris said. "And we actually surfed all through two winters without any suits at all. It was about three or four of us that used to surf at Tolcarne," just up the coast from the Newquay beaches. "And the guy that owned the sport shop on Tolcarne Beach was good enough to clear out his hut. The hut had an electric point outlet, and we used to put the electric fire in there. But we all had chilblains on our hands from standing in front of the fire after a surf."

To make wetsuits they handed around tailoring patterns and ordered rubber from a sports shop. But the rubber didn't stretch. Nylon-rubber blends like neoprene would come later. When they did—making wetsuits light, breathable, and easy to peel on and off— the crowds followed. "Wetsuits have just opened it all up, to everyone in this country," said Chris. One reason surfing later boomed around the world, from southern Chile to the north of Scotland, was the march of wetsuit technology.

In the early '60s the Beatles still wore slim black ties. It was an era of beach parasols, sun hats, and Punch-and-Judy shows on the sand. Essentially the 1950s. Off the Newquay beaches people water-skied and rode plywood bodyboards, which had been known at the British seaside for decades. Then a younger style started to invade British society, less dark but just as subversive as the mod and rocker movements in London and Liverpool, and for a while the coolest thing a British schoolboy could do was listen to the Beach Boys and try to skateboard or surf. "Suddenly every city kid without a wave to his name tuned into a youth cult that stormed out of California and rushed around the world," wrote Doug Wilson and Rod Holmes in their book on British surf history, *You Should Have Been Here Yesterday*. Surfing prefigured the true '60s in Britain.

I asked if British culture had grown less uptight, or less refined, since surfing first took hold. "Well, if you just talk about Newquay," he said, "it's made it more cosmopolitan. There's people from all over the world here. From all over Britain as well. You won't hear too many Cornish voices in Newquay. Most people don't even consider it Cornish anymore." He gave a dark laugh. But he was ambivalent about the changes. He hated the nightclubs downtown and the fact that his own children couldn't afford a house. On the other hand, he lived here. He couldn't hate it. He seemed to accept the changes the way anyone in Britain accepts bad weather.

Jack Lydgate, who let Chris ride his first foam board, was an American who belonged to the hard core of older surfers around Newquay in the early '60s. But Chris also got to know Bill Bailey, an Englishman and cofounder of Bilbo Surfboards. "I personally regard him as the spiritual father of surfing in this country," Chris said. "Very clever bloke. He could turn his hand to anything. He taught himself how to blow foam. And there was nothing he wouldn't tell anyone, about anything. If they wanted to know about surfboards, it was 'Come in and have a look.' And he built Bilbo up from workin' in a little garage into really quite a large company."

Bailey pioneered the British surf industry. He started shaping custom boards in a Newquay garage while a visiting Australian, Bob Head, started conducting fiberglass experiments of his own in a chicken shack up the coast. Soon the two men joined forces and sold boards under the "Bilbo" name in the mid-'60s. The name combined Bill's and Bob's first names and referred, not by accident, to Tolkien's main character in *The Hobbit*, Bilbo Baggins. Bill and Bob had some hippie in them, but they weren't middle-class dropouts from London. "Surfing was a comparatively working-class thing to do," Roger Mansfield had said. "It was a bit like California in the early days. Some of the first surfers were engineers and inventors like Bill."

Chris learned to shape from Bailey. He surprised me by saying the old man was still alive, retired on a farm south of Newquay in a village called Goonhavern. Recently he'd built an "elephant gun" and strolled into Chris's shop to ask for a custom bag. "This thing was like a cannon," said Chris. "He'd made it himself. He'd taken a tube and machined it into a hexagon, rifled the inside, then assembled everything else. And he wanted me to make a bag. I don't know where he learned to do it. But that's what he's like. If he doesn't know how to make something, he'll figure it out."

We talked a little more, and then Chris surprised me by picking up his phone and dialing Bill's number.

"Hello, Bill, 'ow you doing? Yeah, good stuff. Bill, I've got a gentleman here from California, he's doing a book about surfing. Wouldn't mind a chat with you. Maybe you could arrange to meet with him sometime, I don't know."

He nodded into the phone.

"Want to have a quick word now? . . . Okay, I'll pass you over."

So it was set up like that, without formality. Bailey died in the meantime, so the interview was a stroke of luck. To get to his house I had to drive down a winding, foggy road and through the middle of Goonhavern. Beyond the village I found a narrow path leading deep into a plot of pastureland where rabbits hopped across the rutted road and the Baileys owned a green-slatted farm house. "I told Bill no one would be able to find him if he lived up there," said Chris Jones. "He said, 'Well, that's the point.'"

Bill was a pouchy old man wearing a knit cap to keep his bald head warm. He wore bifocals and a faded flannel shirt. The house felt like a ski cabin, with framed photos on knotted-panel walls. We sat in armchairs next to an electric radiator, and his wife Lil made tea while Bill showed me ammunition for his massive homemade gun. One bullet was ten centimeters long and looked like it might pierce a tank. "I change what I do about every five years," Bill said. "Otherwise I get bored. I've been lots of things, but it's the surfing everyone wants to hear about."

He was so well known in surf circles that he could custom-shape a new board whenever he wanted an infusion of cash. But it was a small part of his life, he said—he'd founded Bilbo in 1963 and was out by 1970. Now he wanted to prospect for gold in Canada. He owned a plot of land in British Columbia where he and Lil could live in an RV and pan for gold nuggets and flakes. On his first visit he'd found a nugget in some river sludge. "I've always been interested in that kind of thing," he said. "I like to make jewelry, so I'd like to find some nodules of gold, to put on chains . . . " He shrugged. "It's just havin' the time. Seventy-five, what else am I gonna do?"

I asked Bill whether he still surfed. He laughed and lifted his old flannel shirt to show me a colostomy bag.

He'd discovered surfing as a Newquay lifeguard in the early '60s. He formed a surf club and joined a world network of lifeguarding clubs, which brought crucial information from Australia that was otherwise hard to find. "We had a blue book for lifesaving," said Bill, "and a brown book for equipment." Based on details from those booklets, he started building surf skis, cigar-shaped paddleboards. "We built those, but almost overnight they were redundant, because then the American came"—Doug McDonald—"and then the Australians. And they had something they called a zip board."

A zip board was just a Malibu longboard made from balsa and

highly maneuverable. McDonald had a new foam-core version that was about to revolutionize surfing. Every surfer in Newquay wanted to buy it, Bill included. "What happened was, he'd run his yellow van into a sand dune and popped the gearbox," Bill said. "I got the board by offerin' to buy both. Which saved him a problem. And I ran it for a few years, you know. Every summer I used to live in the old van. I had a full-sized bed in the back, that kind of thing. My first son was conceived in it."

The foam board started Bailey on the next phase of his career. To make an imitation, he mixed chemicals from commercial kits and learned to blow, or expand, polyurethane foam into rectangular blanks.

Foam is the most poisonous as well as the most convenient aspect of surfboard manufacture. Liquid chemicals for the foam—mixed right—will expand within a concrete mold and harden. Then you have a pliable blank to whittle into a surfboard core, which, compared to using balsa wood, is like shaping butter. A shaper then coats the core in liquid resin and fiberglass cloth, which seals into a hard shell. But the process of blowing foam is so difficult and potentially so dangerous that most shapers buy blanks from specialists. Gordon "Grubby" Clark in California monopolized the foam business in America from the 1960s until the end of 2005. He had about eighty concrete molds in his Clark Foam factory in Laguna Niguel, which supplied the world surf industry with its standard range of blanks. These were the fundamental sizes and shapes of most surfboards in the United States and around the world, the Platonic ideals of the modern board.

"I built my mold—a wooden mold—in half, like a board split right the way through the middle," said Bill. "So that in the event of a catastrophe, I would only lose one half the system. . . . Anyway, the first blow was quite surprising. It went all over the place, I couldn't shut the mold in time, all sorts of things. But you pick up an awful lot that first time. And I only lost half a board. What was left made a bellyboard that I used to lend to Roger Mansfield. He was down with his father one day, and I gave him the board and said, 'Go on and show me what you can do.' And he stood up on it."

One compound involved in making foam is an isocyanate, which foam specialists tend to buy ready-made from companies like Dow. "You can make it yourself," said Bill, "but it's extremely dangerous because it gives off a gas that they used to use in the First World War. And that's what killed thousands of Indians who were all camped around the factory in India." He meant the Union Carbide disaster in 1984, which killed at least eight thousand people living near a pesticide plant in Bhopal. A cloud of methyl isocyanate leaked from a holding tank one night and crept through the tent city. Union Carbide had manufactured the chemical for pesticides, not surf foam, but the story shows how nasty the elements of a modern board can be. It was this nastiness that explained the sudden demise of Clark Foam in 2005.

Clark shut his business without warning, faxed an explanation to his clients, and ordered his workers to smash his concrete molds. William Finnegan wrote in the *New Yorker* that shapers and surfers "made pilgrimages to the concrete recycling plant where the broken molds were dumped—piled askew, like huge robbed caskets. A local shaper could still identify, for his companions, which molds had produced the blanks for boards that were ridden to world championships."

Clark mentioned isocyanates in his fax, but there was no legal action against him, no pending investigation. He'd been sued by employees over cancer-causing chemicals, and the threat of more suits may have been enough to shut him down. Laws regarding isocyanates and other chemicals had simply changed in California, and Clark Foam hadn't. "As I understand it," said Bill, "you know, California is very big on environmental things, and as soon as somebody was informed that he was using isocyanate, that was it." He gave a bitter laugh. "Overnight. I mean, that was it."

Clark's closure rocked the surf industry. The price of boards went up within days. But Clark's near-monopoly on blanks also collapsed, and now more shapers use foam derived from a safer kind of isocyanate. "The sad part about it is, Clark could still be going now had he switched to developing an MDI foam, like we have in England," said Bill. "HomeBlown, they've developed this white MDI foam, which you can pour without a mask on," meaning the foam itself doesn't give off aerosols. "It's very safe."

At least for shapers—still not safe for people who might live in tents near the chemical plant.

Bailey was a cheerful but phlegmatic man with a high voice. He was physically slow but full of curiosity. Lil was different, like a bird compared to his buffalo. She had a slim small body, rectangular red glasses, and a polite piercing voice. When Bill couldn't remember something she chimed in. When I mentioned the Severn Bore, he said, "Oh, we surfed the bore in the '60s. Whatever wave was around, we tried to surf it. . . . Jack Lydgate was there. All the Australians were there. And we used the double ski [a two-man kayak] from the surf club. It's a very slow wave. Just watch out for dead sheep."

I blinked.

"I keep hearing that. What does it mean?"

"Well, when the river rises, it washes everything off the bank. I remember Warren the Australian and I, we launched the double ski, and we were in the middle of the river. Two other guys were on the sides because they were psyched out about ridin' it. But the wave was biggest by the banks, and there was so much water that year, one of these guys rode quite a long way. But in the end he got swept up on a bank. Then he was on a farm. He had to run across a pasture, and the bullocks chased him."

When Suzy and I left Cornwall, the sun alternated with huge cottony gouts of black-edged cloud. I drove her to the airport and continued on alone toward the Severn. That night a freak and silent spring storm dumped more snow than anyone had seen in the Midlands in twenty years. On the open highway through Gloucestershire the next morning, snow and rain spat and seemed to float in white drifts through patches of sunlight, against a watercolor backdrop of brush-grown hills. Parts of the road were lined with white-frosted trees and low banks of snow. It was like going skiing.

The Severn River is the largest waterway in Britain. It's as important to the West Country and the Midlands as the Mississippi is to the American South. The road along its northern bank is narrow and winds along green pastureland and the occasional stone-church village. Later I would see the funnel of the Severn estuary from a plane, and at low tide it was a glistening brown expanse of rippled mud. At high tide—no matter how high—the seawater covers these mud flats and surges upriver. The Severn narrows quickly enough to give the surges momentum, and sometimes they change the river's flow for a few hours. "With the aid of a good tide," wrote a retired cargo boat skipper named B. A. Lane in a 1993 memoir about navigating the river called *Time and Tide Wait for No Man on the Severn,* "the time between Gloucester lock to the Upper Lode lock at Tewkesbury could be cut by at least an hour. No river man worth his salt would miss the opportunity of running with a good tide."

The Severn Bore Inn is a tavern on the river at a village called Minsterworth. It has high, gabled farmhouse walls and brass lettering. The bartender was a short, mischievous-looking man with white hair, bad teeth, and a wrinkle-folded smile. His name, I learned later, was Derrick. Fooled by the word *inn,* I asked if they had any rooms. "Naw, we don't do that," said Derrick. "It's too expensive to run it as a bed 'n' breakfast." The damp countryside along the Severn would prove to be studded with these old public houses, flickering in and out of use like candles.

"Will it get crowded here tonight?" I said. "Because of the bore?"

"I shouldn't think so," he said. "It isn't very big this year. Only two stars. It's meant to be bigger on Tuesday."

Free schedules for the bore lay in front of him on the bar. The times for each tide also gave a size rating. A two-star bore was the biggest of the year; some bores rate four or five.

"Do people take off from outside the inn?" I asked, and here Derrick the bartender told a congenial lie.

"Oh no, they go from Newnham," he said. "It's wide there, and it's so shallow you can stand in the water and wait ferrit."

By the end of the next day I would know better. But I thanked him and kept moving down the highway until I found a tavern at Westbury-on-Severn, closer to Newnham. The building was a damp, shambling public house with a white-tablecloth dining room. A cemetery outside was overlooked by a daggerlike church steeple, slate gray, with a brass clock face. In the distance I heard the bleating of sheep.

I was here for the highest bores of the year, but since the bore depends on the tides, the size of the wave rises and falls in a predictable nine-year cycle. I'd turned up at the bottom of the cycle, which was disappointing but hard to remedy.

I'd never seen a tidal bore, so I drove back to Minsterworth that night to watch the first one pass. It was bitterly cold. About twenty-five people collected on a patch of frosted grass behind the Severn Bore Inn, atop a high muddy bank. We could see the dark water reflecting a faint wash of light in the sky—either the glow of a distant town or the remnants of a late northern twilight. The landscape felt Wagnerian. A family near me stared out at the water.

"It's a bit like watching paint dry, isn't it?" the man said.

"I just don't know what we're waiting for," said his wife. "Can't be too exciting, can it? Just a big ripple of water?"

"Well, it says two meters. If it's a two-meter *wall* of water, that should be interesting."

A surfer wandered out on a grassy bank with a green glowstick dangling from his board. We watched him stroke to the middle of the river and begin to float away from us, downstream. (The Severn flowed to our right, toward the ocean, about twenty miles away.)

Soon a boat came downriver and moved a searchlight over the bank, inspecting us. Then it sped upriver again.

"It's late," the man complained. "Two minutes."

"Well, we can't leave now. It's the second-biggest bore in the world. You have to come see it in your own backyard, don't you?"

Two more surfers climbed down to the water, paddled out, and disappeared gently with the current.

At last we heard the crashing, stately march of the bore as it rounded a bend in the river. Dark swells wavered. A shout came from a surfer. A mass of whitewash disturbed the glassy surface and the rushing grew loud and something smacked the bank in front of us and water exploded twelve feet high. People screamed. No surfers had managed to catch the wave, as far as I could see, but suddenly the river was different. A messy flow ran behind the head of water, rippling at least four feet above the previous level like a river in flood, but moving briskly in reverse.

"It sweeps off sheep sometimes," I informed the family.

"It nearly swept one of us off."

The next morning was clear and cold, with frost on the church steeple and the cemetery grass. I had a quick breakfast at the pub, wearing my wetsuit, then drove ten minutes to Newnham and parked near another pub which was perched on a high concrete bank. Glinting brown water stretched at least a hundred yards to cow pastures on the opposite side. The current moved with a placid, lazy force to my right. I climbed down the bank on a wrought-iron ladder that obviously had not been installed for surfers, launched my board from a mossy rock, and let the current glide me downriver. Half a mile farther, a line of surfers in colorful wetsuits waited in the waist-high water.

The first surfer on the Severn was a World War II veteran named "Mad Jack" Churchill, an Englishman who learned to surf in Australia during the '40s and had a number of unusual talents. He learned to play the bagpipes in Burma, where he served with a British regiment in the Burma Rebellion. Later he learned to shoot a bow and arrow well enough to represent England in world-championship contests. He hired himself out as an archer in Hollywood films, and during World War II he shot Nazis dead with feathered arrows. He also took prisoners with his sword. "Any soldier who goes into battle without his sword," he once declared, "is improperly dressed." German troops caught Jack and even sent him to the concentration camp at Sachsenhausen, but he escaped by sneaking past the guards one night and crossing the Brandenburg plain for eight days with only a rusty can for cooking stolen vegetables. "Surf pioneer," in other words, ranked near the middle of Mad Jack's list of attainments.

But in 1955 he took a handmade board to a muddy bank of the Severn and slipped into the water at Stonebench, farther upriver from Minsterworth and the Severn Bore Inn. A local farmer watched him ride the wave, but no one knows how long he lasted. The next people on record to surf the river were Bill Bailey and his friends in 1962.

My heart began to trot. Waiting for the bore could be nerve-racking. The stained concrete bank stood thirty feet high and resembled the hull of a battleship. It was a formidable work of flood control, pocked with rusted drainage valves in case the river slopped over the edge and threatened the inn. A line of damp green scum showed where the river had flowed the night before—about a third of the way up.

Soon the rushing whitewater began to march into view. I heard hoots. The bore advanced with a steady, streaming, ineluctable rush. I saw the whole line of surfers begin to move. Like a single creature they combed upriver. By the time it reached me most of the wave was mushy and broken, only two feet high, but I paddled in front of a glassy rolling section and took off.

Then I was standing among twenty other surfers, old and young, plus a number of kayaks. "Alright, mate," one of them said, and made room. Since the bore was a limited resource, no one felt possessive; they observed a level of camaraderie I'd never seen in such crowded conditions. People adjusted their boards for new arrivals and just kept moving. We cut back and forth; we tried not to get caught in eddies or whirlpools or dead spots where the stately push of the water might slow. The force of a wave like this would be determined not just by rocks and contours on the bottom of the river, but also by the curve of the banks and the power of the opposing current. Some people dropped away; others arrived. At last I hit an eddy and fell. At first I was in denial—I thought I would just catch another wave. A few swells followed behind the head of the bore and I paddled after them. But nothing was really there except a high, rising, soupy volume of water. The next wave wouldn't be along for twelve hours.

I paddled to the bank and landed on a set of slippery, slowly disappearing rocks. I grabbed long reeds to climb up. At the top of the bank a man with a cup of coffee and a white beard, the owner of the property I was about to cross, was waiting.

"Y'alright, then," he said.

"Fine."

"She moves fast."

One thing about a tidal surge is that it can't move as fast as a car. Other surfers in the parking lot strapped their boards to their roofs and hurried down the road. I emulated them. (There was a reason these people were called bore chasers.) By car it was twenty minutes to the Severn Bore Inn; the wave would take an hour to travel the same distance. I parked in a muddy yard, pulled on my boots and gloves, unstrapped the board, and tromped across the grass.

The landscape was no longer bleak in the daylight, but green and English pastoral. People stood on the frosted deck in coats and gloves and watched the water move placidly between banks overgrown with bending trees. The inn itself hadn't opened, but soon whole vans of surfers unloaded in the lot. A few had soft, white, numbered helmets.

I said, "Is there a race?"

"Hey? No." He laughed.

I pointed to my head to indicate his helmet. "Just keeping track of yourselves."

"That's right."

They turned out to be members of a water-polo team. The helmets helped them distinguish each other in YouTube videos.

I followed a muddy path along the top of the bank. Gnarled old trees grew from the waterline; the bank was an overgrown cliff. I looked for a way down until I saw a man I recognized from the previous night at the inn. He was a large guy with youthful but graying hair, a stout neck like Chris Jones's, and a habit of putting what looked like a plastic cigarette filter in his mouth, as if he wanted to light a cigarette. After a few minutes the filter went back in his pocket. He had talked knowledgeably about the bore, and I had gathered his name was Neil. He turned out to be a bore enthusiast who posted videos of the wave on discussion boards and participated in heated debates. A tidal bore, I realized, was like crack cocaine to people with trainspotting instincts. Not only was there a regular schedule for the wave to deviate from; there was weather, wave height, flotsam, a gallery of river-surf celebrities, and even the occasional world record to note and discuss.

"Hi there."

"Hello."

He pointed to a slick narrow muddy chute running fifteen feet down to the water.

"Forget your dignity," he said. "Everyone slides."

I shrugged and took two steps down the chute using weed-grown footholds. Then I lost my balance and slipped on my butt straight into the water. There was a graceless splash. My board clunked down after me.

Neil Law and his friend Stuart Ballard turned out to be interesting people. Not only did they collect details about the bore, they'd also organized against a plan to build a "barrage," or turbine-powered dam, across the river to exploit the Severn tides. At first glance tidal power sounded like a brilliant idea, of course, but in the Severn there was a serious problem with silt. The few experiments with tidal barrages and barriers in Canada had been ruined or hindered by silt. The dam wasn't a new idea in Britain—an engineer called Thomas Fulljames first proposed a mile-long masonry barrage across the Severn in 1849. But the idea was controversial.

America's only tidal bore once hassled steamboats on the Colorado River. The Hoover Dam stanched the river in the 1930s, and now the tidal surge from the Gulf of California—called a *burro* in Spanish—just floods the salt flats south of Arizona.

Anyway, I stood around with a handful of surfers near a wide bend in the river. The river had green, thickly hedged banks on both sides, with trees overhanging the water. The river bottom had a slick oily feel. "Wipe the mud off your feet," someone said as he laid flat on his board to paddle. "Slippery."

A few surfers in numbered helmets discussed whether the wave would hold its power around the bend. Another, named Paul, floated downstream as far as the elbow of the river. Then we heard buzzing outboard motors. A boat appeared, followed by two inflatable dinghies. And then we saw the wave, which had resolved over the last hour into a deliciously clean, three-foot rolling face.

"This first bit?" one new surfer shouted to his friends.

"Yeah, mate. There's nothing else."

Then a number of things happened at once. The wave, since it was rounding a turn, piled up on one side of the river, with its clean face crumbling into whitewash on the left. This whitewash sucked Paul against the bank and before the wave reached us we saw him tumble into the mud and his board bounced up into the brooding trees. The boats zipped by on the right. I took off near the middle of the river, trying to avoid Paul's mistake but aware that the wave would lose power away from the bank. Just then the wakes from the boats rippled the wave and we all missed it. There was a mad scramble for the slippery bank. The streaming, quickly rising water had a faint odor of cow manure.

Afterward, in the lot, Neil turned up with his camera.

"Now I have photographic evidence of what a boat can do to the bore," he said. "It was in good shape until the wake crossed it. You would have been on it," he said to me. "Those were pilots who should have known better. They know this river. Although I think Gordon Ramsay was on one of the boats."

"Was he?" someone said.

"He's doing a show about the river."

Gordon Ramsay was another TV chef. A rumor had gone around that he was filming an episode about a local fish smokehouse on the Severn and about English seafood in general. He had a reputation for swearing too much on TV and telling restaurant owners what they were doing wrong.

A few of us crowded around Neil's camera to watch the replay. Then a surfer came up and said, "Somebody passed a fridge-freezer above Newnham."

"Oh, so that's where it is," said Neil.

"Moves up and down, does it?" said another surfer.

"Yeah, every bore someone has a fridge-freezer sighting. It's been floating up and down for at least two years. Allegedly," he said, "*allegedly*, somebody even rode it one year. He said he fell off his board and found this fridge-freezer floating next to him, so he climbed on it and rode it some way like a bodyboard. Allegedly."

I took this opportunity to mention dead sheep.

"I've heard that too," said Neil. "But I've been surfing and following the bore for two years, and I've never seen any dead livestock."

That night I sat at the bar of the Severn Bore Inn with a few British surfers and a jowly old man with white hair and wide, unfocused eyes. He held forth about "elverin'," fishing for baby European eels, which swim upstream with the bore for six weeks or so in the spring. They're also called glass eels. Tiny, wriggling, clear, and born in the western

Atlantic, they drift on long currents across the ocean and swim up rivers in Europe and Africa to mature. After a stint in freshwater, the eels migrate downriver again to catch the Gulf Stream and mate in the warm Sargasso Sea.

British monarchs have shifted position on elver fishing for centuries, back and forth, between declarations to allow it and prohibitions to "conserve" the eels, which seem almost ridiculously cautious now, in light of the modern population collapse. A doctor in 1858 described elver fishing on the Avon:

> They were so numerous that the river appeared solid with them for a considerable distance around, and there were a great number of persons, men, women, and children, dipping them out by means of fine sieves, baskets covered with very coarse bunting or muslin, or other contrivances, and depositing them in pails, pans, and washing tubs; many large ones I saw more than half filled.

Now elvers are caught in the Severn by the thimbleful, using fine dip nets the size of large buckets. The populations have fallen by more than 90 percent since the '70s. The fates of the young eels are therefore regulated: 40 percent go to restaurants; the rest have to be sold live to breeding farms around the European Union. Almost all are exported. If I wanted fried elvers, I'd have better luck in Japan.

"We get all kinds of things in the river," said Derrick the bartender. "Canadian sea bass, lampreys, porpoises, an' once we had a baby whale. But that died. The whale and the porpoises died."

"When we used to catch elvers as kids," the old man shouted, "you couldn't get rid of the bloody things. You couldn't get rid of 'em!"

"On a wheelbarrow, 'round the street," said Derrick.

"How much do you get for them now?" I said.

"Two hundred pounds a kilo," the old man said.

"Jesus."

"Because in Japan, they eat 'em like a delicacy," said the old man. "A bit like caviar. So everyone's fishin' 'em out of the river. You need a license to get 'em now. But they're not breedin' anymore. They're not growin' up."

"How many can you catch in a night?"

"Well, not too many, because they're all fished out," he said. "But we used to get, fer a pint of elver"—he reached across the bar to demonstrate with a glass. "This is a pint."

"Yeah."

"For a pint of elver, we'd get a tenner."

"A tenner a pint!" Derrick echoed.

"That's old money, that," said the old man.

"They had elver-eatin' competitions in all the pubs," Derrick said. "Who could eat the most elvers."

"Live or dead?"

"Oh, you had to eat 'em cooked."

"There's elver with bacon and egg," the old man said. "You get some bacon, plenty of fat on it, put the elvers in, put the lid on it, fry it, then put an egg in."

"Baby eel fried with egg?"

"Yup. It's all right."

"My gran told me this," Derrick said, imparting a cherished tradition. "Use the bacon fat, and she used to put—I'll tell you what—baked beans in the thing. Bacon in a pan, you put yer egg in next, right, *then* you put your elvers in so they don't explode. And you mix it all together."

"There ya go!" the old man shouted. "You're larnin' off the locals."

One of the surfers at the bar was Paul; the others were clean-cut guys from Cornwall. They talked about home. but Derrick shook his head. "Don't like Cornwall," he said. "Got no use ferrit."

Derrick was a Gloucestershire local, and Gloucestershire has enough pride of its own; he couldn't take the Cornish attitude seriously. Gloucestershire is known for low rolling hills and pork sausage. It has seen Roman roads, Celtic and Saxon kings, and Viking raids up the Severn. The name of the river comes from Sabrina, or Hafren, a pagan Welsh goddess. Near the tidal estuary, she used to relinquish influence to an ocean deity, Nodens, who resembled Neptune and is shown sometimes riding a horse on the crest of the rushing bore. He's a reminder that the British Isles were once as wild and strange as Polynesia, no less thick with half-naked tribes and weird superstitions.

"Did you surf today?" Derrick asked.

"Today and yesterday," I nodded. "I was surprised the wave was so clean."

"Yeah, but not so big this year. I mean, this was a two-star bore this year. But when there's a four- and five-star bore . . . " he implied with the grim set to his mouth that the wave could be very impressive. "The force of the bore is greater than anything in the sea. It's far greater than any surf in Cornwall," he declared, "and probably in America." I didn't contradict him. "And when you actually get on it—what a great experience."

Derrick, I think I've said, had white hair and a wrinkly smile, rotten teeth, a wrestler's build, and a generally puckish manner that belonged in a Dickens novel. I couldn't picture him on a surfboard. Maybe he was exaggerating. It was hard to tell because most of us were drunk; we'd managed to close the place down. The darkness and damp of the Gloucestershire countryside seemed to weigh on the pub windows like a winter fog, and between drinks I felt extremely far from home.

Then I made an observation that lifted my mood a little. The Severn Bore Inn was an elephant of an old alehouse with polished oak and a phalanx of beer taps—a more traditionally British establishment was hard to imagine. But a majority of the people in it were surfers.

When Captain Cook dropped anchor near an island called Huahine, off Tahiti, during his first voyage in 1769, a band of canoes paddled out to meet the ship. One carried the island's king and queen. They boarded full of bewilderment. "They seemed surprised at whatever was shown them, but made no enquiries after any thing but what was offered to their notice," reads a contemporary history of Cook's voyage. "After some time they became more familiar; and the king, whose name was Oree, as a token of amity, proposed exchanging names with Capt. Cook, which was readily accepted."

The Englishman became Captain Oree, and the Polynesian took the name King Cookee.

6

ISRAEL AND THE GAZA STRIP:
TWO OPPOSED IDEAS

"MR. MOORE?"

"Yes."

"What was the purpose of your visit?"

"Surfing."

"But there are no waves in Israel," the uniformed woman told me.

"Oh yes there are."

"Where else have you been?" she said, flipping through my passport.

"Morocco and Indonesia," I said, knowing she'd see those stamps.

"Also for surfing?"

"Yes."

She was an airport attendant, not a government official, and I was trying to leave Israel, not enter it. But rockets had been flying along the Gaza border.

"Did you meet anyone in Morocco?"

"Of course."

"Who did you meet?"

I made up a name.

"And how do you know this person?" she said.

This line of questioning had to be repeated three times before I could put my luggage on the conveyor belt.

"This was months ago," I said. "What could it have to do with Israel?"

"We want to make sure you aren't being used by somebody. This person gave you nothing to carry to Israel?"

"Of course not."

I moved on to "primary inspection"—bags through the conveyor belt—and a humiliating secondary inspection, which involved a number of young women unpacking my bags to swipe every surface for explosive powder. I don't mind people rooting through my underwear, but it raised my hackles to watch them inspect my books. *To Jerusalem and Back* by Saul Bellow roused no suspicion. Neither did *The Middle East,* by Bernard Lewis. But *A History of Modern Palestine,* by Ilan Pappé, had the wrong title. The woman read the rear cover and sifted the pages. She read scrawls on one of my bookmarks. My heart pounded. No one, until then—no one in uniform—had ever scrutinized me for my ideas.

She showed the book to her boss and they talked in Hebrew while the other women wheeled my surfboard away for tertiary inspection.

"Okay. Thank you," the woman said at last. "Do you want to repack your bag, or should I do it?"

"What was that with the book?" I said.

"Nothing. We just have to be careful."

"I'm from America," I told her, as if that made any difference. "These things make me nervous."

"Yes."

"Would you have kept me off the plane if I had the wrong kind of book?"

She thought for a minute. "No. We just have to be careful. You understand."

"I'd rather not have someone say that to me in my own country," I said. "You understand."

"Yes."

The others wheeled my surfboard back and I was free to check in. There were three more passport inspections, two more wipe downs of the laptop, one more security line. Then I could sit for a while around a splashing circular fountain in the elegant marble atrium of Ben Gurion Airport.

"I find that no other question," Christopher Hitchens wrote about Israel and the Palestinians around this time, "so much reminds me of F. Scott Fitzgerald and his aphorism about the necessity of living with flat-out contradiction. Do I sometimes wish that Theodor Herzl and Chaim Weizmann had never persuaded either the Jews or the gentiles to create a quasi-utopian farmer-and-worker state at the eastern end of the Mediterranean? Yes. Do I wish that the Israeli air force could find and destroy all the arsenals of Hezbollah and Hamas and Islamic Jihad? Yes. Do I think it ridiculous that Viennese and Russian and German scholars and doctors should have vibrated to the mad rhythms of ancient so-called prophecies rather than helping to secularize and reform their own societies? Definitely. Do I feel horror and disgust at the thought that a whole new generation of Arab Palestinians is being born into the dispossession and/or occupation already suffered by their grandparents and even great-grandparents? Absolutely, I do."

Israel, we need to establish from the very start, exists. It's a modern, functioning, bustling state, with traffic jams and bureaucrats and public parks. For some reason people love to debate Israel's existence—should it exist, can it exist, will it stop existing—until the topic resembles a make-work program for journalists as well as politicians. President Mahmoud Ahmadinejad in Iran made headlines by asking why the Middle East had to accept a state of Israel "because of" World War II. Why not put Israel in Alaska, he wondered, and the number of people who took him seriously—I know this from reader mail we received at Spiegel Online—is astonishing. As if Zionism hadn't existed before Hitler! So let's get a few things out of the way. Israel exists, and should exist, because even before World

War II most societies on earth could turn suddenly lethal to Jews, not just in Europe. Israel also isn't going anywhere. No matter how often its conservatives, or its enemies, try to invoke the prospect of its destruction, the end of Israel would be a disaster as unthinkable as the destruction of fourteen cities the size of New Orleans, or the sudden collapse of an American state the size of Maryland. None of Israel's enemies can manage that disappearing trick, not without a nuclear bomb. But Israel's existence is still a deep contradiction, so understanding it requires a tolerance for paradox. "The test of a first-rate intelligence," said F. Scott Fitzgerald, in the aphorism Hitchens referred to, "is the ability to hold two opposed ideas in the mind at the same time, and still retain the ability to function."

Okay.

I stayed in a cheap hostel on Ben Yehuda Avenue, which runs parallel to the beach in Tel Aviv. The deck of my room overlooked the street and was overlooked in turn by two of Tel Aviv's white towers. My first five days in town were plagued by a rare and violent storm. The rattling rain and hail and whipping winds found every gap in the windows and walls of my room. Ben Yehuda Avenue itself is a boulevard of misshapen olive trees, crumbling stucco apartment buildings, and a lively assortment of cafés, trinket shops, bookstores, shoe stores, dress shops, white-lit bodegas, falafel joints, Laundromats, and hotels. Old air conditioners studded the windows of flaking apartment houses. Flamelike Hebrew letters glowed from dusty, electric-lit signs. The street smelled like exhaust from straining buses and sometimes the dissolute odor of the sea. But the neglect had energy; it was almost deliberate, as if people had better things to do than keep up the neighborhood.

The state of the buildings surprised me. I had had the impression that Israel was a triumph of Jewish labor, a poor outpost of the Ottoman Empire cultivated by the settlers into a sort of smaller California. But the littered sidewalks, the monumental pebbledash walls, and the soaring, rain-smeared, almost Soviet concrete made me think not of California so much as the modern edges of booming ex-colonial cities like Jakarta and Casablanca or neighborhoods of Berlin rebuilt after 1945—places thrown up in a hurry. Tel Aviv was designed by Bauhaus architects from Europe, some persecuted by Hitler but influenced by Lenin. They had turned the city into a feverishly modern showcase of the international style, a "White City" that declared: We are as advanced as any nation in the world. And now it seems to be falling apart.

Not that Israel isn't advanced. Tel Aviv is not a lie. But it felt like a city on welfare. The only reason this mattered was the story I'd heard, over and over, in the United States. Over and over you saw billboards and editorials in America claiming that Israel is the only nation in the Middle East with a) true Western freedoms, b) true racial diversity, c) a free press, or d) whatever else might convince Americans to lend support or send cash. In Israel I realized that the point of these assertions, before they became political tools during the wars against Islamic terrorism after 2001, was to lift the country's image out of the old cliché of shepherds and communal farms. "Israel's modern," a white-bearded, American-born Israeli named Danny Guberman told me in Jerusalem. "People don't realize that." But his generation had learned to think of Israel as a nation of *kibbutzim*. That was his point of reference. Mine was the reverse. Both ideas are false. They are the wrong way to approach Israel, entirely.

◆◆◆◆◆◆◆◆◆◆◆◆◆◆◆◆◆

The walk to Arthur Rashkovan's apartment took me past a wheel-shaped concrete building, an ugly work of '70s architecture that seemed to have landed with ill intentions on top of Ha-Yarkon Street. It was a gutted nightclub. But a huge surf ad hung on the curving windows, with a surfer standing in a beautiful, tubing blue wave for Tel Aviv traffic to see. Drivers ignored it. Israelis thought they had no surf.

Arthur had buzz-cut hair and a bleary mischievous smile. He spoke English with a Slavic accent but looked like an American skateboarder.

His bachelor pad was bare but comfortable; from the top of his building he could check the surf at Hilton Beach. "I just looked, and it's choppy," he said. "Storm surf. But it should be good tomorrow." He handed me a cup of instant coffee. "This is how it is in Israel. You get a storm, then a day later the surf comes."

Arthur had grown up on the beaches of Tel Aviv, the son of a Moldovan soccer star. He'd been sponsored as a surfer "basically by every brand that ever came into Israel," he said, and he still had skateboard sponsorships. But his contest career had remained on these shores, and now he worked for his father's liquor-distribution company. He found and promoted Israeli wines from vineyards in surprising places, or surprising to me, like the Negev, the Galilee, and the hills around Jerusalem. "I went to a settlement in the West Bank today," he said. "They have a vineyard out there, believe it or not."

A friend of Arthur's called Matt Olsen, an American surfer, came over. Suddenly—though I didn't know it—I was at the center of Tel Aviv's surf-activist community, the small nexus in Israel of surfing and politics.

"I got some wine for your girlfriend," Arthur told him. "It's settlers' wine. I don't know if she'll drink it."

"She'll drink it," said Matt. "She won't buy it, but she'll drink it."

"Is there enough water in the desert for a vineyard?" I asked.

"There should be," said Matt. "They build settlements over aquifers. In fact if you take a map of the aquifers under the West Bank and a map of Israeli settlements, they match up almost exactly."

Matt was a slim, intelligent guy with dark short hair and wide-set eyes and an open American manner. Since he spoke fluent Hebrew I assumed he was Jewish. But he was a Scandinavian goy, raised in Maine, with an apartment in California. His father had been a US envoy to Gaza during the 1990s, so he'd attended high school in Israel. For him the peace process was a family tradition. "We're a family of Maine fishermen," he said. "So I work on ocean-related things." After Israel's pullout from the Gaza Strip in 2005, he tried to win fishing rights for Palestinians out to forty miles from shore, where the fish are. Twenty nautical miles was the limit set by the Oslo Accords. "But right now they've only got six miles," he said. "That's not far enough. All they can do is fish the breeding grounds, and that's wiping out fish populations."[1]

Matt had the somewhat loony idea of helping Palestinians found a surf club. An American named Dorian "Doc" Paskowitz had flown in from California that summer with the equally loony idea of bringing surfboards to the Gaza Strip, and now a handful of Palestinian surfers had equipment to ride. Paskowitz was Israel's surf pioneer, a California surfer who had introduced the sport to Tel Aviv in 1956. Arthur and Matt were his friends. They intended to build on the momentum from his visit by establishing a Gaza Surf Club to receive more donations. They'd already established a group called Surfing 4 Peace to maintain contact with Gazan surfers and send equipment across the border; it was easier to arrange donations if you had organizations on both sides. The idea was simply to make friends with Palestinians and start a small surf economy. "Israel has a surf industry of two billion dollars' worth of goods each year," Dorian Paskowitz told National Public Radio after his trip in 2007, "and I know, sure as God made little green apples, that the same thing will happen in Gaza."

Paskowitz is an American Jew with a medical degree from Stanford, born in Texas but raised in Depression-era California. He'd surfed with Gard Chapin in San Onofre and Miki Dora in Malibu. He was also the patriarch of an eccentric, itinerant family of nine children. He has a white mustache and a lean, sagging, still-strong frame. His mission to bring boards to Gaza—at the age of eighty-six—had started when a story appeared in the *Los Angeles Times* about two Palestinian surfers, Mohammed Abu Jayyab and Ahmed Abu Hasiera. A picture showed them posing on Gaza Beach with a single board. "They just looked so

---

[1] The limit has since been narrowed to three nautical miles, to prevent weapons smuggling, Israel says.

forlorn," he told me. "So my son David and I said, 'Well, let's go take 'em some boards.'"

Arthur helped Doc and his family find about a dozen donated boards and other equipment from shapers and surfers around Tel Aviv. They also arranged to meet Abu Jayyab and Abu Hasiera in the massive terminal building at the Erez crossing. Arthur informed the media, and a pack of TV and print journalists turned up at Erez on a warm day in August. "Everybody was there," said Arthur. "Al-Jazeera, CNN, NBC, CBS. The whole world was there."

The picture published in most newspapers that day showed Paskowitz bowing under a gate with two surfboards. At that moment he was flouting orders. Arthur said he could technically have been shot by a guard. But he was saved by the legion of cameras as well as a lack of clear regulations governing a surfboard incursion into Gaza. "That's the thing about the occupation," said Matt. "There's no rules. So if you can convince someone that your rule is worth following for five minutes, they'll follow it for five minutes—even at the border. They don't have a rule that says 'No one can go through with a surfboard.'"

Paskowitz found the reporters annoying. "They were there in droves," he told me, "and they created havoc, so much so that the guards didn't know what to do with us. I got kind of pissed and I went in to the terminal and talked to the main guard. I *shmeikeled* him." Doc kept after him, in fact, for two hours. "The guard said, 'You can't come through here. Get out of here.' He was a very powerful force," Doc said. "His history went back very far in the Gaza Strip. He was the man in charge of the safety of all the settlements that had sprung up in the Gaza territory, which Ariel Sharon uprooted by force in 2005. So he, Eli, was a tough nut. But he had such a beautiful Jewish face, and a long ponytail, and I'd grab him and I'd kiss him, and he'd say, 'Get away from me.' And I'd say, 'Look, I'm an old Jewish man. I came halfway around the world. You wouldn't turn me away.' And he said 'They [Abu Jayyab and Abu Hasiera] can't come in here.' And I said, 'They're fifty feet away!'

"Then David said something in Spanish, like 'What the fuck's going on here?'

"And then Eli turned to him and said, 'You speak Spanish?'"

Doc said Eli and his son spoke Spanish for a while, "and that was it."

Abu Jayyab and Abu Hasiera were allowed into the terminal, and the Paskowitzes handed off the cart with a dozen boards. They never met face to face. But it was the start of a long-distance relationship.

"It was a love story," said Doc, "amongst enemies."

The *Los Angeles Times* reported that Abu Jayyab was "sympathetic to Hamas," which damned the effort for a lot of people. Hamas was like a four-letter word. Hamas kidnapped journalists, Hamas trained suicide bombers, Hamas allowed rockets to be launched from Gazan olive groves into Israeli towns. No one I knew could stand Hamas. *I* couldn't stand Hamas. Now Paskowitz wanted to grace them with not just surfboards, but a whole surf economy?

"The account of this blinding idiocy continues for several more paragraphs," one American blogger wrote in reaction to the story of Paskowitz's border crossing in the *New York Times*. "Being of a certain age, I've paddled in the hot pools of the sybaritic lifestyle that has boiled Paskowitz's brain to cream cheese; I know that he means well, but still have a rough time conjuring a jam-wearing Yasser Arafat shooting the curl, unless it involved a pistol and a Hasidic Jew."

"Only the broken brain of a Jewish libtard could dream up such nonsense," jerked another knee. "Murdering a retired Jewish doctor would really bring those Gazans together."

But Shifty Shifren, the surfing rabbi, was more precise. "Dorian's an idealist," he told me. "He doesn't quite live in this world. For Dorian to give surfboards to the Palestinians is like if I handed out Popsicles to drug addicts. I mean, it's a nice idea, but it's not gonna help."

Of course, nothing else had helped, either. "People in Israel ask me, 'What do you think you're gonna change?'" said Arthur. "And I say, 'Nothing much.' I'm just making a few friends and giving them a little bit of quality of life. And then maybe—in a few hundred years—something'll change." He wasn't fazed by Abu Jayyab's sympathy for Hamas. "It's actually more efficient, what we did. Because now they've actually recognized receiving boards from Israeli surfers—Hamas supporters."

Matt said, "The way it can work in Gaza is like this: A mother has two sons, and one of them joins Fatah, and the other joins Hamas. Then the family receives protection from both sides, and subsidies from both sides. So it's not always political."

The Gazans may or may not have hated Israel, but when Doc said "enemies," he meant it. He told one reporter that in a war he would "want to take a gun and shoot" an Arab, and the Arab would want to shoot back. He was a surfer, but also a Jew. They were enemies. So be it. But at least Dorian Paskowitz, with boiled cream cheese for brains—patron of surfing in Israel, bringer of surfboards to Gaza, condemned to death by more than one American blogger—could hold two opposed ideas in his head.

"So many people look at what I do as sort of mealymouthed," he said, "some sort of saccharine thing for peace. I don't give a fuck if Arabs shoot at me. The important thing isn't peace. It's *peacefulness*. There is no peace. I've been married forty-seven years, I fight with my wife all the time. There is no peace. But *peacefulness*. It means contentment, having enough to eat; having someone to care for your wife if you're gone; having streets paved, that you don't walk through the mud. That's peacefulness. And we can have that during the bombing. We don't have to stop bombing. Let them shoot missiles at Sderot. The question is what we can give them, and what they can give in return. That's the only way. All this other shit, with Condoleezza Rice coming in there, is as effective as a fart in a whirlwind.'"

The part of Paskowitz's magnificently strange life that can't be narrated here involves two divorces, a suicidal depression, and a decision to drop out of his medical career to travel the world and live, eventually, in a camper van. There was a further decision to raise nine kids in the camper van with his third wife, Juliette, and there were years of trying to provide for them by running a surf camp—before the world had heard of surf camps—on San Onofre State Beach. A film called *Surf-wise* deals with their surf-gypsy lifestyle and its effect on all the kids. "I have gone into the water literally ready to blow my brains out," he says in the film, "and come back out of the water a warrior."

Before all that started, after his second divorce, Doc headed for Israel. He wanted to learn about manhood, maybe become a para-trooper, "and get killed." But he took a longboard just in case the Mediterranean had waves. He was surfing alone at Ashkelon, near Gaza, when he heard mortar fire *crump* in the south. The year was 1956: It was the start of the Suez War.

Doc tried to volunteer without thinking that an American Jew might need Israeli citizenship to fight for Israel. "I volunteered in quite a Hollywood kind of manner," he told me, "so much so that the recruiter in Tel Aviv laughed and said, 'You must have seen too many John Wayne movies.' He shook me up so bad I said, 'Fuck him, I'm gonna get my board and go surfing.' So I paddled out at Frishman Beach, which was the Santa Monica of Israel at that time, meaning there was a great lifeguard culture there. The lifeguards were absolutely awed. So I went from a very demeaning situation with the military, to the beach at Frishman Street in Tel Aviv, where my counterparts the lifeguards simply fell in love with surfing. And I realized that Israel didn't need me to be John Wayne. It needed me to bring surfing."

The lifeguards climbed down from their towers to meet him. Shaul Zinner and Shamai "Topsi" Kanzapolski had heard of surfing, but had never seen it done. Shaul borrowed Paskowitz's board, paddled out, and stood up on his first wave. Doc was so impressed that he left the board behind. Some time later, he sent a shipment of six boards to Shaul and Topsi from California, seeding Israel's surf industry.

Tel Aviv's beaches are now tamed by a system of rocky breakwaters.

Hotels cluster along a heavy pebbledash boardwalk, and in postcards of high season you can almost smell the suntan oil and hear the crying kids. But in 1956 the beach was lined with fishermen's shacks. Shaul's son Gali showed me pictures. "The fishermen and the very poor families that couldn't afford to live in the city, they lived on the beach," he said. "That was the worst place to live. It was cold and wet, and they didn't have good homes or nothing." Tel Aviv had a bidonville. "This was the beginning of Israel," said Gali. "We still had austerity measures. There was nothing here, only camels and sand."

Gali was a burly man, a former lifeguard who made regular trips to Hawaii to surf big waves. He'd grown up on the beach in Tel Aviv because of his father's job. The whole family learned to surf after the shipment of boards from Paskowitz arrived; Gali said even his bris was held under the lifeguard tower. "It was a way of life, not a hobby or something," he said. "It was seven days a week, twenty-four hours a day. My father was never home" at their house in the city. "When we finished school, we went down to the beach. All the family was there."

The Middle East, oddly enough, is one of the few regions outside Hawaii with a stand-up surf tradition of its own. Israeli lifeguards still use flat-bottomed fiberglass boats called *hasakes* (CHA-sa-kays) as rescue craft. They're broad and leaf-shaped, ridden upright with a double-bladed paddle. "It's very, very old," Gali said. "It comes from the Arabic side, from Egypt, I believe. But when they built the first lifeguard stations in Israel, they had to have something, and that was the lightest and the easiest." Jaffa, the ancient port just south of Tel Aviv, was and still is an Arab town, and fishermen used hasakes there. "My father used to make them," said Gali. "He was very talented with his hands. He used to make them from wood and fabric and paint."

Shaul's partner in the tower at Frishman became Israel's iconic "first surfer." Topsi Kanzapolski used the first handful of boards to start a rental business on Hilton Beach, then commandeered a storage space for them under a concrete staircase at Frishman. It was just a doorway that opened onto the sand, with Hebrew graffiti on the walls, but it became the center of Israel's fledgling scene. Topsi learned to shape boards and started working on an outdoor table on the beach. Since polyurethane foam was hard to come by, he used blocks of green foam from local florist shops for the blanks.

Topsi was a bearish, middle-aged man with a thick, reddish brown beard. Anyone who's seen the movie *Big Wednesday* will remember Bear, the renegade shaper who worked under a California pier, who was based on Dale Velzy in Manhattan Beach. Topsi was Tel Aviv's Bear. His son Orian said he'd learned about surfing as early as the 1920s, from a newsreel. "He told me that as a child, he went to the cinema," said Orian, "and he saw news from overseas—that somebody surfed on a surfboard. So later he took an ironing board from his mom and he tried to catch a wave. I have a picture of it. But he didn't stand."

Surfing tends to flourish when a society starts to change. It remained a fringe sport in Tel Aviv until the 1980s, when the children of Topsi and Shaul led a new, rebellious, "cool" generation of surfers. "That generation in Israel," Matt said, "growing up in the late '70s and early '80s, was the first generation that wasn't based on a kibbutz. Israeli society was based around the model of a kibbutz for the first thirty or forty years. Then suddenly Tel Aviv livened up in the '70s as an urban center with a Western urban style. So you had the first generation of Israeli kids who grew up in Tel Aviv as a city."

Some Israelis said that in the '80s the country's orientation seemed to shift from Europe to the United States. The old socialist intellectualism fell away, and fashions from America took hold. During the '80s young Israeli soldiers were also coming home disillusioned from the war and occupation in Lebanon. "We got video players, we saw America, a new lifestyle, TV shows," said Arthur. "People started thinking more about themselves." The old guard of Israeli surfers, like Topsi, who had a potbelly and a receding hairline, started giving way to a fit, cool, hedonistic new generation. The emblematic day for this shift may have come in 1983, when Israeli surfers held their first national contest in Tel Aviv.

Until then local surfers had ridden waves in a slightly old-fashioned style, heading straight for the shore instead of pulling fancy maneuvers. But the South African champion Shaun Tomson made a celebrity appearance, and the sight of a Jewish professional tearing up smallish Tel Aviv surf turned the Israeli sport into something modern and new.

"I grew up in Tel Aviv," said Arthur, "in an area that lived and breathed a kind of California lifestyle—skateboards, surf, parties. I knew everybody. I was like a little beach-boy bum. My first day surfing was Topsi's last day surfing. Me and him were sharing the same peak, and he was yelling at me. I didn't know what I was doing, so. Maybe I dropped in on him." Arthur laughed. "That was the summer of '93. And then he died of cancer."

<hr />

The storm rattled Israel for five days. Tel Aviv became a city of rain-whipped streets, sodden olive trees, and unexpected plagues of hail. My blankets were too thin; the mornings were frigid; it was the worst storm anyone could remember in years. Arthur's text messages kept promising surf ("Tomorrow. Bring your wetty"), then calling me off ("No way").

To make myself useful I talked to a woman named Maya Dauber, Israel's first professional surfer. I thought she might have something to say about learning to surf in a society that still, on its conservative edges, tries to keep men and women apart. Tel Aviv has a "separated beach," where a high concrete wall runs from the sand into the water. Orthodox Jews avail themselves of the beach to swim without breaking mitzvahs against mixing with the opposite sex. On certain days only women can swim there; on certain other days, only men. "They will be very disappointed if you try to surf there at those times," an acquaintance of mine, Yoav, had said.

Maya was thirty-four, broad-shouldered, with soulful brown eyes, long hair, and freckles. She said she had to compete against boys during the early years of surf contests in Israel because no one had bothered to form a women's division. "Sometimes I competed with boys, yes," she told me. "They didn't like it."

"Why?"

"I don't know, it was a shame." She smiled. "I didn't want to hurt their feelings."

In 1986, when she was twelve, she started riding for Israel's national team. They went to France the following year, and she learned (a) that grown women surf in other parts of the world, and (b) that she could beat them. But her break as a professional came when she met Doc Paskowitz by chance in California, in the '90s, after the Israeli national team flew there for a contest at Huntington Beach. "It was very exciting to meet him," she said. "He was like our godfather. He told me, 'You're going to be the first professional surfer from Israel.' Don't go back to Israel. You go to Hawaii now. I was twenty-four, and I thought, 'Wow, Hawaii.' It was a dream come true."

She spent two seasons in the World Qualifying Series, the professional minor league where surfers compete to join the major world surf tour. She trained in Hawaii during the winter and traveled for the rest of the year. It was a glamorous life for an Israeli surfer. Even without breaking into the world tour, she accomplished more on the world circuit than anyone before from the Middle East. "Doc said, 'I don't have a lot of money, but I do have connections. You'll get some sponsorships, and go on the pro tour.' And he did that for me."

She grew up in a coastal village called Michmoret, near Haifa in the north, remote from the Tel Aviv scene. Its remoteness was an advantage: No one ever told Maya that girls weren't supposed to surf. "But I had to wear my brother's shorts," she said. "So, yeah, I was a tomboy. . . . My brother was a great surfer. That's why I started. He's a tube charger. He's big, and he's tall, and he's considered one of the best tube chargers in Israel. Amir. He become religious six, seven years ago."

"Did he stop surfing?"

"No. . . . If you talk to some religious people, they would say that if you go in the water, you get fresh. It's good, and they do it. So it's not necessarily against religion. Like my brother, he still surfs, but he wouldn't travel someplace like Indonesia, where he couldn't find kosher food."

The surfing rabbi, Shifty Shifren, upholds the minority argument in Orthodox circles that surfing and scripture blend perfectly well. He grew up around Los Angeles and Malibu as a secular Jew, but converted to Hasidism as an adult. He'd spent years reconciling the early, beach-bum part of his life with the later, religious part. He'd studied Torah in Israel and lived as a settler in the West Bank, but his surfing-rabbi shtick still made him a renegade. "Anything physical is seen as a waste of time from Torah study," he told a Jewish magazine called *Guilt and Pleasure,* where he also invoked Maimonides to defend his exercise regimen. He used to jog through the orange groves near Ramla before his morning classes. "It was my way of surviving. We were sitting twelve hours a day in a dimly lit room. I wanted a fresh mind. The days I didn't run, I didn't learn as well."

Surfing stirs a lot of people to transcendental speculation, but the most elaborate system of marine metaphysics I've ever heard comes from Shifty. "Jewish scripture talks about powers that are manifest upon the earth," he told me in LA. "Well, the biggest one is the ocean. Which is to say that through the waves, and by the ocean, God's presence is felt on the earth." Mystical Judaism described "emanations" of energy radiating from a single divine source; water could be seen as a medium for these emanations. "The water we surf in now—hasn't changed. Water doesn't change. The same water that God created in the ocean on the first day of Creation is with us now." Of course water constantly evaporates from the sea, turns to cloud, blows around the globe, and precipitates again as rain or snow, but there is conservation of matter; very few molecules of water have arrived in the world from outer space. "It's something very unique that only surfers have. Not skateboarders, or cross-country skiers, or scuba divers. . . . I mean there's always some joker, like a snowboarder, who will say, 'Sure, I feel it too.' But that's a bunch of bull. No real surfer will say that anything else comes near the high you get from surfing. It's just a real, awesome manifestation of power that comes through the ocean, by means of the wave. It's all part of these supernal messages about God's emanations in this world."

Anyway, Maya said the crucial problem for Israeli girls who want to surf is not religious, but social. More women than ever surf in Israel now, and the reason has to do with social expectations. Wetsuits cut for girls have helped, and so has the movie *Blue Crush*, a flick about female surfers in Hawaii that has possibly done more around the world to encourage girls to surf than any single professional woman. "It's like the egg and the chicken." Maya shrugged. "Now surfing's cool for girls. For a teenager, fourteen, fifteen, what society thinks is very important."

Maya was probably a force herself. She taught both boys and girls to surf at a school in Herzliya, north of Tel Aviv. She said the decision to come back to Israel, after her shot at an international career, was difficult. She'd been teaching American kids to swim in Los Angeles, where she could be near consistent Pacific waves, but she missed Israel. "I knew I would have to give up surfing, to a certain extent," she said. "But I think many Israelis feel like this. They have a strong connection to their home. Family is very strong, and your friends. Israel is still like a big kibbutz. Also, the language. And I thought that to teach surfing in LA, this is not very special. In California I could teach young California boys to surf. Anyone can do that. But in Israel, I can help girls to surf, and this is special. So I feel I belong here."

She encourages girls to surf with boys because she knows from experience that it forces them to improve. "I tell them, 'Don't surf together so much. Surf with the boys. Try to compete with them.' You have to fight in the waves. Not just in Israel. You have to prove yourself every time you go out. . . . But male surfing is more powerful. A woman's surf style is more round. I think it's okay, that a woman surf like a woman, and a man surf like a man. The boys do much more radical than the girls, and the women still do it much more like men in the '80s."

She meant the fluid, stylish grace that Tom Curren demonstrated in the '80s before Mark Occhilupo and his friends made everything explosive and radical. That's what women do now.

"Yeah. But in California, the women are becoming more radical. Some of them do it now. It's a matter of belief, you know. If a woman thinks she can do it, she can."

On the fifth afternoon of the storm in Tel Aviv, the rain blew off and the sun began to shine. We went out in rough surf at Frishman Beach. The sky was marbled with soft, storm-blackened wads of cloud, and from the beach the waves looked like pure chop.

Tel Aviv beaches are protected by a series of breakwalls, long lines of boulders arranged parallel to the shore like a series of dashes, to protect casual swimmers. They make the water and currents more complicated, since the waves have to bend around each wall and meet on the beach at an angle. During the '70s some Tel Aviv surfers tried to sabotage their construction. ("Pouring sugar into the bulldozer gas tanks, stuff like that," Gali Zinner said. "It didn't work.") Stories of larger waves off Frishman in the 1950s and '60s belong to surf lore now in Tel Aviv.

We walked out through the swimming area, where ridges of whitewater collided in a perfect V form, splashing up in zipping lines. Paddling into the waves from behind the breakwall was like going onstage, literally entering a theater of action. The surf was rough and unpredictable. Peaks kept shifting, and the soupy water hid the boulders of the jetty, then exposed them in a streaming rush of water that could suck you into the rocks the way a sinking ship can suck down boats.

The surfers joked in Hebrew. When a large wave rolled through, they shouted. Sometimes a wave broke into a violent froth at the top before tilting over, so we took off in whitewater. But there was logic in the rough conditions. As the sun set over Tel Aviv I saw one guy catch a fat, seaweed-colored wave, run down the thick face and back up to the lip, then slot himself into a tube section and let out an ecstatic whoop.

Later we tried surfing at Gordon Beach, just to the north, where twenty surfers jostled for short peaks in a narrow space between a breakwater and a stone jetty. Compared to Frishman it was a kiddie pool.

"There's a lot of people in the water," I said to Arthur.

"It's kookville." He smiled, squint-eyed, and shook his head. "This is what my adolescence was like."

Most of the surfers were young, with no sense of how to share the waves.

"Once I got hit in the face by some kook's board," said Arthur. "It cut me really deep, right over my eyebrow, like a boxer? It made my whole eyebrow flop down, only I couldn't tell because there was so much blood. So I turned to the guy and said, 'What do you think you're doing?' He looked at me and threw up in the water."

"Your skull was showing?"

"Yeah."

Later we walked back to Matt's car and peeled off our wetsuits on the street. Two young Orthodox men approached, with full beards and sidelocks and broad black hats. They had surprisingly soft and tender faces. I thought they would step around our boards and keep moving, but one stopped to deliver a speech. "Shabat shalom," and glory to God, he said to Matt. It was a request for money. "Sorry, I'm not Jewish," Matt told him in Hebrew, so they turned to Arthur, who stood by the open trunk of the car in a sweater with a green hood over his face, looking in no mood to hear a pitch for charity.

The Orthodox man was persistent. He placed one hand on the open trunk and talked with tender solicitude. Traffic on the street streamed by. Without turning, Arthur reached for his wallet, produced a twenty-shekel note, and held it out between two fingers. Pure insolence. At first I was shocked, until I imagined a surfer in California besieged by Christian evangelists.

"Shabat shalom."

"Shabat shalom."

"You're such a good Jew, Arthur," said Matt when they were gone.

The Mediterranean went flat again after two days, so I boarded a bus for Jerusalem, hoping to get a pass to Gaza that would let me see those boards Doc had donated to the Palestinians.

Yoav, a Jerusalem-born medical student I had met in Tel Aviv, said he preferred Jerusalem for the same reason a lot of people prefer New York to San Francisco. "It really is tolerant," he said. "There are so many different people there, you basically have no choice [but to be tolerant]. In Tel Aviv people tolerate you as long as you're hip and sort of left-wing, or homosexual. But Jerusalem has true diversity."

He was right: The Old City is a mazelike medina of narrow lanes and market stalls that fill, every day, with people who despise each other. It's like the New York subway. Arabs pushing carts and wearing kaffiyehs mix with bearded Orthodox priests who tend the Church of the Holy Sepulchre and local Jews headed for the Western Wall as well as Christian pilgrims disgorged by buses from Poland. Armed Israeli soldiers, armed Palestinian soldiers, backpack-wearing tourists, and exultant, sidelocked, black-suited Hasidim knock shoulders. There should be wars every day. But within the walls, people tolerate one another with a sort of restless energy.

The Old City is so cramped and small that you think the centuries of wars and miracles must have passed somewhere else. Some of them did; ruins of older Jerusalems are just down the hill. Now the Old City encompasses the last standing wall of Herod's temple complex at Temple Mount—the "Wailing" or Western Wall. Islamic tradition claims Temple Mount as the spot where Mohammed sprang up to heaven on his steed Barack, and the current Old City also envelops what Christian tradition calls Golgotha. This, in a nutshell, is why people fight over Jerusalem.

But on the slope below Jaffa Gate, outside the Old City, I also found a hyper-modern mall with terraces of pale new stone. Glass-walled restaurants with a view of the newer city are happy to overcharge you for tea, and one terrace has a Billabong Board Shop with clothes that look like a cheap New York interpretation of the "surfing aesthetic." But where are the boards? I looked everywhere, and the only surfboards in evidence were on top of miniature toy VWs and station wagons.

Anyway, Jerusalem was fun to explore. The Western Wall plaza had the same jumbled nervous energy as the rest of the Old City, but in this case everyone was Jewish. People showed up not just to pray, but to assert. Young Hasidim with broad black hats swaggered like gangsters in a Bellow novel. Plump American hipsters in flannel and sneakers put on cardboard yarmulkes and walked flat-footed past old men with tangled white beards chatting on cell phones. Arab-looking Israel Defense Forces soldiers with shoulder-slung rifles tied tefillin to their arms, and Russians, Tajiks, Armenians, Arabs, Ethiopians, and Poles all ignored each other but strenuously showed their devotion under the crumbling ancient wall.

An older tradition claimed the Western Wall as a remnant of the Second Temple, built under King Herod on the site of Solomon's Temple. Archaeologists now think it's an outer retaining wall from Herod's complex, not from the temple itself. It rises over a plaza of modern stone surfaces like the walls of LA's Getty Center, and at sundown this remarkably peaceful, open, ancient-modern space fills with murmuring Jews. The swaggering Hasidim looked anxious to get to the wall, then fervid in prayer once there; sometimes they lapsed into a trance. They reminded me not just of Bellow characters, but also of what Rabbi Shifren had said about Mike Purpus: "The Kabbalah tells us that the heart is a place of 'fire,' enthusiasm." Every day it seemed to be the business of a Hasid to locate this fire, and the mood around the Western Wall was *spritzig*, effervescent, undampened by the soldiers or the metal detectors. After prayers they seemed content to stand around with friends and socialize, as if they'd just eaten a decent meal.

I left the plaza and turned up a vault-roofed alley that was also an Arab souk, its food stalls and shops just shuttering for the night. Two Palestinian soldiers stood at the top of a flight of stairs. They were talking to a few men at an open doorway. That seemed interesting, so I tried to go through. "Sorry, sir. Closed," the soldier said. Through the door I saw part of the golden Dome of the Rock.

"Closed?"

"Yes, sir. It will open again at seven tomorrow morning." He was very polite, but insistent. "This gate is only for Muslims."

The other men were Arabs, showing their passports. I was learning that the top of Temple Mount had gates for the clean and the unclean. I was unclean, like a leg of pork.

"Okay, thanks."

"Thank you, sir."

A tour group of Mexican Catholics congregated not far up the lane, at the foot of the Via Dolorosa, a kitschy lane of pizza joints and souvenir shops along the supposed path of Jesus's final march. The pilgrims huddled around a framed square of reddish beige stone set in the gray wall of a shop. The stone has been polished smooth by Christian hands.

I suspect the guides for these tours are no more scrupulous than they were in the 1860s, when Mark Twain paid a visit. The framed piece of reddish stone touched by two dozen Mexican grandmothers may even have been the continuation of a confidence trick described by Twain. "We saw a deep indentation in the hard stone masonry of the corner of a house," he wrote in *The Innocents Abroad*, "but might have gone heedlessly by it but that the guide said it was made by the elbow of the Saviour, who stumbled here and fell. Presently we came to just such another indentation in a stone wall. The guide said the Saviour fell here, also, and made this depression with his elbow."

The Church of the Holy Sepulchre was a few hundred yards away. Soon I stood in the incense-heavy gloom of an old cathedral, waiting in a line of tourists for a glimpse inside a "tomb monument," a rocky, broken-off shrine from an even older church, where we would come as close as modern mortals possibly could to seeing something or other that was distantly related to the tomb where Christ's body was laid to rest. I can't remember what. The shrine is ornate inside, slathered in candles and holy icons, cramped and sparkling with candlelight. It replaced something that had replaced something that had replaced the stone sepulchre itself (supposedly), which in 1009 had been destroyed by the mad Caliph Hakim. A weak provenance, but hordes of Christian pilgrims are convinced that Christ was shut up in his tomb *right here*.

I went downstairs to a Byzantine chapel hewn from raw stone, and a family of tourists came running down the steps behind me in noisy sneakers. They all had cameras. They looked at me, then at the altar of the chapel, then at a floor mosaic, to see if any of it was worth photographing. No—they kept running. On the next level down was another raw stone cave where Saint Helen, the mother of Constantine, claimed to have found the true crosses of Jesus and the thieves. I could hear the family's sneakers shuffling around in the darkness.

They reappeared later, by the main entrance upstairs, near some kind of holy slab set in the floor—perhaps not unrelated to the stone where Christ's body was anointed after the crucifixion. Pilgrims genuflected at the long pale stone, murmuring prayers. The father of the harried family shouldered a pilgrim out of the way and knelt with his camera and backpack and waist-tied windbreaker all in a blur. He laid his palms on the slab and looked impatient while his wife flashed a picture. Then they hurried out.

Constantine had the Church of the Holy Sepulchre built over the actual peak of Golgotha to preserve the rock. Up a ladderlike flight of stairs a cramped chapel covers the very top of the hill, and this holiest of Christian sites looks unchanged from Twain's visit.

When one stands where the Saviour was crucified, he finds it all he can do to keep it strictly before his mind that Christ was not crucified in a Catholic church. He must remind himself every now and then that the great event transpired in the open air, and not in a gloomy, candle-lighted cell in a little corner of a vast church, up-stairs—a small cell all bejeweled and bespangled with flashy ornamentation, in execrable taste.

All this history—these historical layers of mythmaking over what might have been legend or truth—fascinated me. A day later I went to the Church of the Nativity in Bethlehem, where a silver star laid in a basement grotto showed the *exact spot* where Christ was born, at least as far as church fathers could determine in 1717. I stood in a long nave with red marble columns while Orthodox priests chanted and jangled a censer. Sunlight filtered in from high windows. The church was empty and peaceful until the mother from the harried family from the day before appeared through an inner doorway—in tights, a bouncing camera, and sunglasses—and bolted at top speed for the door.

She was undignified, but she wasn't the silliest thing the church walls had witnessed. Sometimes Orthodox priests waged broom fights in Bethlehem over which denomination got to clean what. The Armenian and Greek divisions of the eastern church both had historical claims over parts of the church, along with Roman Catholics, and when one priest swept the wrong step, or leaned his ladder against the wrong patch of wall, or intruded on someone else's ceremony, it could lead to nasty gang fights. Twain mentions the same brawls in the Church of the Holy Sepulchre. It was another abbreviated version of the Holy Land—factions fighting over real estate.

Hershel Shanks, a biblical archaeologist, has written books about the probable history of the region that might have spared the world a number of wars if more religious leaders had been infected by more of his rational doubt. Jesus, for example, probably was not born in Bethlehem. "He was supposed to be the scion of David who came back and gave us salvation," Shanks said in the *New York Times,* "and since David was born in Bethlehem there was a desire to put Jesus there. This doesn't reduce the power of symbolic stories, but it's not historic reality." So much for the Church of the Nativity; so much for several crusades.

Shanks argues that the Church of the Holy Sepulchre could in fact mark the rough locations of Golgotha and Christ's tomb. But he says Mohammed couldn't have risen to heaven from Temple Mount because there was no mosque near Jerusalem until fifty years after his death. (Tradition only says it happened at the "furthest mosque." So much for the Al-Aqsa Intifada.) Both the Dome of the Rock and the Al-Aqsa Mosque date from the seventh century, but they've been rebuilt several times, and the current golden dome is really gold-plated anodized aluminum, financed by modern Gulf states to remind everyone of Islam's claim on Jerusalem.

And the Western Wall has become so holy in the Jewish mind that some people take biblical tradition literally and believe both temples were built on the *very spot* where God scooped up a clod of dirt to make Adam. Also where Abraham almost slew Isaac, and where Jacob dreamed about his celestial ladder—as if this place of places had special conducting properties to heaven. The wall's holiness (and its mistreatment by Muslims, who dumped garbage at its base) is one reason Israeli forces took the Old City during the Six-Day War.

How is an outsider supposed to sympathize with all this conflicting literalism? If the heart is the place of fire, how does a truly religious person justify slaughtering even one human heart to save a relic, or a piece of land? Most of the supposed holy sites are more than a thousand years old. Their worth is psychological and political; their reality is guesswork. For the Christian sites there are semireliable records back to Saint Helen, who "rediscovered" them only three centuries or so after the Crucifixion. "She traveled all over Palestine and was always fortunate," wrote Twain. "Whenever the good old enthusiast found a thing mentioned in her Bible, Old or New, she would go and search for that thing and never stop until she found it."

The other problem with fundamentalism is that it can drive people, and nations, to self-destruct. At a grim Holocaust memorial chamber on one edge of the Old City I met an American Hasid with a thin brown beard, very friendly and informative, who said the Holocaust, like all of Jewish destiny, was contained in the books of Moses. Hitler had simply fulfilled the book. "People talk about political causes and the reasons the Holocaust happened," he said. "As religious Jews we don't see it that way." They focus on God's intent. That's more than understandable. If you believe in an all-powerful God, then it makes no sense to view an evil historical fact as contrary to God's will—in fact it may be the only way to face genocidal loss without permanent rage and other forms of damage to the soul. But his insistence on literal scripture suggested a way forward for Israeli politics that might not be palatable to the Palestinians, descendants of the Arabs who (after all) were here when the first Jewish settlers arrived.

His talk on Jewish destiny reminded me of an English-born professor who wrote about meeting Saul Bellow in Jerusalem in the '70s, "the very Orthodox Professor Harold Frisch":

> He tells me fiercely in his Oxbridge voice that we American Jews are not Jews at all. It is a strange experience to hear such a judgment in such an accent. "You will say," he adds, "that we may be annihilated by the Arabs in reclaiming our land according to God's promise. But history sometimes gives us no choice. It is shallow to argue with one's fate. If this be our fate as a people we must prepare to accept it."

Bellow's conclusion—moderate, genial, American-bred—was that Zionism had changed after the Six-Day War from a practical settlers' project to win *a* homeland into a messianic religious ambition to win the *entire* homeland, *Eretz Israel HaShlema*. By 1976 Bellow was no man of the left, but Israeli politics have shifted so far in the meantime that he now reads like a hopeless peacenik.

"Why do you want to go to Gaza?" asked the woman at the press office in Jerusalem.

"Like it says there, to meet surfers."

She made a face. "But you don't have an assignment from a newspaper."

"No, I have a letter from my publisher."

"But you are a journalist."

"Yes."

"Can I see your press pass?"

"Of course."

The office was plain and bright with sunshine, a normal dry bureaucratic office except for a display of twisted rockets in one corner. They'd been fired from Gaza's fields and olive groves into Israeli border towns like Sderot.

"Yes, but the problem is that we only give credentials to journalists with specific assignments. Specific reasons to be in Gaza."

"But I have one."

"Not from your news organization."

"But from a publisher," I said.

"We are only for newspaper journalists," she said. "As a rule we deal only with correspondents."

"How do filmmakers get in? Or other authors?"

She smiled and handed back my press pass. "We don't have an office for them, as far as I know," she said. "I'm sorry. It's difficult since Hamas took over."

For a minute I considered paddling to the Gaza Strip. How long could it take? Just jump in the water north of the armistice line and—well, hurry. It seems the same idea had occurred to Dorian Paskowitz. "Doc said, 'What if we get a group of surfers and paddle across the border?'" according to Matt. "And all I could think of was the guards there opening up on him with a fifty-millimeter. For a kilometer out into the water there it's like a free-fire zone."

That evening I met a former settler, Danny Guberman, who traveled the world as a fund-raiser for a school called Kadima. He had a long white beard, glasses, and a slight frame, and he spoke English in flat, Missouri-bred slang. He'd moved to Israel in the early '80s. He seemed cheerful and young-minded. The idea of surfers in Israel was new to him, but not a surprise. I wanted to know if he'd noticed a change in Israel since American culture started trickling in.

"We didn't move here until 1982," he said. "I do remember seeing stores with American names on them in the late '80s. And I remember in the late '80s how radio stations would play the same type of music you would hear in the States. Today it's all over the radio stations." But he was noncommittal about whether the change was good or bad. "I look at things from a religious point of view," he said. "Anything that takes away from keeping or making a person religious is not a benefit."

He wanted to know if I could put him in touch with Ralph Giordano, a Jewish German writer whom Guberman and his wife had met in a West Bank settlement almost twenty years before. Danny seemed to feel duped. Giordano had been kind in person, but negative in print. In his book *Israel, Um Himmels Willen, Israel* (*Israel, in Heaven's Name, Israel*), he mentioned an Israeli soldier in the West Bank who showed no remorse about killing Arabs. The inhumanity was a betrayal of Israel's promise, Giordano had written. Danny wanted to chat with him. He agreed with some of Giordano's judgment—he and his wife had quit being settlers—but, he said, "after you live in Israel awhile, you begin to see how things are. From the outside, you may have the impression that Palestinians are so oppressed, but when we pulled out of Gaza, you'd think we could have got something in return. You know, like, they could stop shooting missiles at us."

Homemade missiles were falling every day in Sderot. As a rule they were yard-long pipes loaded with gasoline and fertilizer, lethal if they hit a person but impossible to aim. "Where in the world is that normal?" Danny said. "You begin to think of the Palestinians as like teenage kids. You give, and they just want more."

He also said there were towns in the West Bank, like Ramallah, where it was dangerous to show your face as a Jew. "If you look too Jewish, you can get killed," he said. "Where in Israel is it that dangerous to be an Arab?" He meant outside the Territories. "We have Arabs here, and we're used to them. Unfortunately they get harassed at checkpoints and so on, because, also unfortunately, they're the ones who bring in the bombs."

A suicide bomb had exploded that day in Dimona, a city in the Negev where Israel runs its nuclear reactors. One victim had died. It was the first suicide attack after a year of calm. Danny said he almost felt relief. "You start to worry when it gets quiet for that long, like 'Where's the next one gonna be?' Because you know quiet isn't normal."

I liked Danny. I didn't have to agree with everything he said. The religious Jews I know have always been *menschlich* and conversational, earthy as well as sophisticated. Except in the matter of a literal Promised Land, Judaism seems far more sensible than the Catholicism I was raised with. It is less ornamented and more honest about human nature. Danny's religion was not just scripture and rules; it had also made him nimble minded, gentle, and free.

<hr>

"Mr. Moore?"

"Yes."

"What is the purpose of your visit?"

"Surfing."

"Surfing? But you have no board."

This interrogation opened my third trip to Israel, my second as a journalist on assignment from Spiegel Online. I was still in the Berlin airport. I'd been advised not to mention Gaza.

"I can borrow one in Tel Aviv."

"Do you know people in Tel Aviv?"

"Yes."

"What are their names?"

"Arthur Rashkovan . . . "

When you check in for an El Al flight in Berlin you have an interview with an airline official at a little portable desk, and the official, a fleshy, black-haired man with a false smile, struck me as meddling. "If we go to a computer, can you show me e-mail from this Arthur Rashkovan," the attendant said, "that proves you intend to surf?"

No, I said, sorry. I wasn't about to let some airline apparatchik read my e-mail.

"Do you have his phone number?"

"Yes."

"Do you mind if we call him?"

"I suppose not."

So they called Arthur, and Arthur mentioned Gaza. The official came back with his boss. "We have just talked to your friend, and he told us a different story," with the mild air of a good cop cross-questioning a suspect. "Are you planning to go anywhere else, related to surfing?"

I said yes, perhaps Gaza City.

"Why didn't you tell us this before?"

"It isn't definite. Who knows if I can get in?"

"Okay."

They took me to a room, unpacked my bags, wiped everything down, emptied my pockets, read my notes, and searched me for weapons. The experience was irritating, but I got over it.

At Ben Gurion Airport, the problem escalated. The border authorities forced me to sit for several hours while they ran background checks. During the first hour they quizzed me about my business in Israel. This interview went badly. I still couldn't admit the power of airport authorities to oversee what I planned to do in a supposedly free nation, and I wasn't aware of which ministries—or which links to El Al—were behind the interrogation. So I didn't mention Gaza. It broke no laws to visit Israel and write a story about surfers without declaring myself as a journalist, and when I did register for a press pass, to reach Gaza, I would be honest about my plans. I was trying to glide through the border regime.

Bad mistake. The woman managed to confiscate six pages of printed e-mail from Matt Olsen that gave the names of Gazan surfers.

My German passport didn't help, but neither did the American one: two passports were suspicious. The border authorities in Israel are also notoriously unreasonable. This particular bureaucrat was attractive— short and nerdy and hip, wearing glasses and a pair of jeans—but when we established that I was a journalist she turned against me, and when I continued to fail to mention Gaza, she called me "stupid" and gave me one last chance to declare my true reasons for entering Israel.

Well, I said, "if I can," I'll go to Gaza and write about surfing there.

That *if I can* set the woman off. She was *pissed*. She called me a liar and banished me to the waiting room. A British man simmering there had been waiting for two hours. He worked for a humanitarian organization. "If they don't want us to go back with bad reports about Israel," he said, "I'm not sure why they do this." Soon police also put an agitated Orthodox man in the tank with us and even cuffed his hands.

I called the *Spiegel* correspondent in Jerusalem, Christoph Schult. He was very helpful. "I know someone at the Foreign Ministry, they have an office at the airport. They can put pressure on them. This is ridiculous."

He said Shin Bet was investigating me—Israel's answer to the FBI. Now I think El Al had reported the contents of my bags, including that e-mail printout, to the Interior Ministry.

After a while I was summoned to the police desk and handed my passports and a gate pass by a woman in uniform. "Thank you, Mr. Moore," she said. "Enjoy your stay in Israel."

Great! But hang on.

"Do you have my other papers?" I said.

"What papers?"

"Some e-mail printouts were taken from me."

I saw them in the hands of a large plainclothesman at the end of the counter.

"Those papers there," I said. "I need them."

"You can have them on the way out," the plainclothesman said.

"On the way out of Israel?"

"Yes," he said. "Maybe."

I called Christoph again.

"No, they can't do that," he said. "They can photocopy the pages, but they can't keep them."

I insisted on the papers. The man just waggled his fingers for my passports and asked me to wait. After half an hour a middle-aged policewoman in glasses said I no longer had permission to enter Israel.

"Why?"

"Because you lied about your reasons for wanting to enter. You were talking to the Interior Ministry."

"But you just gave me permission. The only difference is that I demanded some personal papers. I still have the gate pass in my pocket."

"You have your gate pass?"

"Yes."

"Give it to me."

I straightened up.

"No," I said.

"You will give it to me, or we will take it by force," this policewoman said. "You are no longer allowed to enter Israel!"

"I don't accept that," I said.

"You don't accept that?"

For the second time in one evening I had awakened the wrath of a petty bureaucrat, and I felt the rage of an official who sees her over-reach of power go unrecognized.

"Then you will go into this office and we will take it by force," she said. "You are not allowed to enter Israel!" She pointed into a small clerical office, and when I didn't move on command she hollered, "*Go!*"

And they sat me in the office with a pretty uniformed guard by the door. No one tried to take anything by force. It felt like being sent to the principal's.

I called Christoph.

"They're guarding the door," I said. "I can't tell if I'm under arrest."

"This is harassment."

"Is there anything we can do? They're trying to rescind my permission to enter."

"I'll call the Foreign Ministry."

After fifteen minutes the policewoman who had shouted at me for not accepting my banishment from the Holy Land called me to the desk and handed over my passports, my flight ticket, and my printed e-mail.

"Enjoy your stay in Israel," she said.

·························

The road to Gaza City ran between shambling concrete buildings in far worse condition than the buildings in Tel Aviv. Strings of green Hamas flags fluttered over the traffic. A concrete center divider had sporadic trees and more than one burnt-out hulk of a car. "Israeli missiles," said my driver, Ahmed.

You can watch the IDF videos on the Internet: A car runs along a road, carrying—perhaps—a gang of Palestinians preparing to fire rockets into Israel. A white set of crosshairs follows the car on the grainy screen until a sudden explosion erases it, silently. Cars around it swerve and brake.

It was more than a year since my first visit to Israel, and several months since the Gaza Strip had been shut to journalists in preparation for the bombardment that came to be known as Operation Cast Lead. (My bad luck; that was my second attempt.) "Cast Lead" is an interesting phrase. Traditional dreidls are cast from lead, as are bullets; at New Year's parties in Europe it's also a tradition to melt a lump of lead in a spoon and toss it into a pot of water. The shape taken by the lead indicates your fortune for the year. Israel's fiery roll of the dice in December 2008 and January 2009 might explain the military-state behavior at Ben Gurion. Two months earlier a massive incursion by Israeli tanks and F-16s had killed between nine hundred and fourteen hundred people. Gaza had become a free-fire zone, a hermetic patch of desert with the torpor of a ghetto where houses and cars detonated without warning.

"Look," said Ahmed. "The Pepsi factory."

A steel door facing the street bore a Pepsi logo. The yard behind it, where trucks would have backed up for crates of bottles, was filled with dusty boulders of concrete.

Now and then we passed a similar pile of rubble where a building had been. But the city bustled. There was a sense of survival, not desolation. Trucks and cars made room for trotting donkey carts, the sun angled over concrete tenements, and robed women led children through the dusty streets. The smells included salt air, dust, and garbage smoke.

David Hare, in his play *Via Dolorosa,* writes that passing from Israel to Gaza "is like driving from California to Bangladesh." Exaggeration. Israel isn't quite California, and Gaza isn't quite Bangladesh—the bridge between the cultures was narrower than I had been led to believe. Gazans weren't starving. The illegal tunnels from Egypt provided a low but stable standard of living. Even the shambling quality of the buildings in Israel and Gaza was a continuum, a shambling quality of the whole Middle East. "Arabic and Hebrew are like Spanish and Portuguese," said my main contact in Gaza, a man named Mohamed Alwan, that night over dinner. "They're very closely related."

Mohamed was a loping, middle-aged man with a brushy mustache and hair slicked back around his ears. He worked for CARE International as a fresh food manager, making sure produce went where it was needed and sold for a fair price. (Most of the Gaza Strip is farmland.)

Mohamed had started to work as an intermediary for Surfing 4 Peace when Dorian Paskowitz was in Tel Aviv. He had long-suffering brown eyes and wore loose gray suits. He didn't surf, but he reminded me of other formal people who were carried by an abiding curiosity into odd situations. Mohamed knew every surfer in Gaza.

Arthur had given me four wetsuits to give to the surfers. The surfers knew Matt, but Israelis were barred from Gaza, so Mohammed Abu Jayyab and Ahmed Abu Hasiera, to Arthur, were just two lean guys in their thirties with rough black beards standing (in the *Los Angeles Times* photo) next to their single board on Gaza Beach. They were quoted in that article about the feeling of freedom in the water, which released them from the sense of imprisonment. "When I'm surfing," Abu Jayyab said, "I feel like I'm flying."

Mohamed and I had dinner at a hummus restaurant with long tables and fluorescent lights, where men sat around the tables in groups. A few of them wore large, squarish, flowing beards that looked almost Babylonian. We received a dish of hummus, a dish of bean paste, and a stack of pita bread, but no plates. Instead of Coke we drank Pepsi. "It comes from Egypt now," said Mohamed, "through the tunnels."

He used his phone at the table to call a few surfers. The Gaza Surf Club was up and running now; it had two factions and about twenty members. In the meantime, Israel had established rules at the border saying no "sea-related equipment" could cross to Gaza. So Surfing 4 Peace couldn't move its donations. Getting even four wetsuits across in my bag—scanned by Israelis in the Erez terminal, athletic young guards who were, perhaps, surfers themselves—had been a matter of luck.

"Did it go smoothly?" Mohamed asked.

"No problems. Well, not with the wetsuits. They questioned me at the airport, though. They kept me for almost six hours."

"Really?"

"They almost sent me back to Berlin."

"What happened?"

"I don't want to talk about it."

The power cut off before we finished dinner. The restaurant owners rolled out a small generator. "This is normal," said Mohamed. Gaza City shuts down at night because of the sporadic blackouts, except for a number of restaurants and corner shops with rattling generators on the sidewalk. Whole dusty streets were desolate. The blackouts were either the result of a shortage of fuel caused by the Israeli blockade, or a tactic by Hamas to blame the blockade, or both.

The recent bombardment was still on people's minds. Mohamed said the destruction had been unbelievable. At the height of the siege, the shooting came from every direction—the air, the ocean, the street. F-16s bombed the buildings, tanks and warships fired cannons, helicopters sprayed phosphorus flares, which burned people on the ground. Mohamed hid with his wife and daughters in a basement. Their house wasn't damaged, except for some windows blown out when planes bombed the parliament building. But he knew one family whose young daughter had been burned by phosphorus and died in the open; later the family saw her charred body being eaten by birds.

The bombardment had support in Israel because the constant rockets from Gaza had worn down people's nerves. After prime minister Ariel Sharon pulled settlers and soldiers out of the Strip in 2005, the violence only continued, which had disillusioned Israelis about the dream of "land for peace." There was rhetoric about precision weapons and targeting only Hamas militants, but the storm of fire visited on Gazans during those twenty-two days was collective punishment. Mohamed said it had strengthened Hamas outwardly by giving them a victory of resistance under tremendous Israeli firepower. But within Gaza, people were angry. They blamed Hamas for provoking the attack. Mohamed told me this in low tones. He didn't like Hamas. He didn't consider them real Muslims. He was also not entirely free to speak his mind. "I am a Muslim, I pray every day," he said. "I fast and observe the holidays. But I can get along with everyone—Christian, Jewish." The provincial attitude of radicals like Hamas was not religious, in his opinion. "A little while ago two tourists were captured," both from Europe. "Hamas announced they had converted to Islam." Mohamed shrugged. "What good is this?"

So the shock of the bombardment may have worked its strategic purpose; it may have weakened Hamas from below. But it had also sown hatred for Israel.

By now we were having coffee at the restaurant in my hotel, the Al Deira. Under the window of my room, when I checked in, I had noticed Mickey Mouse and Tweety Bird hugging children on their way into the restaurant. (That was one of my first impressions of Gaza: big felt costumes of American cartoon characters.) Now musicians packed up their instruments on a small stage and waiters cleaned the tables. A full-blown party for children called the Al Deira Happy Meal had just ended. The Mickey and Tweety costumes were gone, but I mentioned them to Mohamed because I knew about the Hamas-produced TV show starring a Mickey knockoff named Farfour, who squeaked out Islamic-supremacist slogans and anti-Semitic bile. "With you we are setting the cornerstone for world leadership under Islamic leadership," Farfour told the kids in one episode, before his show had to be canceled under international pressure and the mouse was martyred onscreen by an agent of Israel.

Mohamed didn't know whether the costumes I had seen were meant to be Mickey Mouse and Tweety Bird or Farfour and some sort of friend. He said the "Happy Meal" was probably meant to buck up the children's morale. "Since the bombing, they are afraid to come out of their homes," he said. "But this was a terrible show." He nodded. "They had propaganda against Fatah, too."

A waiter delivered a narghile and set burning lumps of charcoal on top with a pair of tongs. Mohamed took a long draw from it. He seemed contemplative and slightly depressed. "The problem is," he said, "we all know what has to be done to achieve peace. Both sides know. All the talking has been done." He puffed out a cloud of the cloying smoke.

"And if Palestinians put all the money we spend on weapons into research and technology," he said, with some exaggeration, "we could someday be the strongest Arab country in the Middle East."

The next afternoon we drove to Sheik Khazdien Beach, about a mile south of the hotel. It was a winter day, and the beach was deserted except for a group of about twenty surfers waiting near a lifeguard tower. In the summer these beaches thronged with families. Women swam in the shorebreak wearing abayas and head scarves. Tents and umbrellas could be rented, camels roamed on the sand, and lifeguards worked in magnificent, shambling towers made of wood and draped in faded sheets to keep off the wind and sun. "What is there to do at home?" a Gazan taxi driver wrote for the Israeli news service YNet. "Watch TV? It's all the same anyway. Watch the news? It's all bad. What's left? The beach."

The reception from the surfers overwhelmed me. The near-complete membership of the Gaza Surf Club was there. I gave a speech explaining that I had four wetsuits from Tel Aviv, and only four, but Arthur and Matt would try to get more across, along with a number of surfboards. Then we climbed a wooden ladder into the sprawling life-guard shack and sat around on plastic chairs. It was like sitting in a big treehouse. The surfers—mostly grown men—were as enthusiastic as little boys.

They said the first Gazan surfer was Salah Abu Khamil, now a dignified-looking man in his forties with short salted hair and a wres-tler's build. He made his first board from a wooden plank in about 1983. "He was working in Israel, and he saw surfing on Israeli TV," said Mohamed, who translated. "But he started here, in Gaza." He painted his homemade board and used knives for fins.

"Knives, really? Blades?"

I didn't quite buy that.

"Yes."

"How did the board surf?"

"He started on his stomach, but step by step, slowly-slowly, he learned," Mohamed said.

Among Gazan surfers there are divisions and factions, so Salah probably was not the first Palestinian surfer in the history of the world but the first in the history of the Gaza Surf Club—a broadening, fairly central surf community. He was certainly not the first surfer in Gaza. Before the Israeli pullout in 2005, the beaches between Gaza City and Rafah had a Jewish surf culture. A friend of mine in Berlin, Ze'ev Avrahami, spent part of his childhood in an Israeli settlement called Yamit, just over the Gaza border in Sinai. Now it's in Egypt; the Israeli government cleared Yamit after the Camp David Accords in 1982. But until then it was such an important Israeli surf town that *Big Wednesday* premiered there instead of Tel Aviv. "The city was between some dunes, and near us were some bedouins," Ze'ev said. "We had nothing to do but surf."

It says something about the state of war between Israelis and Palestinians that their surf histories exclude each other. The main exception is Paskowitz; members of the Gaza Surf Club speak of him with affection.

Anyway, Mohamed said a few kids imitated Salah on wooden boards after his first attempts to surf in the early '80s. By 1987 three long sailboards had found their way to Gaza Beach, and a small generation of Palestinian surfers learned to ride them, including Al Hindi Ashoor, an enthusiastic bearded lifeguard sitting near me who was more or less the leader of the Sheik Khazdien crew. But sailboards (without their sails) are difficult to maneuver on a wave.

Mohammed Abu Jayyab and Ahmed Abu Hasiera interrupted. They were the surfers written up in the *LA Times,* and they headed the Beach Camp crew, from a settlement near the Al Deira Hotel. "It was difficult to get real surfboards," Abu Jayyab said, "because we had no money to buy them. But Ahmed's brother was working in Israel, and he bought one board, a small one, and brought it here."

This board had a distinctive cartoon shark and happened to belong, once, to a friend of Arthur's in Tel Aviv. It was the first real surfboard in Gaza. "We surfed on this one board for nine years," Mohammed Abu Jayyab said—until 2007, when Paskowitz saw it in the newspaper.

Mohammed Abu Jayyab had green eyes and a bright smile. His beard was rough but he had a voluble way of talking, with a high, shallow-chested voice. He was perfectly kind. I had to remind myself he was "aligned with Hamas," especially since another surfer in the lifeguard shack, Taha Bakir, was "aligned with Fatah" and was said by Mohamed Alwan to have lost twelve family members in fighting with Hamas. Taha had long, tightly-curled hair and wore his kaffiyeh with an almost European fashion sense, as if it were just another scarf.

How did it feel to ride a wave?

"It is the best thing in life," said Mohammed Abu Jayyab.

"We can express our love and our energy this way," said Taha Bakir.

"I've practiced most sports, but this is the best."

"I wish to have someplace to practice," another surfer said. "I dream of surfing on an ocean, which would be better than this sea."

"What do other Palestinians on the beach say, when they see them surf?" I asked.

"They still think it's strange."

When Matt first organized the Gaza Surf Club, in the half-year after Paskowitz brought his fourteen boards, he estimated there were "nine or ten" Palestinian surfers in Gaza. Now there were "fifty to sixty," according to Mohamed, including the twenty or twenty-five club members who sat around us, percolating with enthusiasm.

"How many boards do you have," I asked, "for the Gaza Surf Club?"

"Four," Mohammed Abu Jayyab said.

"Only four? For all these surfers?"

No; the northern Beach Camp crew had four surfboards, while the southern crew, here at Sheik Khazdien, had six, stored in the lifeguard tower. Getting boards to the right people was a problem. In fact the

Paskowitz mission, in strict terms of merchandise delivery, had been a fiasco. Since the Gaza Surf Club had yet to exist, another group called the Palestine Sailing Federation got involved with the handover at Erez, and "distributed them to their own friends," according to Matt. "Pretty typical of Palestinian politics."

Two boards were handed over to the Palestinians by Surfing 4 Peace shortly before Paskowitz's big day at Erez; Arthur rustled them up from his friends in Tel Aviv to show his group could deliver. Mahfouz Kabariti from the Palestine Sailing Federation served as a reliable middleman and gave them to Mohammed Abu Jayyab and Ahmed Abu Hasiera. Two days later, though, Kabariti and the others all turned up at Erez to receive the twelve boards from Doc. This time, according to Matt, "Mahfouz Kabariti said, 'Thank you, now these boards belong to the sailing federation,' and [Mohamed and Ahmed] never saw the boards again.

"Mahfouz cut all contact with Mohammed and Ahmed and found another group of kids at Sheik Khazdien beach that he would groom to become his surf team. He distributed the boards out to the kids and they quickly broke and damaged most of them."

Since then Matt had visited Gaza himself, bearing a load of equipment. That visit accounted for most of the boards. He'd also spent time teaching members of the club to surf, and more than one of them told me they wanted more of that—coaching, encouragement, tips. Some Gazans suspected Matt of being an "Israeli agent," I learned later, so these visits involved a measure of risk and mistrust.

Hamas, as an organization, is one of those corrupt gangs that masquerade as "religious" in the Muslim world to strong-arm Israelis as well as other Muslims. I have no respect for them, but I also didn't quiz the surf-club members about their politics. I did notice that the surfers, individually, were like people all over the world. They understood kindness.

Although the Mediterranean looked about as flat as Lake Michigan, I invited Ahmed Abu Hasiera and a few other surfers to paddle out with me the next morning. Ahmed turned up at seven in the lobby with a board. The concierge announced him skeptically to me on the phone ("Shall he wait in the lobby, or the restaurant?"), and we walked down to the beach—past the black-dressed Hamas brigadiers on plastic chairs, past the white rubble of a house leveled by an F-16, past Arabic graffiti. Near a jetty Ahmed set down the board, and we looked at the hopeless surf.

He was quieter than the other surfers, more watchful, with a darker beard and sullen eyes. He spoke no English. A cousin of his interpreted. I tried to ask about the TV show *Baywatch*. "Like the other Gaza surfers," the original *LA Times* piece had said, "[Mohammed Abu Jayyab] watches reruns of 'Baywatch' episodes. But he doesn't ogle the bikini-clad lifeguards on the show, he said. 'I close my eyes and watch through my fingers,' Jayyab said, laughing as he held his hands in front of his eyes to illustrate. 'We think of the joy of surfing, and how to develop our style.'"

I found that hard to believe. But I'd forgotten to ask Mohammed about it. Now I tried to describe *Baywatch* to Ahmed and his cousin. "A TV show about lifeguards in California? With blonde women in swimsuits? Running on the beach?"

"I don't know."

"There's nothing like that on TV here?"

"I have never seen it."

"Well, what about those Hamas guys with guns on the street corner? Do they come down and enforce sharia law on the beach?"

"No." They looked confused and shook their heads. "It's okay."

"Don't men get harassed by the police for not wearing shirts? Or for flirting with girls?"

I'd heard both stories. Ahmed knew the one about the girls.

"Some men were bothering them," he said. "So they go up to the guards and ask for help. The guards take care of it, no problem."

Okay. Under a roof of dried palm fronds Ahmed opened a door to a storage shack and produced the famous board with the cartoon shark.

He wanted to send pictures of it back to Arthur, Matt, and "Dorian," as all the surfers called Paskowitz. He also handed me a gift for Kelly Slater, the American surf champion who'd lent his name and celebrity presence to Surfing 4 Peace. It was a glossy photo of Slater himself, folded into thirds like a big greeting card, signed by Ahmed and Mohammed. Fan mail.

Al Deira Beach was wide and dirty white, not pristine but pocked with chips of shell and tufts of grass. On our left was a small harbor for fishing boats. The jetty consisted of concrete rubble, slabs and chunks of it, mixed with tetrapods (four-pronged, concrete weights that look like jacks once used by some extinct race of giants). The beach at Al Deira was also "one of the most polluted in the world," according to Matt, because of Gaza's degraded sewage system and an outflow pipe near the hotel. But today the water looked blue.

Since the surf was nonexistent, Ahmed suggested paddling out on a *hasake* instead of on surfboards. We carried it to the waterline. Ahmed threw a board on the deck for good measure, and we pushed off. Hasakes are absurdly easy to ride. I stood at the front while he paddled with a long, two-bladed oar. We slapped through the waves and watched fishing boats putter out from the harbor.

It was a silent, cool, peaceful morning. When he'd paddled about two hundred yards Ahmed said, "Okay, Mike?" and let the hasake coast. I had no idea what we were doing. He threw the surfboard in the water and jumped in after it. We both swam for a while, treating the hasake as a diving platform; then Ahmed paddled the surfboard to the beach shore and I caught a wave on the heavy, all-but-unsteerable board.

More than one person in Gaza told me that fresh fish from the Mediterranean used to be abundant as well as delicious; but since the Hamas takeover and the Israeli blockade, a staple of the Palestinians' diet had collapsed. Still, while we were on the water that morning, boat after boat puttered out to sea. There were small motorized fishing cutters as well as larger yachts, all shambling and old, with flaking paint and a peculiar swerve in the bow. They were fishermen, so they fished.

I heard a sound in the far distance that was like a machine gun, an irregular pulsing combustion, but I figured it was just the sporadic chugging of some old yacht motor. On the beach afterward, we still heard the noise; Ahmed's cousin said it was gunfire. He pointed out the white ships to me, Israeli coast-guard vessels far out on the horizon, and I remembered what Matt had said about fishing limits.

"They are enforcing this limit," Ahmed's cousin said.

"They do it every morning?" I said.

He shrugged. "Is normal."

Critics of Paskowitz who said surfboards would never solve much were right; Surfing 4 Peace had accomplished very little. A backlog of donated boards and wetsuits had piled up in Tel Aviv, and politics on both sides of the border had a chokehold on the flow of charity. Surfers in Gaza liked to mill around in groups and talk about surfing, they liked to pose for photographs, and the effervescent growth of the sport since Paskowitz's gesture at Erez involved a lot of froth. Surfing was a topic in Gaza, more than a thriving sport. It was a way to forget politics for a while so that enemies—Hamas and Fatah, Arab and Jew—could be friends. In that sense Paskowitz was brilliantly right. These awkward relationships across the militarized Gaza frontier would not have existed without his surfboard mission. They were halting friendships, pen-pal relationships, ripples working to mitigate the powerful tides of racism, hatred, and ignorance.

Guards at the Erez terminal searched me twice on my way back to Israel—once before an official read my passports with their confusion of airport stamps, and once, more thoroughly, afterward. I stood in my underwear and submitted to a wave of the magnetic wand, even between my thighs, to be sure Mike had no bombs in his colon. Two women inspected every item in my luggage by hand. They dusted for explosive powders, poked toothpicks into my shaving cream, and peeked between the layers of my tire-tread sandals from Bali. After two hours I walked like a free man into the glaring lot. A driver I had called ahead for, about an hour too soon, sat behind the wheel of his car.

"I been waiting here, forty minutes," he complained.

"Sorry, Shmulik. They gave me the complete procedure."

Shmulik knew nothing about the mess at the airport. I didn't bother to explain. But his sunglasses watched me in the rearview mirror. We drove through the bright dry ancient desert south of Ashkelon, a city with roots in the Bronze Age, when the Canaanites around here worshipped Baal.

After a while Shmulik said, with deadpan irony, "Maybe you look too much Hamas."

I snorted. "Maybe so."

7

CUBA:
LA OTRA REVOLUCIÓN

···*Calle 70, Havana, 2009*

IN A BEACHSIDE neighborhood I flagged down a powder blue Cadillac with fins.

"*¿A Habana Vieja?*"

"*Sí, sí.*"

No room in back, so I sat in front. The dashboard had cheap wooden panels and backlighting provided by old pale bulbs. A Cadillac eagle logo rendered in steel reached its wings over my knees. Most of Havana's *máquinas*, or gypsy cabs, are old American iron. They're run by Cubans for other Cubans, and visitors aren't supposed to ride them. But there was almost no way to move in Cuba without breaking the law.

"American?" the driver said when the car was almost empty.

"Yes."

"What brought you to Cuba?"

I should mention that some máquinas have a rotten energy and can't be romanticized—a driver in one was so drunk he gave me a five-peso rebate. Another driver was either on morphine or believed his car would collapse if he leaned on the gas. He crawled through the night with his friend riding shotgun, both of them clean-cut, muscular, and intolerably slow. His friend talked above the roar of the motor in rapid molten Spanish, but the driver kept saying, "*¿Hay?*"

But cruising Havana in a good máquina put me in a rare fine mood. You rumbled along a boulevard where crumbling ruins of colonial Spain alternated with Communist cinderblock. The seductive, gorgeous, fading tropical light was tainted green by tree ferns and African baobabs. The leaden stink of exhaust leaked through the windows and floors, and the car trembled in places new cars don't even have.

"But Cuba has no waves," my driver said.

"Cuba has a surf club. *Una asociación de surfistas.*"

"Where?"

"In Miramar."

Miramar was a grid of trees and broken sidewalks west of central Havana where hotels and embassies stood along the water. We were driving from there past the Malecón, Havana's great seawall. The ocean slammed against the wall with spectacular plumes that could have made the driver think twice about his judgment of Cuban surf. Instead he asked a peculiar question.

"Is surfing a hobby, or a sport?"

"What?"

"Is it more of a hobby, or more of a sport?"

I didn't understand. "For me, more of a hobby," I said. "I'm not a professional."

That seemed to satisfy him. But later I realized he wanted to know surfing's official status in Cuba. Did it qualify as a sport, under the athletics ministry INDER—the National Institute for Sports, Physical Education, and Recreation—or was it more of a thing people did? The difference mattered, because one achievement of the revolution was a well-disciplined athletics department. "The slogan for these guys is 'Sport is a right of the people,'" said Eduárdo Nuñez Valdés, president of the Havana Surf Club. "So they have to recognize everything. Even the sports they don't like, they have to put someplace official."

From an official point of view, surfing was recreation. Until it became a sport there would be no surf team, no international contests, and no travel to other parts of the world for Cuban surfers. "Even dominoes got more status than we do," Eduárdo said. "I mean, dominoes? Is just a game. But the government says it's a sport. They got a federation, a national team, they got everything. They go to the regional championships of dominoes in Venezuela and Brazil."

"Athletes get passports," I said. "But not regular Cubans."

"You got it."

We drove into the rotting core of old Havana. It reminded me of East Berlin, where the Soviets in 1961 had walled off part of a city still shattered by World War II so the smashed bridges and churches, yards full of rubble, and regiments of unrepaired tenements were simply frozen in time. Havana had the same halted quality. There were the columned Spanish palaces crumbling in the sun; the proliferation of antique American cars, like clanking ghosts of the Batista era; the alien concrete tower of the Soviet embassy in Miramar—these traces of empire—and, of course, the movie theaters. Cuba is a nation of film buffs, and you could almost date the revolution by the state of its flaking cinemas.

"Do you like Cuba?" my máquina driver said.

"The country is beautiful." I wondered what else to say. "Do *you* like Cuba?"

He shrugged and gave an ambiguous smile. "I would like to travel."

We turned down the crumbling leafy Prado, with its stone lions and central promenade, while the sky blued over Havana and the sun began to disappear. I got out and wandered out of curiosity to a crowd that had gathered to watch some dancers. Drummers played for Afro-Cuban women wearing bright parrot colors. I assumed it was a show for tourists, but soon a bunch of teenagers cheered from a balcony across the street, on a building called El Centro de la Danza. One of Havana's dance schools was showing off its students. "They call that *folklórica,*" Eduárdo told me later. "Or *folklórica yoruba.* It's the stuff from Africa." His girlfriend taught ballet, so he knew about dance. Another triumph of the revolution.

Tourism has inflated since the Soviet collapse, and Europeans treat parts of the island like a Caribbean playground, which is *not* a triumph of the revolution. Grinding poverty mixes in central Havana with fresh luxury. Restaurants here take convertible pesos, the hard currency issued for outsiders. A convertible weighs in somewhere between a euro and a dollar; it buys exactly twenty-four Cuban pesos. Average Cuban salaries hover around two hundred pesos a month—less than ten convertibles—and the difference between domestic and tourist prices is so stark that people talk about "tourist apartheid."

It's the worst aspect of a visit to Cuba, a sign of decadence as well as a crack in the dictator's blockhouse. Fifty years after the fall of Fulgencio Batista, you can stay in a selection of luxury hotels on the Varadero peninsula, where Batista himself once maintained a mansion. Fifty years after Fidel and Che fought down from the Sierra Maestra, you can walk through a maze of dark streets in the tenement core of old Havana, under the rotting lightless hulks of Spanish townhouses, where stores sit empty and streetlights flicker and men play dominoes on fluorescent-lit stoops and laundry flaps from sagging cords in the darkness overhead, where it's hard to believe anyone but pigeons live, and emerge onto the restoration triumph of the Plaza Vieja, with murmuring restaurants and a plashing fountain. Waiters bring glass columns of frothing beer to the outdoor tables at one restaurant, and the columns have little toy taps to let customers help themselves. Another place has lobster. Elegant lights accent the arches and columns of restored colonial buildings and the plaza is far more alluring and modest than any colonial revival in Miami or LA, where they would have wrapped ropes of light around the palms and incorporated a multilevel parking garage. But after a walk through the tenements, it's enough to ruin your appetite.

Eduárdo lived with his mother and grandfather in a house near Miramar that served as a headquarters for the Havana Surf Club.[1] He was a friendly surfer with round eyes and black hair curling below his ears, a bright smile, and a soul patch under his lip, mellow but excitable, sometimes talking in an irrespressible stream. His imperfect English never held him back. His girlfriend Claudia was short and slight, with smooth black hair and catlike eyes. She spoke English too, but let Ed do the talking. Sometimes she stirred, to communicate her shifting mood.

The house had a sun-bright living room with a sofa and a few glazed ceramics on a side table. Surfboards leaned in two corners. He took me down a narrow set of stairs to the shaping room, really the garage, but the family owned no car, so now it was a cave whitened by fluorescent lights with posters of bikinied women on the walls. Someone had spray-painted the club's Web address on the exposed concrete over the garage door. This Web site was crucial to surfing in Cuba. Castro's planned economy provided nothing in the way of boards, wetsuits, leashes, or wax. The government might recognize surfing as a recreation, but it wasn't about to order equipment from abroad, much less devote precious resources to surfboard manufacture. The Havana Surf Club relied on the kindness of strangers.

Q: Can you rent boards in Cuba? [reads the Web site.]
A: No, you will have to bring your own board or bring an old board and leave it for the Cuban surfers.

From this charity Eduárdo had built his shaping room. He showed me folded draperies of fiberglass, an electric sander, a face mask, as well as hacked-up pieces of old boards, recycled fin boxes, leash plugs, fins, and other parts organized in bags and stowed in plastic drawers. American

---

[1] In Spanish, *Asociación de Surfistas de Cuba*.

222 SWEETNESS AND BLOOD

shapers take these parts for granted, but scarcity had made Eduárdo a collector.

The only surfers on earth prohibited from visiting Cuba are American, but most donations come from across the Florida Strait. "It's like 80 percent, we get from America." He pointed to a row of dented, clear plastic water bottles filled with resins and catalysts for the fiberglass. "I'm lucky that I live on this street, because I have a neighbor who works for a guy from Spain who builds floors. He uses epoxy resin to make floors for kitchens. So he steals some of this resin and sells it on the black market. Without him, I'd have to go further from here, to where they fix boats and everything made with plastic. Those guys there have polyester resin."

A Florida donor had fixed him up with an electric sander to shape the foam, as well as a plastic face mask to avoid breathing the dust. "Before, I was sanding the boards without a mask. But if you breathe that stuff in, it's really bad."

One rumor about early surfers in Cuba was that they shaped boards from refrigerator foam, sanded down with cheese graters.

"Is that true about the foam?" I said.

"Sure, man, look."

He took a blank from a shelf and showed me the brittle yellowed core of a future Cuban surfboard. There were fine seams where separate chunks had been fused to form the blank, but it had been sanded into an elegant tapering whole.

"From kitchen refrigerators?" I said.

"No, from big freezers. If you see big kind of freezers in the trash, you see if the foam's in good condition, you come to your house and get some tools, you go take the outer layers off the fridge, and you take the foam."

"Big slabs of it?"

"Yeah. Or, a long time ago, there used to be stores for selling fresh fish? They were made from steel but inside they used to have this foam. The shop worked like a freezer. You step into the store, you were inside a big freezer. But after the Special Period got worse, these places were empty. When the government decided to close them, we'd go there and take apart the walls, and we'd use that foam. This was after the Soviet Union collapsed, in '91. After two years they started closing."

Surfing was all but unknown in Cuba before the "Special Period in Peacetime," declared by Castro after the collapse of communism in Europe and Russia. During the deep economic crisis that followed, the future Havana Surf Club founders saw their first real surfers. Eduárdo was a kid at the time, attending a school near the water in Miramar, next to the Soviet embassy. While he sat at his desk in the early '90s, he saw people walk past his classroom door with surfboards. "People like me, who were skimboarding, we'd see these guys surfing in the water. We thought, 'We got to get a piece of plywood, to try that.' That was my first wave, on my skimboard."

"A homemade skimboard?"

"Yeah, with plywood."

"But how'd you even think of skimboarding?"

"Well, here, people used to go to the streets when it was raining, and they grabbed the fenders of cars and they used to ski on the streets with an old pair of shoes. People figured out that if you rode on a big piece of wood, you were making like a ski."

The first surfer in Cuba, according to Eduárdo, was his friend Tito Diaz, a slightly older man who used plywood desktops to ride Miramar waves in the 1980s. "We put tables from the school into the ocean" is how Tito put it to me on the phone—he now lives in Canada—"because we saw a movie from Brazil, *Maneuver Radical*. But we didn't have a board or nothing. My friend said, 'Oh, we can take the tables from the school.' Desks. 'We can try. Like a Boogie board.'"

Tito first stood up on a board in 1990, when he was about twelve. He and his friends tried to improvise surfboards by nailing wooden fins into the bottom of the desktops. "There was a guy we call Batman because he was a good painter. His name was Edgar, but we call him Batman," because he painted a Batman logo on his desktop. "He was the first one to stand up on the board." But Tito pursued it, and became a good surfer.

Until 1992 the only suggestions in Cuba that people in the wider world rode sleek modern surfboards came from the Brazilian movie *Maneuver Radical* and *Point Break,* the kitsch-violent American film about surfing bank robbers, which ran on government TV. Those two films, more than any single force, brought the idea of surfing to Cuba, according to Eduárdo and Tito. Around the same time—in 1992 or '93—Eduárdo met a surfer from Spain named Ricky. He was the first foreign surfer their circle of friends knew. "Then Ricky got in an accident," Tito said. His board broke apart. "And we saw what's inside—foam. Everybody said, 'We can cover this with epoxy, no problem.' So we started to make boards. But very horrible ones."

So the arrival of modern surfing in Cuba coincided with two big trends: economic collapse and experiments by restless kids. The kids, as usual, were ahead of the government. A surge in demand for fiberglass and resin around Miramar drew the attention of Cuban officials, and one of Tito's friends even went to jail. "He was buying the material from the government," Tito said, "and they was thinkin' we was going to use these little boards to go to the United States."

Tito had his own problems with the law. The police threw him in jail for a week when he tried to surf after a hurricane. "It was crazy. One week, just investigation," meaning the police never charged him. "I always get in trouble because I surf. There's no way to do anything in the ocean in Cuba, because they think you're tryin' to go somewhere. Or if you sleep at night on the beach? They think you're waiting to help someone to the United States. But it's nice when you sleep on the beach, you know. You make a nice fire, dancing, chicks, drinking, party. After that the waves are very, very nice, before the sun comes up. This is the most beautiful moment, when the sun starts to come. Man, it's unbelievable. It's a little dark, and then everything is clear and the wind is not so strong in the morning. After eleven o'clock, the waves is no good in Cuba."

Insane as it may sound, there was a reason for the police to worry about people floating in the shorebreak. After the Soviet collapse, tankers of cheap Russian oil quit arriving in Havana. A long-standing contract to sell Cuban sugar at comfortable prices to the Soviet bloc also had to be renegotiated. The twin pillars of the economy wobbled, and people started to starve. To contend with the shortages, Castro declared the Special Period which Cubans remember now the way Americans remember the Depression. Some built rafts out of any near-seaworthy assortment of junk—oil barrels, wooden planks, zinc roofs, inner tubes—and set out for Key West.

At last, in '94, Castro announced that Cubans who wanted to risk the Gulf Stream on a raft were free to leave, and people put their lives at the mercy of nature or the US Coast Guard, whichever got to them first. The Coast Guard scooped them out of the water and sent them to Guantánamo Bay, where a lottery let some of them into America as legal immigrants. Others had to go home.

Castro decided to throw open the doors to tourism for the same reason, but it was a bargain with the devil. Keeping the number of pleasure seekers down to a trickle of Canadians and Russians during the cold war had been a point of revolutionary pride because Batista and his friends in the Mafia had run the island as an international playground before 1959. As soon as a regular stream of rich foreigners started arriving in the '90s, Eduárdo said, "that was the start of the new era. People started to see that the reality outside was not what the government said—that Cuba is a paradise, or that in other countries people are dying, or hungry, or they don't have a job. And all the Cubans that left Cuba back then, none of them want to come back."

The new tourism brought not just disillusionment but also first-world corruptions—more drugs, more prostitution, more crime. The Communist fabric began to unravel. Eduárdo's generation, born since the revolution, says *I*, according to conventional wisdom, as opposed to their parents and grandparents, who believe in the communal dream of Castro and Che and feel embarrassed not to say *we*. "It's a big, big difference," Eduárdo said. "We still feel that human side, of wanting to help each other, but when you talk about goals for your own life? Cubans are more independent."

<center>~~~~~~~~~~~~~~~~~~~~</center>

Miramar has palm-lined sidewalks and chain-linked yards, mansions along the main boulevard, and a smattering of schools with white plaster busts of José Martí, the poet and martyr of the war of independence in the 1890s. I stayed in a *casa particular,* an apartment in a small family home. My hostess was a generous madwoman named Marta. She had youthful braids in her gray-frosted hair, hazel eyes, and a taste for brown-printed blouses with nothing on underneath. She lived in the furnished rooms next door with her quiet teenage daughter and her ancient mother.

My clean kitchen contained a fridge, a table, and nothing else. No oven, no hot plate, no electric kettle, nada. Cubans called their refrigerators *cocos,* because they're hard-shelled and empty. I had a sparkling new white coco.

Marta called me "¡*Migue!*" and kept finding reasons to knock on my door.

"Do you need a table for the sitting room?" she said.

There was a bare but sun-bright front room with two comfortable chairs.

"I don't think so."

"You should keep the door closed," she said. "Open the window if you like the sunlight."

"Oh? Is that better?"

"You need anything else?"

"I'd like to rent a bike," I said. "And make a phone call."

She said something in galloping Spanish that I took for an invitation to come around and use the phone when I was ready. Fine. It wasn't urgent. But after an hour she returned with a telephone and a workman who fed an extension line through my window. This generosity with items from her side of the house continued until I had an electric cooking coil, a frying pan, and a small pot for boiling water. Soon I felt like a king.

I was reading *Islands in the Stream* late that afternoon when an old black street peddler came down Marta's sidewalk pulling a woven basket on a hand truck. "*¡Caliente tamales!*" he shouted, and whistled a repetitive tune. He was like an ice-cream man. I went over and handed him a convertible. "*¿Son más caliente?*" I said. Are they too hot to carry?

"*No, pueden en la mano.*"

I took five scalding tamales in my hand and went back to stock the larder. The man kept walking.

It's easy to see why Hemingway loved Cuba. The weather boils away your need for luxury. His ranch south of Havana was more than a casa particular, of course. It was a walled compound with a view of Havana from its stucco observation tower—and a pool where Ava Gardner once swam naked—but it would have been cheaper than a comparable estate in America in the 1940s. You might say the wealth of Cuba consists not in its sugar or rum, not in its magnificent cigars, but in the sun and clear water and hot fertile land. Cuba's brilliant yellow days promote a simple life that feels leonine.

Miramar is upscale for Havana, but most of it resembles lower-middle-class LA. It has dead lawns and broken-down máquinas by the curb. Modern plaster and stucco houses alternate with terra-cotta-roofed Spanish houses. Children walk to school in khaki slacks or skirts, uniformed like Catholic-school kids except that Cubans rarely go to church. Around four or five in the afternoon a number of boys would gather on Marta's corner to play baseball with a stick.

I'd flown here from Berlin, using my German passport, so it was a shock to recognize the island as a natural part of North America. If I'd flown from Mexico I wouldn't have noticed; but the sere fields around the airport had a brushy smell familiar from my earliest California childhood, a smell that doesn't seem to exist in northern Europe. Cuba, of course, is the corner of North America that Columbus really did discover. His landing marked the start of the Atlantic slave trade, and now Cuba has American-style problems with race. (Obama's election challenged the creaky revolution, since no Cuban could imagine a black *líder máximo*.) There's a tradition here of cattle, rancheros, "Indians," and hell-raising. Baseball stretches back to 1857, when a young Cuban named Nemesio Guilló brought it home from New York.[2] Politically, Cuba is the anti-America, the empire's subversive underbelly. But it hardly felt foreign to me.

It's even full of Hemingway fans. "His friends were fishermen, jai alai players, bullfighters," one Cuban told Chris Baker, a travel writer. "He never related to high society." That goes against his American image as a bohemian expatriate and sport hunter who died with great wealth and an international circle of friends. But Hemingway's Cuban novels deal with bare-knuckled smugglers, hard-drinking laborers, and, of course, the old fisherman from Cojímar. His American reputation gives him a Hugo-like stature—Victor Hugo without the social conscience—but his Cuban image, reinforced in every school, emphasizes his social conscience and even plays up his communist sympathies. Cubans learn that Castro carried a copy of *For Whom the Bell Tolls* in the Sierra Maestra.

Hemingway's parting words to the island in 1960 were "We are going to win. We Cubans are going to win. I'm not a Yankee, you know"—which is the closest he came to declaring support for Castro. The British writer Norman Lewis flew to Havana in 1957 to learn what he could about the big man's tardy novel, which later became *Islands in the Stream,* as well as his affiliations, if any, with the revolutionaries in the mountains. Lewis first met an odd New Zealander named Edward Scott, who lived in a still-standing hotel near the Prado called the Sevilla. In those days it was the height of international glamour.

---

[2] Probably. There are several stories.

We passed first of all into a small anteroom, in which stood, elegantly posed, a quite naked negress. At first, I took her to be a statue, but in passing I could not help noticing the goose-pimples produced by the chill of the air-conditioning. Scott glanced at her as we passed into his office.

I learned later that Scott believed frequent intercourse to increase mental creativity, and I wondered if he had simply forgotten that the girl was there. He kept a register in which he entered the details of several thousand encounters over the years. It was a compulsion he shared with John F. Kennedy, who occasionally popped over to Havana for random excitements of this kind, and Scott had had the pleasure of showing him round.

"Why do you want to see Hemingway?" he asked.

"Because Ian thinks that he and Castro may be working together."

Scott gave a bellowing laugh. "Hemingway, of all people!"

"There's some story that he met Castro when he was hunting in the mountains."

"The only mountain Hemingway hunts in is the Montana Bar. He's a burnt-out case. Any time you want, you can see him in there. His friends bring him king-sized prawns. He chews them up and swallows the lot, shells and all."

Lewis happened to be on assignment from Ian Fleming, then an editor at the *Sunday Times*. "Ian had told me that James Bond was an amalgam of four actual persons," Lewis wrote, "one of whom was Scott."

At Hemingway's ranch, instead of a magnificently aging author, Lewis found a sloppy drunk who reminded him of Massart, the one-time revolutionary hero in *For Whom the Bell Tolls*. "Now I was amazed that a writer who had understood how greatness could be pulled down by the wolves of weakness and old age should—as it appeared to me—have been unable to prevent himself from falling into the same trap."

When Lewis found a way to ask Hemingway his opinion of Castro, the Big Unshaven Man said, "My answer to such questions is bound to be that I live here."

Lewis was unimpressed. He wrote back to Fleming:

> This man has had about everything any man can ever have wanted, and to meet him was a shattering experience of the kind likely to sabotage ambition. . . . You wanted to know his opinion on the possible outcome of what is happening here. The answer unfortunately is that he no longer cares to hold opinions, because his life has lost its taste. He told me nothing, but he taught me more than I wanted to know.

"*¡Migue!*"

"*Sí, Marta.*"

"How many days you want to rent the *bicicleta*?"

"Just for a couple of days."

It would prove difficult—actually impossible—to rent a bicycle in Cuba. During the Special Period the island had swarmed with ten-speeds from China, but now the economy had revived and people rode buses again.

"Be sure to close this window whenever you go out," she went on, "because someone could reach in and open the door."

"Okay, Marta."

"And I need to clean in here. Want me to do it today or tomorrow?"

She did not need to clean. I'd been in Cuba for three days. But when I returned from a surf the next morning she was scrubbing the shower and washing the floor. She'd also rearranged my kitchen items to her satisfaction. The dish drainer and hot plate had been left in the wrong positions on the counter by the clueless American bachelor, and even a carton of mango pulp, which I kept in the fridge, had been moved to the counter. Mango pulp was good on crackers, and I'd learned for myself how hard it could be to spread when refrigerated. But I was trying to keep away flies.

The feeling of regal simplicity at Marta's casa would wear off in less than a week. My hot plate began to malfunction. Whenever the coil turned red a surge protector on the power strip would snap off, so it was impossible to boil water without sitting over the power strip to snap it back on every two or three seconds. When the water had boiled, the remaining heat would fry a strip of bacon, then eggs in the grease, if you tended now and then to the switch. But you needed the power strip—the wall sockets were dirty and required a grounded plug—and the dream of preparing instant coffee while taking a shower (for example) vanished over the horizon of first-world privilege.

~~~~~~~~~~~~~~~~~~~

The main surf beach in Havana is a shelf of jagged, pitted limestone called *dientes de perro,* dogs' teeth. Massive tourist hotels line the waterfront here, but no one ever lazes on the sand, because there isn't any. It's perfect for surfers. Beach crowds won't be a problem for at least two million years.

Waves arrive in western Cuba like clockwork a day or so after any cold front, provided it brings a deep low-pressure system, and the surfers congregate at "Seventy," the end of Miramar's Calle 70. "Without a *frente frio,* we got a shadow from the Bahamas," Eduárdo said. The windward islands block deep-ocean swells from the Atlantic. "That's why it's so flat." The wind had been chilly the previous night, but as we walked across the beach I said the weather was warm. "Man, for Cuba?" said Ed. "This is cold. This is winter." Summers are so hot a spinning fan feels like a furnace blast, he said, and the regular squalls of rain raise steam from the baking streets.

A huge work of graffiti claimed Seventy for the club—HAVANA SURF, painted in bulbous blue letters on a concrete wall. We stepped across the rock with our boards and Eduárdo pointed out clusters of sun-bleached feathers and bone. "Wherever you see that? It's a sacrifice by people who follow Santeria. They have to kill birds as a sacrifice to Yemayá. She's, like, the goddess of the ocean. They clean it up with fruit, melon or something, and our guys, sometimes they take the good part of the fruit afterwards and eat it." He laughed. Fruit is hard to come by in Cuba. (Most of it is exported.) "The chickens sometimes, too."

A Catholic church devoted to Yemayá is on the far side of Havana Bay. Later I went to see it. She is a Yoruban goddess identified with the Virgin Mary, and a wooden figure of a jet-black virgin has pride of place above the altar. She wears a silver crown and a halo of stars. Her baby Jesus is white. It's no contradiction to Santeria devotees; they consider themselves full Catholics as well as followers of certain African gods. Yemayá is Yemayá but also la Virgen de Regla, patroness of sailors, fishermen, and Havana's harbor.

A Santeria follower stood on the limestone at Seventy with a maraca. He had a black plastic doll with him, wrapped in blue velvet; someone explained to me later that such dolls represent the souls of certain ancestors. Devotees keep these dolls in their homes, dressed in hand-sewn clothes, but sometimes they have to be cast away almost like an exorcism. The man with the maraca left his doll behind, along with a couple of gutted watermelons.

Other surfers arrived, one by one, on foot or by moped. One surfer had a brother with a beautiful old turquoise Chevrolet, which they'd used for atmosphere in some scenes for a Spanish documentary about Cuban surfing called *Havana Surf*. But most of them were too poor to own cars. "If we had cars, we would explore," Eduárdo said. The documentary director had sent a handful of surfers on a road trip across Cuba, and for the first time they went to Baracoa, an Atlantic-facing bay in the far east with excellent waves. "I had no idea my country was so beautiful," Eduárdo said.

Soon about twenty people were in the water. They had Cuban crew cuts or Caribbean dreads; they rode yellowed secondhand boards. One lean surfer with a bright aggressive smile, on leave from the military, was considered the club's best surfer, but he'd injured his foot. "They put these sharp traps around the army base to defend it," said Ed. "And if you go out at night for a party or something, it's dangerous coming back. He stepped on one of these traps and got like a nail through his ankle." He could surf, but he couldn't show off. "So there won't be a show today."

I asked if everyone floating in the water had equipment from the Havana Surf Club.

"All of 'em." Ed nodded. "We distribute the stuff as it comes in."

The club turns out to be a centrally planned, equitable distribution syndicate. It has about ten district bosses around Havana who feed requests up to Eduárdo. Big donations, like boards, come from visitors in person—I'd brought Gregor's board, for example. (I thought Gregor would like it to retire in Cuba.) Smaller equipment like leashes and wax might come in the mail.

"The first guys here who ask for something, they're usually the first ones on my list," Eduárdo said. "But the gear goes to whoever needs it most. So if it's a good surfer, he might get the good board."

No one pays a peso for equipment in the Havana Surf Club. They just have to learn to surf.

I thought about this while we floated in the water.

"You run the place like a communist," I said.

Eduárdo smiled.

That night I met Circles Robinson, an American journalist living full-time in Havana. A slight, excitable, nebbishy man with gray and black hair, a wild beard, and terrible eyesight, he carried a knit shoulder bag and looked like every radical Jew I had ever met in California. But as far as I knew he was a goy from Arizona. We went for dinner at a patio restaurant in his neighborhood near the Karl Marx Cinema. Circles wrote in English for the Latin American division of the Inter Press Service; his editors were in Uruguay.

Circles had left the United States in 1971 for two reasons: to avoid the Vietnam draft, and to escape the mentality of people like a high school job recruiter who took a dislike to his bush of hair. "Why do you want to have hair like a nigger fur?" the man had said. "I'm not going to get you a job looking like that!" So he moved to Colombia, then back to the States for a stint in an Arizona mining town. He'd picked fruit in Europe and observed the Sandinista revolution in Nicaragua, where he now had residency. (He spent three weeks every year in Nicaragua to refresh his Cuban visa.) But his given name is John, his family is Jewish, and he'd been raised in Beverly Hills.

"So your mother was Jewish?" I said.

He shook his head. "Changed at immigration. We were from Russia and Romania."

"And 'Circles'?"

"I changed that myself. I got tired of turning around anytime someone said 'John Robinson.'"

He was likable, intelligent, and generous. He was also the only person I met who defended the Havana regime. "I agree with the goals of the government," he said. "I just may not agree with its methods. In that sense it's like Israel to me." Both countries were on a military footing, which had derailed each government in different ways. "In Havana they know there are invasion plans on some shelf in the Pentagon. Maybe a high shelf, but they're very aware of it, so they try to be prepared. That's a big drain on any third-world economy."

Circles grew up with anti-Castro rhetoric around the dinner table. As a teenager he couldn't believe that a sweltering little island near Key West could pose such a devastating military threat to the United States. So he made a point of coming to Havana, and fell in love. "One thing I like about the country is that it's not run by corporate money," he said. "And it isn't a military dictatorship. Journalists from America make the mistake of comparing Cuba to the US, but I mean, it's still a third-world country. They should be comparing it to other nations in Latin America. The government tries to invite some comparisons, like to its health care system, its education system—it likes to try and compete with the developed world. But it's still a third-world country."

No American journalist reporting on Cuba had failed to mention the ban on Cubans entering tourist hotels, he said. It was the most famous example of tourist apartheid, an example of the repressive Cuban state. But it wasn't a law, said Circles. It was an *orientación* from Fidel, an executive order, passed over the heads of the parliament and other lawmaking bodies. The distinction mattered. "Everyone reported on this in the American press, but I don't see why it's such a big deal. Most Cubans don't care if they go to these places. Do you ever go into a Marriott in Berlin? I mean, who cares?"

I said the problem was the lack of freedom. Why shouldn't I go into a Marriott in Berlin?

"Well, sure. But the reason anyone complained about this at all in Cuba is that some Cubans used to meet their lovers in tourist hotels. It was sort of a tradition—once a year, you take a vacation to one of these hotels and you have an affair. Normally with another Cuban. The old people missed this tradition and complained to the journalists. No one explained that part of it, at least not that I saw. Anyway, the orientación went against the Cuban constitution. It was actually illegal. And now Raúl has lifted it. I don't think that's been reported in the American press. But this is what I mean about liking the goals of Cuba, rather than the implementation. If someone could get the government to obey the Cuban constitution, things would be better. A few organizations are challenging the government in court"—like Oxfam, the international human-rights organization where his wife worked—"but the process is slow."

I think Circles was tolerated by Havana because he'd left America behind. He told one story about a salesman from the Middle East who had his business ruined in America because he'd traded with Cuba. He told another about James Sabzali, the Canadian fined ten thousand dollars for violating America's "trading with the enemy" act by exporting Canadian-built water filters to Havana. (Sabzali was living in

America at the time, and the filters included American chemicals. But the Canadian government complained about an overreach of American law.) These insane third-party sanctions, or "tentacles of the blockade," as Circles put it, helped explain Cuban poverty to Cubans. It wasn't the whole story, but it made good propaganda. For years Cubans believed it was America's fault they were poor.

But Circles was realistic about the Special Period. He said the Soviet fuel shortage had paralyzed the island. "They couldn't even run buses. That's why they imported so many bikes." Construction workers he used to chat with on a site near his first apartment in Havana told him horror stories that rivaled anything Americans tended to hear about the Great Depression. "They told me pets kept disappearing." I thought he meant the animals had starved. "And then there were no *pigeons*."

" . . . They had nothing to eat?" I said.

"They were getting eaten!"

I wonder if President Kennedy knew that by signing the blockade order in 1962 he would slow the spread of surfing to the island by several decades.[3] Hippies exploring Morocco in the '60s laid a foundation for surf culture by leaving equipment behind, and an American hippie trail through Cuba would have worked the same effect. It still mystifies me that British, French, and Australian surfers seem to have missed Cuba. Maybe they didn't entirely, but I've heard no stories of foreigners leaving surfboards on the island in the first thirty years of Castro's revolution.

Cuban surfing has followed a Latin American pattern. Historically, Latin Americans don't need much encouragement to surf. Califor-

---

[3] Kennedy's press secretary, Pierre Salinger, has a famous tale in his memoir about the day the president asked him to order as many Petit Upmann cigars from Cuba as possible. The next day he asked how many Salinger had rounded up. Twelve hundred, the secretary said. "Fine," said Kennedy. "And with that," wrote Salinger, "he pulled out the decree establishing the trade embargo with Cuba and signed it."

nians in the '40s brought the sport to Mexico in a highly predictable way—they tossed boards into a truck and drove to Baja—but in Peru, a sugarcane heir returned to Lima in 1939 with a Hawaiian-built board after taking lessons from Duke Kahanamoku. His successors imported modern boards from California, and a visiting Argentinean teenager carried one home in 1963 to spread the gospel there. The first surfer in Brazil was probably an anonymous American in 1928, but surfing got started when a pair of teenagers in 1939 followed a *Popular Mechanics* article to build their own Tom Blake–style boards. Thirty years later, a Chilean marine biologist invented a board to use as a vehicle for studying mollusks. And so on. Wandering Americans and Australians helped things along, but as a rule the Latin American urge to surf has required very little foreign intervention.

Some surf historians argue that the true roots of the sport lie in Peru. Evidence of Peruvian surf boats now called *caballitos* goes back some three thousand years. Caballitos are canoes made from tough yellow totora reeds, densely bundled and bent upward at the front to push through an onrushing wave. They buck up like horses when the whitewater hits them, and a skilled modern caballito oarsman can spring to his feet and navigate the canoe like a surfer on a wave ski. At least one stone artifact showing a man fishing from a reed boat is no doubt older than Polynesian surf culture. But did the ancient Peruvians stand? Or, to put it another way: Did they use caballitos for anything besides catching fish? "There's no proof that they ever did it recreationally," the surf writer Sam George told me. "It's like the Vikings. I mean, Viking ships were designed for coming in and out of the surf—they were fantastic surfers. But they didn't do it recreationally. That's how I make the distinction."

Bob Samin is a cheerful but guarded Australian with crew-cut gray hair and a mustache. He works for British Petroleum in two-month cycles, one month on the job in India, one month surfing in Cuba. He made

Cuba his de-facto home base a road accident in Africa nearly killed him. He was driving across a bridge one night in Ghana, in the mid-'90s, when an oncoming timber truck lost a log from its cargo bed.

"I didn't even see it coming," he told me. "The truck had an overhanging log which collected the Toyota and spat me off the bridge," tearing off the top of his car in the process. "I was lucky. I should've died, but it just dislocated me back." He spent three months paralyzed in a hospital, frightened of losing everything he valued, starting with his "mobility." By then he'd been to Cuba more than once; he'd met Eduárdo and Tito. But he still had roots in Queensland, including a load of material things that suddenly felt superfluous. "I didn't own the things, the things owned me," he said. "It was like a lightning bolt from God, who said, 'If you don't change your life, I'm going to take that life from you.'"

"I had a farm and everything, I sold the yacht, the only thing I kept was me photo albums." He gave those to his sister. "I said, 'Keep them for me, they're the only things I can't get again.' And I just pulled up and left." Now he feels like an outsider in Australia. "I've lived in third-world shitholes for most of my life; Australia's weird to me now. Here I got my bicycle, my surfboard, and I'm happy."

Bob has served as a godfather for Cuban surfing. In 2002 he set up the Web site for the Havana Surf Club, which gives real information about surfing in Cuba and explains the equipment dilemma to foreigners. The government restricts Internet access for Cuban citizens, so Bob's contribution as a Web master has opened Cuban surfing to the outside world the way Matt Olsen and Arthur Rashkovan have opened the scene in Gaza.

He spends most of his time in Baracoa, on the wild northeastern coast. In *Havana Surf,* the Spanish documentary, the town looks wild and tropical, with muddy red goat trails, thatched wooden houses, and men with machetes walking shirtless under green burdens of plantain. "Surfing was all new to them down there . . . and it's a very poor region of Cuba," Bob said to the director of the film. "But they're only poor in assets; their actual life is quite good. They live out of the ocean, they live off their gardens, they actually live very well. . . . And they probably have the best break in Cuba right in their front yard. But they haven't taken a shine to [surfing] like the guys in Havana."

He has a small motor for his bike to propel him around Baracoa. "Foreigners can't own scooters," he told me. "They can rent them, but they can't own them, so I just run a little motor on my bike and I get around fine. You see a policeman, you just shut it off and pretend to pedal."

Bob used to have plans to retire in Cuba, but he's changed his mind. The law against owning a moped was one problem; another was a law against owning land. Someone had given him a patch of property in the Baracoa countryside, but he couldn't live there because of a law against foreigners settling outside town limits. The lack of freedom chafed. "I had a couple American visitors in Baracoa and they couldn't even *bike* outside the town limits," he said. "One of 'em was a teacher, really nice guy, just wanted to help, didn't even drink. They hounded him. The police did. They stopped him biking outside the town, and finally they hounded him until he got on a plane. Now I tell my American friends, 'Look, it's nothing personal, but around here there's guilt by association.' I'm surprised they haven't thrown *me* out yet."

I'd made reservations to fly to Baracoa to see Bob, but for paperwork reasons he had to be in Havana, so I met him there instead. The plan to surf in Baracoa broke down entirely. Eduárdo said the plane to Guantánamo province, in the far east, tended to malfunction. "You might not get your flight home," he said.

"The flight lands at Baracoa airport," I said, glancing at my papers, "but I come back from Guantánamo city. That's how we did the reservation."

Eduárdo shrugged. "It's the same plane."

The other reason to visit Guantánamo province is the US Naval Base, but that's closed to outsiders. The easiest way for an American to get there—if not by joining the Taliban—is by plane from Florida. The land approaches are defended by an armed perimeter fence and a minefield stocked with Cuban as well as American ordnance. The American writer Tom Miller paid a visit in the '90s, as a journalist with authorizations from both Washington and Havana. In those days the base existed mainly to show that a US base in Cuba could go on existing, and Miller managed to walk in from Guantánamo city. But even then the perimeter was militarized, like the border between East and West Germany. The two sides held war games, but it was obvious who was in charge of the island. Gitmo's commanding officer at the time, John Boyd, told Miller, "If Castro wanted to, he could tear down that fence in no time flat. At first we'd hold out until help came from up north. We have weapons that can fire twenty-five miles into Cuba if need be."

US Marines first captured the bay in 1898, during Cuba's war of independence with Spain. Washington posed as Havana's loyal neighbor, but the island reminded some American businessmen of Hawaii—a sugar plantation!—and the next few years would make it clear that America wanted to move in as Cuba's colonial master. The subsequent tussle for sovereignty led to a Cuban constitution with an American amendment. This Platt Amendment established Washington's right to rent Guantánamo Bay for pennies per acre.

The amendment had expired, but the base remained because of a lease that couldn't be terminated without a mutual handshake. America kept the lease alive as a deliberate irritant to Fidel, and Fidel made a grand production of not cashing Washington's checks. "The United States is in the enviable position of an imperious tenant," wrote Miller, "who establishes the rent, controls the lease, and ignores the landlord."

And then builds a torture chamber in the yard.

The base lies on forty-five square miles of land around the marshy bay, enough space for bunkers and firing ranges, a modern harbor, family housing, a high school, a golf course, the notorious Camp X-Ray, other prisons called Camp Delta and Camp Iguana, a cemetery, two airstrips, and a museum devoted to the station's history. Windmill Beach is the main surf spot. It faces south, not north like Baracoa, so the waves wouldn't be Cuba's finest, but companies like Quiksilver have flown pro surfers to host "clinics" there since about 2002.

Craig Basel, who worked at Guantánamo for the Navy's Morale, Welfare, and Recreation department, told me by phone: "We sponsor different groups to come down and interact with the soldiers and sailors and kids, because we're isolated and remote and they have no other place to go. So we might contact Quiksilver and Roxy a couple times a year and see if they can come down and do some surfing clinics. . . . We take care of [the military's] entertainment needs, so we sponsor these guys to come down and entertain the troops."

Now that "Guantánamo" is a synonym for the recent induced coma of American values, it's hard to think about soldiers playing in the surf while prisoners languish in the detention camps. These prisons were designed to be a legal netherworld like the system that kept Pramoedya Ananta Toer from his freedom in the 1960s and '70s. Institutional confusion over what to do with certain prisoners in Jakarta is what banished Pram to Buru. Suharto's Indonesia—now as in the past—is filthy moral company for the United States to keep.

But surfing at Gitmo isn't new. Soldiers have surfed Windmill Beach for a good long time. "When I first got here in '93," Basel said, "we had a club called the Guantánamo Bay Surf Association. It was made up of military members and some dependents, some civilians. They had little get-togethers out at Windmill Beach, [and] that lasted until right around 9/11. After that the complex changed a lot, with the camps and that kind of stuff, so the club kind of filtered away. But we still have a good amount of surfers here. And MWR, my department, actually rents surfboards. We sell the wax and the leashes and that kind of stuff."

"What happened after September 11?" I said.

"The people changed over. They were replaced with single guys, or people that were only here for three months or six months on deployment, instead of being stationed here permanently."

"And then it made sense to have these clinics come year after year."

"Absolutely."

"Do you know when the first serviceman paddled out at Guantá-namo?"

"The best that we could figure out was, probably early '60s to mid-'60s. We say that because there's a an old longboard out in the museum."

"There's a date scribbled on it?"

"No, from the style of the board. We had the pros go out and look, and they figured it was probably mid-'60s. Maybe late '60s."

So the first surfers on the island of Cuba, probably, were American soldiers. "Back then it was a different navy, it was a different base," Basel said. "A lot of single kids lived here, rather than families. Especially after the missile crisis, it took them a while to have dependents here." Of course. And frankly it's hard to imagine bachelor marines from Hawaii or California receiving orders to Guantánamo in those days *without* trying to smuggle in a surfboard. It would be like Alan Shepard, on Apollo 14, forgetting to pack his golf club.

Yaíma Espinosa Martínez was living with her parents in a western suburb of Havana. She's a former Cuban sailboarding champion and the founder of two surf clubs, Surfing Oeste for kids and Cubanitasurf, consisting of eight or nine women. At first glance the Cubanitas seemed to be female members of Eduárdo's syndicate, since they shared space on the Havana Surf Club site. In fact they formed a rival faction. The relationship was complex. If Cuba is the mouthy and inconvenient relative in the basement of American history, the all-American anti-America, then the scourge of the Havana Surf Club, who irritated Eduárdo on a regular basis, was Yaíma.

Women's groups from Florida to Australia had sent donations to Cubanitasurf and the group worked as a charity, but Yaíma asked for money rather than equipment. She used the money to stock up on boards. In practice this meant buying equipment out of the Havana Surf network. It was a capitalist model, and it messed up Eduárdo's scheme.

"She pays our guys like a hundred convertibles a board," he complained. "It's a problem. Where else are they gonna get so much money? They get the boards from us for free, then they sell 'em to her." He accused her of trying to ruin the unity of Havana's surf scene. "Surfing Oeste is, like, for one break, over at Santa Fé, but the good thing about surfing in Cuba is, right now, there's no localism." If the surf community splintered into smaller clubs all centered around individual breaks, he said, the communal aspect would be gone, and his syndicate would fall apart. He accused Yaíma of not surfing well. He said she posed as a surfer to find a way to leave Cuba. But he was determined not to let her bother him. "We don't worry about her, basically. She's not a big problem."

Yaíma had shoulder-length black hair and an engaging smile. Her family home was the rear of a duplex in a long row of houses with chain-linked yards along a major avenue in Santa Fé. One of the thin woven bracelets on her wrists said CUBA. "I am so proud to be Cuban," she said, "and I am so proud of my country." She was a student at the national athletics institute (the school connected to INDER), and was working on a special project to find a legal way to make surfing a sport. Her certificate, when she graduated, would let her work as a government coach. "Maybe for windsurfing, maybe for swimming," she said. "I don't know yet."

Yaíma was smarter and more serious than Eduárdo portrayed her. But marketing, self-positioning, was absolutely her game. She showed me a longboard in her room, shaped by a donor in California. It had personalized messages scribbled in pencil along the spine—PARA YAÍMA, LA REINA DE LAS CUBANITAS, and ONE LOVE. "I looooove Bob Marley," she said, unnecessarily, since her walls were covered in posters. Later she showed me an album of Marley pictures clipped from magazines and assembled by her boyfriend.

Her ambition, she said, was to change the status of surfing in Cuba and get in on the formation of an international team. She had a detailed plan to push surfing through the bureaucratic maze. First, an advocate had to show a circuit of contests where a Cuban team could compete. Latin America has a regional circuit as well as top contests on the world tour, and Yaíma had professional friends in Venezuela and Brazil who could write letters of support. But INDER authorities also had to believe in Cuba's native talent. So she had to estimate the number of medals a national team could bring home. "When the team travels, you got to pay for all the players, the coach, the doctors. . . . The government has to see that it's gonna be worthwhile."

Surfing has never been an Olympic sport, which has hurt it's status in Havana. But Yaíma was hopeful. She seemed to understand the bureaucratic problem better than Eduárdo; at least she was better prepared with paperwork. She showed me sheaves of notes and forms in a binder.

"How is it being a female surfer in Cuba?" I said, and she laughed.

"In Cuba, a woman is supposed to be at home. So just think: When people see a woman going to the beach, walking without shoes, with a board on your head maybe or under your arm—you can feel how they look at you. For that reason it's hard. But it's getting better. People are used to it in Santa Fé and Miramar," these western districts of Havana. She hoped that when surfing earned real athletic status in Cuba, "people will see surfing on the TV news, and say, 'Oh, I remember that crazy girl.'"

Cubanitasurf was a small team of eight or nine women who surfed together and had meetings once a month, sometimes "parties." But they didn't seem to clash with Eduárdo's club. Yaíma's other project, Surfing Oeste, did. "We call it Surfing Oeste because it's surfing in the west of Havana. It's just for children. From sixteen years and younger, they can be in the club. I don't teach them, because I'm not good enough to be a teacher. It's just to give them the opportunity. And maybe to get a future surf champion of Cuba."

The clubhouse for Surfing Oeste was just the borrowed backyard of an ordinary stucco home near the beach. We went to see it. The house had a dry lawn and a yapping dog. Near the patio, in the rear, the famous Korda portrait of Che hung in a crooked frame on a storage-room wall. It was easy to imagine groups of kids milling under his militant gaze, and a row of eight or ten surfboards hung from the underside of the patio shelter.

"When there are waves," Yaíma said, "the children have the opportunity to come to the club and use these boards. When they are finished, they put the boards back."

"So you don't hand them around, like Eduárdo does."

"*Well,*" she said, intending to set the record straight. "They don't give the boards to everyone. That is what they say in Miramar. But the truth is, they send the boards to Santa Fé, to one guy named Raúl—he is my friend—and then he *sells* the boards. So I have been buying all the boards from him. I pay a hundred and fifty convertibles for each board."

I wasn't about to inflame an argument between Eduárdo and Yaíma. But their spat expressed one of Cuba's contradictions: Yaíma, who surrounded herself with patriotic symbols, ran her club with cash donations that threatened to spoil the finely balanced, quasi-communist syndicate of the Havana Surf Club. It put Eduárdo—who was open about his disdain for Castro—in the position of party chairman.

I never figured out the purpose of Surfing Oeste. Why did kids need a club with boards doled out by a young woman who couldn't quite be their coach? Eduárdo was unemployed in the Cuban system; he lived off of perks from his surf-club syndicate and had the counter-cultural opportunism of surfers all over the world. Yaíma appeared to be a loyal patriot, angling for a career in athletics. But she wasn't as loyal as she seemed. She mentioned the working title of an upcoming

Spanish-language film about Cuban surf culture, *La Otra Revolución*.

"I think that's a good title," she said. "Don't you?"

While she gave me a tour of the yard, a man named Arnaldo watched us. He wore Hawaiian surf shorts and a pair of reading glasses. He had a long tanned face and spidery hands. I took an interest in the Che portrait and he grew very excited. He brought out another framed picture, showing Che with his young kids, and set it on the patio table for me to photograph. He stood reverently aside, but when I motioned for him to sit at the table, next to his hero, he placed his hand on his heart in a show of great humility, and complied.

Until that moment, Che was just an old cliché to me. You found him on T-shirts and buttons at street protests in the States; you saw him on propaganda billboards in Havana as well as posters hung by hipsters in Morocco. I remembered the bad painting of Che at a hippie vegetarian café on my college campus. But in Cuba he wasn't just a symbol of the revolution; he was also a subversive memory. Havana uses him the way it uses busts of José Martí—the government prefers to pepper the streets with images of dead revolutionaries, rather than overdo the cult of Fidel. But Che was shot in 1967, the same year Castro linked the island's fate to the Soviet Union.

The long period of compromise and disappointment can be dated from about then. So a Che portrait can express both patriotism and protest; nostalgia for Che is also nostalgia for the days before Fidel started to forge the repressive rules (or "orientaciónes") that every communist leader has to forge. The early years of the revolution— bloody as they could be—are still infused with romance, which may serve as a warning against romance in politics generally. Jean-Paul Sartre had come to Havana to interview the swaggering young guerrillas; they were the toast of the world's frustrated Left; they even had supporters in the CIA ("My staff and I were all *fidelistas*," wrote one desk officer).

Richard Gott, reporting from Havana for a leftist London paper in 1965, sketched a very different island from the one I saw. "Amazing self-confidence is reflected in every facet of the Revolution, now about to enter its sixth year," he wrote. "Many things make one unhappy about Cuba, but one can never get away from the central fact of the Revolution, that it is still wildly popular." Later he met Che at a Russian reception in Miramar. "Guevara strode in after midnight," he recalled, "accompanied by a small coterie of friends, bodyguards, and hangers-on, wearing his trademark black beret, and with his shirt open to the waist. He was unbelievably beautiful. Before the era of the obsessive adulation accorded to musicians, he had the unmistakable aura of a rock star. People stopped whatever they were doing, and just stared at the Revolution made flesh."

8

SÃO TOMÉ AND PRÍNCIPE:
THE STERN OF AN OLD CANOE

····················The author's surfboard, Porto Allegre, São Tomé, 2008

PORTUGUESE HAS ALWAYS sounded to me like a softer, more sinister Spanish, and the Portuguese passengers on my plane from Lisbon to the islands of São Tomé and Príncipe all looked like compromised businessmen. There was the man with a graying head of flowing hair and stylish glasses who talked in a clever bray and wore a business blazer draped over both shoulders. There was the game retiree in overlarge glasses and a candy-striped shirt who smiled like an old rooster vacationing at Hefner's estate. There were the dark-browed Mediterraneans, grave with machismo, who wore square-toed leather slippers that would mark them, in America, as gay. Later I would wait for them in a taxi to finish cigarettes in front of the Pestana São Tomé, one of the island's luxury resort chains. They had the manner of Pestana executives just down to check on the help, and they made me think of a phrase: golf-course piracy.

São Tomé and Príncipe is a two-island nation in the Gulf of Guinea, the great bend in Africa's west coast. The islands belong to a volcanic archipelago that was probably just a lush home for birds before about

1486, when the Portuguese established São Tomé as a colony. European sailors called it "the center of the world," because in Western navigational terms there was no more central landmass. The main island lies on the equator, or 0° latitude, a few degrees to the east of the prime meridian, or 0° longitude.

Imagine a colony run as a slave outpost by homesick Portuguese traders in the 1500s. Sailors, pirates, whores, and slaves. Plantations, malaria, miscegenation. (Rum, sodomy, and the lash.) São Tomé is not an African nation so much as a prototype for the colonial Caribbean. These were the first islands colonized by Europe in the tropics, and they propagated an early creole culture of Africans, Catholicism, and Portuguese. Their history is stark and elemental. São Tomé is one of the poorest countries in the world, with an economy ruined by the slave trade, Marxist mismanagement, and harsh colonial exploitation lasting into the 1970s. But Santoméans are mellow and pleasant.

In a bus at the airport I saw that Portuguese tourists had brought pens for the kids who hung around the taxis and vans. They were strong- but poor-looking teenagers who begged with the weak eyes of junkies. Knuckles knocked on my window, disconsolately, and made writing motions. One woman erupted in pens as she boarded the bus. I wondered why pens were so important. I'd heard of children in São Tomé asking for sweets by yelling *"Doce! Doce!"* at tourists—in fact, I'd been told not to bring sweets so I wouldn't indulge such dependent behavior. ("Don't turn São Tomé into an island of beggars!") But the begging at the airport was rote, not desperate, as if what the kids wanted, more than pens, was the attention of a stranger.

On the way to the capital our minibus crossed a bridge over a fresh stream near the ocean. People bathed in the water. A tall woman the color of black coffee wiped her wet hair with both hands, naked as Diana, with young breasts the size of cognac snifters. She was surrounded by muddy riverside trees and laundry strewn on the rocks and grass—a sudden vision of beauty in the middle of a normal African day. Then more kids on sputtering scooters, the acrid smell of garbage smoke, the muggy malarial heat.

I was here for a strange reason. The first stand-up surfer on São Tomé, as far as anyone knew, was a Californian called Sam George, who flew here in 2000 with the idea of finding waves. Sam is a professional. He used to edit *Surfer* magazine. At first I didn't care about his story, because I instinctively don't care about celebrities who set out to "first-surf" any location. They're promoters, missionaries who don't belong (I thought) to the folk history of surfing. But Sam had found "an indigenous surf culture" in a fishing village on the south side of São Tomé, where kids rode hand-carved bodyboards and even crude wooden surf boats. He returned to make a film about it six years later and learned that a boy he called Shun had hewn and learned to surf his own stand-up board. Sam was delighted. After shooting the film he and his crew left a handful of modern boards in the village. Now there was a very small stand-up surf community on São Tomé, maybe the youngest modern surf scene in the world. The story was still unfolding, and even if it turned out to be a fluke I wanted to know what had become of those fiberglass boards.

The center of São Tomé city has square-cornered colonial buildings with verandahs, and the streets have the comfortable scale of a California gold rush town. It's dusty, hot, and slow. Caroceiro or sea almond trees shade a small central square occupied by a perpetual crowd of loitering men and women selling fresh cassava. The square also has a gas station smack in the middle, but it is small, and the line of motorbikes and cars was somehow not obtrusive.

I owed money to a travel agency in town for a reservation on the south end of São Tomé. Since the island has no bank machines, it's smart to reserve lodging and cars in advance. The sleepy, air-conditioned travel office was run by an excitable man called Luís, who had squarish glasses and a long dark face. I'd done business with his office by e-mail, so we shook hands like old friends.

"Sit down! How was your flight? How do you like São Tomé?"

"Just fine."

"What brings you to the island?"

I gave him a quick rundown, and he said: "Samgeorge! He's a crazy man! Always surfing, surfing."

His office had handled car rentals and hotels for Sam's film, apparently. Luís was interrupted by a phone call. A woman at the next desk, Guitola, who was silent and shy, had worked on all my reservations. She printed my invoice and handed it to me. When Luís was off the phone I asked if I could pay with traveler's checks.

He looked grave. "You must go to the bank," he said. "But I am afraid you may have no luck. It is almost four o' clock, and tomorrow we have a holiday."

"But tomorrow's Tuesday."

"Yes, but it is a holiday here, on São Tomé."

"So if I can't get you the money until the day after tomorrow—," I said.

He waved. "No problem."

São Tomé's central bank was nearby, in a shambling white building on a sad oceanside square. The interior had dark wooden desks and sophisticated computers, but there was an atmosphere of inertia and desperation. Customers leaned against the counter and waved useless-looking bits of paper until someone paid attention. Sharp-dressed tellers talked on the phone and filled out forms. Some ran soft, ragged money through counting machines. One teller sat in front of his computer and taped up a pile of torn old banknotes.

After a long wait I was told my traveler's checks were no good.

"Do you have an account here?" the teller said.

"In São Tomé? No."

"But at this bank?"

"No."

"Then I'm sorry."

We were speaking French. The next-best language on São Tomé, barring Portuguese, is French.

"*C'est un chèque de voyage*," I explained. "American Express. *Je suis voyageur.*"

Traveler's checks, according to everything I'd read, were the way to go in São Tomé. But the man shook his head. The post office could cash my checks and wire the money to this very bank, no problem—if I opened an account.

I remembered having a similar conversation with a teller in small-town Ohio. "Do you have an account here, sir?" said the birdlike woman with a meringue of dyed hair. Utterly bewildering. If I had an account here, *why would i need to cash a traveler's check?*

Instead, I asked for a credit-card advance. He typed on his terminal, waited, did about twenty minutes of unrelated paperwork and finally showed me a printout of numbers. For two hundred dollars I would get more than three million Santoméan dobras. Then he deducted 245,000 by hand.

"This is the telecommunication fee," he said. "Do you agree, sir?"

It seemed like a large commission. I noticed a standard commission deducted already on the printout. I complained.

"Two hundred thousand dobras," the man said smoothly. "Is not that much, sir."

"It's more than ten dollars."

In fact it was more than fifteen. All told they wanted more than twenty dollars to give me two hundred. "If you'd told me this earlier, I would have drawn more," I said. "I can't pay these big fees every time I need cash."

"Oh, monsieur. But telecommunication on São Tomé is very expensive."

I had planned to be generous on São Tomé, unconcerned about money, as long as it went where it was needed. But without bank machines or even banks outside the capital, I might be counting euros and dobras in my head for the rest of the week, just to keep from getting stranded. I felt bitter and walked to an expatriate café on the main square, Café e Companhia, a small wooden storefront built like a barn, with fans in the rafters cutting the sunlight. Two or three laptops glowed on the tables. A white Santoméan called Francesco drank beer with his friends at the bar. He recognized me from the Lisbon plane and we fell into conversation. My story about the bank surprised him, so he retold it in Portuguese, and a fat man on a bar stool, with wide round eyes and stubble that suggested an amiable knowingness about the island, gave a confident reply.

"He says you can change a check at the Parallel Market," said Francesco.

"Where's that?"

"No, the unofficial market."

"The black market?"

"Yes," he said drily. "I was trying to avoid this term."

Of course.

The fat man, Mauricio, knew a man who could give me cash. He said, "I trust this man like my brother."

There was a flurry of chatter and shouting at the door. Soon a young man came in, deep black, unsmiling, alert, but not the man in question. He was a runner. He wanted to see the check. Fifty euros. He went away and returned.

"No problem," said Mauricio. "But he'll get you euros, not dobras."

"Fine."

Euros and dollars were alternate currencies here. Even the bank, I thought, might recognize them. I felt better and ordered a drink. Next to me at the bar sat a young Frenchman from Strasbourg. He was working for six months in São Tomé as an intern from a Paris business school. "I have tomorrow off, so that's nice," he said, lighting a cigarette. "São Tomé is very easy. It's not like other African countries, not so much resentment. There's enough money here for the people, that's why. You know how they say 'levé-levé'? 'Take it easy'? That's because there's enough money."

I nodded, but after seeing the rest of the island I know this must have been true only in São Tomé city.

"There also is not so much begging," the Frenchman went on.

"I saw people beg for pens at the airport."

"Yes, because Europeans come and bring things they think are good for the people. They bring clothes and pens and things for school. School is just opening now, maybe that's why. But these people at the airport, they will sell the pens again. They make money. It's the same thing with clothes."

"But somebody buys the pens. There must be a big market for them."

He laughed. "In São Tomé there is a market for everything."

The runner returned from outside. He talked to Mauricio in Portuguese. Mauricio produced a hundred-euro note from his own wallet and laid it on the bar.

"No problem," he said. "I trust this man."

I blinked at the money.

"Can we do two checks?"

"Yes, of course," he said.

I signed them on the bar and snatched up Mauricio's cash. He smiled and shook my hand.

"Welcome to São Tomé."

The best hotel on the island was the Miramar, worth seeing, supposedly, for its air of corruption, its faded colonial glamour, and its international mix of soldiers, con men, entrepreneurs, oil riggers, would-be spies, diplomats, and international financiers. I stayed there hoping to soak up the flavor of an African country in the process of profound historic change. But the hotel was empty. It had a grand lobby with mahogany furniture and atmospheric port barrels planted with ivy. The glamour wasn't faded so much as dead, inert. The golf-course pirates had cleared out.

A few years earlier the hotel's German owner, Manfred Galland, had talked to a radio journalist I knew in Berlin. He'd boasted that business was good. "Before, we used to be 30 percent, 40 percent full," he said on the radio program. "Now we're most of the time full, full, full. Nobody wanted to know us here, really. We didn't have anything except bananas and cacao. But now with oil, everybody wants to come."

He was talking about the oil craze that swept São Tomé after seismic tests hinted that a bed of the stuff might lie under the ocean floor just north of the islands. Suddenly visions of São Tomé as an oil state danced in the heads of politicians from Nigeria to Washington. The islands were new to the world economy; they were just emerging from centuries of tropical inertia when oil money threatened to jerk them into modernity whether they liked it or not. Politicians realized the oil could be tapped and loaded from platforms in the middle of the ocean without disturbing the people. At the same time the oil might make a *millionaire* of every citizen, including the poorest fisherman or farmer's wife who worked in clearings in the jungle to harvest taro root or cacao. "The amount [of money] is enormous," said Manfred Galland on the radio program. "When you think that there are 120,000 or 140,000 people on this island. Where is it all going to go?" The buzz was so palpable that a team of well-meaning experts sat down to write an agreement for São Tomé to keep the oil from wrecking its economic and social balance the way oil, diamonds, and gold had wrecked the fabric of other African states. The economist Jeffrey Sachs belonged to this team. He thought of São Tomé as a test case. He wanted to see if an African country could be saved from the resource curse, the corruption that followed wealth. Sachs helped draft a set of laws to steer Santoméan oil profits out of the hands of corrupt and grasping politicians and toward development projects, even into the pockets of the people. São Tomé city became an international boomtown. Texas oil wildcatters, Belgian construction contractors, Swedish telecom agents, and financiers all came to the islands looking to profit from the imminent wave of cash, which was set to hit any day now, any minute, just wait till Chevron-Texaco sinks the first test drill—

Chevron-Texaco sank the first drill in 2006 and announced that oil existed, yes, but it wasn't commercial grade. By then São Tomé had signed two rotten contracts for drilling rights, one with a shifty American firm and another with Nigeria, São Tomé's imposing mainland neighbor. There was corruption in the islands, corruption on the mainland, corruption in the supposedly helpful corporations. One former Santoméan minister, Manuel de Deus Lima, had cut a deal with Liechtenstein to forge a São Tomé commemorative millennium coin. Nice idea; but a portion of the profits went straight to him. The minister had studied in East Berlin and spoke German, so when a reporter from *Der Spiegel* wrote a feature about the islands he called Lima for an interview. Lima resisted. In fact he shouted into the phone, "Oil! Oil! Oil! Everyone comes here to write about it, but no one wants to help us get to it!" And hung up.

Meanwhile the diplomats and ministers left town. The Miramar was abandoned. My dinner in the hotel restaurant—a crab *sopa fria* and a fish kebab "with local fruits," meaning a roasted tomato and some pineapple—was boring. The beer was chilled and looked as if its head had evaporated, as if someone had left it in the fridge too long. I wondered why anyone would pre-pour a beer and store it in the fridge. Because the kegs weren't chilled? In the island's most exclusive hotel?

The next day I moved to a cheap hotel on the central plaza, where the owners ran a generator every evening just to turn on the lights. Then I found someone with a motorcycle who could take me to see Ned Seligman, a Peace Corps veteran who turned out to be enormously helpful. Ned ran a nonprofit called STeP UP in a quiet neighborhood outside the center of town, near the bottom of a ravine. The office was a converted old house set below street level. A footbridge, oddly, reached from the top floor out to the sloping sidewalk. The front door was on this upper level. But nobody answered my knock, because, as Luís had said, it was a national holiday. I came back the next morning.

Ned was a gentle, tough-minded man with owlish glasses and white hair. His office was open and sunny and still, with wooden desks and slow computers. He said my timing was perfect—the power had just gone out.

"So you're a surfer," he said from behind his desk. "I didn't even know there was surfing on the island. But my volunteer out there, Sean, he's a surfer, too."

"Really?"

"He's a New Zealander, but he grew up in California," said Ned. "I think he'd like to know where to surf around here. He brought his board with him. He's only been here for a few weeks."

"Good timing all around," I said.

STeP UP did development work. Malaria prevention, reforestation, crop diversity, employment training, school libraries, health clinics. The small staff arranged courses in construction, upholstery, sewing, tailoring, auto mechanics, and English. Ned was skeptical about the promise of oil. "The prime minister from his own lips said to me, 'If it happens, it's not gonna happen anytime soon.'"

Two freestanding prosthetic legs stood under Ned's desk, both wearing shoes and socks. He'd lost his legs four years earlier, after a rare and powerful strain of *Staphylococcus* had infected his blood. He'd lapsed into a two-month coma and woken up crippled. The doctors had to amputate below the knee to save his life. It was like a horror film, a nightmare about claustrophobic third-world hospitals and tropical disease, but it had nothing to do with Africa. Ned traced the infection back to some dental work in California. MRSA is an epidemic staph strain that rages through first-world hospitals because of overuse of antibiotics, and Ned's coma came on three days after a dental procedure in San Francisco. He was remarkably mild about it. "I don't think it was strictly the dentist's fault," he said. "I think he just opened me up, and then I had wounds, and the infection got into my mouth somehow. Then it got into my blood. You can just breathe it in. We can carry it on our skin. I'm not sure why it doesn't happen more often."

So that explained the footbridge. Every morning and afternoon he crossed it on his prosthetics, using a walker, between the office and his car. He had drivers and people to help him.

"You may have noticed," he went on, "that yesterday was a holiday. It was the anniversary of nationalization on São Tomé—when they nationalized the plantations." Slavery was abolished throughout the Portuguese empire in 1838, but private ownership under the Portuguese allowed indentured servitude, essentially slave labor. So after the plantations were nationalized in 1975, people celebrated. They were free. But they were also tired of working the fields, and farm production collapsed. "Things have been going downhill economically ever since."

"So oil's the last hope?" I said.

Ned looked horrified. "Oil is the worst thing that could happen. It would do more harm than good. . . . And nothing *has* to change, the country's proved that for thirty years. But one of the things we're working on"—and here he handed me the shock of the trip so far, after my slow night at the Miramar, after my comedy routine at the bank— "is tourism."

Quintino Quade is a tall, deep-black man from Guinea-Bissau with a handsome easy smile and an almost formal manner. He was Ned's assistant at STeP UP and would be my translator. At the office he wore belted dark gray slacks and a white buttoned shirt—he seemed very conscientious—but in the car to the south end of the island he wore a German soccer jersey and khakis. Sean Buckley, the other surfer, wore a T-shirt and shorts. What they wore would be important later in the day.

Sean was as much of a surprise to me as I was to him: neither of us had expected to meet another Western surfer on São Tomé. He'd just finished a public policy degree in New Zealand. He was spending three months on the island to work in Ned's office as a postgraduate volunteer. He had an earnest intelligent face and wheat-colored scruff on his chin.

When we loaded our equipment into the truck, I noticed graffiti on his board that said ARTICLE 24, with an Amnesty International symbol. As we started out, I asked him what it meant.

"I used to intern for Amnesty," he said. "Article 24's from the Universal Declaration of Human Rights."

"Something about torture?"

"No, it's about workweeks and vacation time. 'Everyone has the right to rest and leisure.' That always seemed critical to surfing."

The highway south of São Tomé city was a paved country road, curving through banana trees and what looked to me like Faulknerian slave shacks, wooden boxes on stilts. "This road has potholes," said Quintino. "But it is better than it was." The island had started cooperating with the Taiwanese, instead of the Chinese, after 1991, when voters kicked out their Marxist leaders and shifted allegiance away from the communist bloc. "The Taiwanese build better roads," he said. "And they did a very good job eradicating mosquitoes. But it is still funny to hear them speak Portuguese."

The highway wound through villages where pigs rooted in the bushes and ran from the car. People walked along the road with baskets of laundry on their heads. One woman balanced a plastic bucket with an enormous whole single fish, head and tail sticking up, like something in a cartoon.

We passed a kid with a truck made of crude blocks of wood, using a stick to move it forward and back. "I've seen a lot of those toys on the south side of the island," said Sean. "I've seen helicopters made out of flayed plastic water bottles and things made out of aluminum cans. Why don't I see them in the city?"

"The city has an airport. The whole north is closer to Europe, so they have modern toys," said Quintino. "The south is different."

The road wound through forests of banana trees, past edges of plantations, where goats nosed through piles of red cacao-fruit husks.

Twice we had to cross a river on a style of concrete bridge that was more like a ford, a heavy white block low on the water, just a stone extension of the road. Later in the day this would become extremely important.

Quintino told us how he had come to São Tomé. Ned had worked in Guinea-Bissau in the '90s, and when he decided to leave the Peace Corps and establish STeP UP on São Tomé, he invited Quintino to work with him. At first Quintino had said no. But a coup in Guinea-Bissau led to a civil war and fighting with Senegal in 1998 and '99, and the job was an important escape. "Now I like São Tomé very much," he said. He'd married a Santoméan woman and had two daughters. "My city in Guinea-Bissau is destroyed."

Sean asked about politics in Guinea-Bissau. Nino Vieira, the corrupt leader who fell during the civil war, had just been reelected. Sean said, "Can't they think of anyone else to elect?"

"There are other politicians, but they have not been in power," Quintino said. "They have not had an opportunity to steal from the nation. So the people voted this time not for the wolves that were hungry, but the wolf that was full."

We passed palm-oil plantations, ranks of huge palms disappearing in military formation into the jungle. But sometimes the forest opened up and carpets of ferns, pierced with an occasional tall, pale tree, gave white egrets and black kites room to glide. Soft bolts of sun alternated with bursts of rain. It felt like a dinosaur film.

Sean knew about Sam George's film, *The Lost Wave*. He'd even e-mailed one of the surfers who had traveled with Sam, a professional from Redondo Beach named Holly Beck. She and Joe Curren, Sam's other companion, are excellent surfers, and the footage of them is one reason to watch it. Otherwise *The Lost Wave* is incomplete. It's dumbed down for surfers—to what some producers think surfers can understand. It tells about Sam's return to São Tomé in 2006, years after meeting and surfing with "Shun." Sam still had a photo from the first trip of Shun balancing buck naked on a longboard with a look of wavering joy. The photo became a talisman for his own lost enthusiasm for surfing. "Something about sharing the stoke with this primal African surfer reaffirmed one of my deepest convictions," he actually says in the voiceover, "that surfers, as a tribe, truly are a special people."[1]

Porto Alegre was a muddy assemblage of stilted wooden shacks and old plantation buildings. Children, pigs, and chickens stood around in the mud. We drove past a massive, empty barracks left behind by the Portuguese, up a slope to a concrete school. Then we were lost. We asked for Shun, and a man sitting under a tree with drink-bleary eyes climbed into our car. He directed us back down the hill. This time a crowd gathered. Somebody ran off.

From the film I knew that Shun's father, Chano, was a lean and friendly black man, about fifty years old, with a severe face. When he appeared, scowling, we showed him a printout of the famous photo. Chano laughed and shook our hands. He said Shun had been in the military, but now lived in the village again. And suddenly there he was, fresh from farmwork: about nineteen years old, with wide-set eyes, a brooding face, and tattoos from his time as a soldier. Quintino said later they'd been pressing sugarcane, which explained the bits of fiber in his short-cropped hair. I'm not susceptible to celebrity—or I think I'm not—but at first I felt nervous. Seeing Shun from the disembodied, abstract distance of a screen, even just on my laptop, had worked a strange power.

Shun and Chano lived in a stilted fishing shack near the beach, where a large gray pig snuffled under the floor. The shack had a series of small rooms with pallet beds and rough furniture. The first room was almost a storage shed with a mess of tools, a bike, and a smoldering fire of dried coconut shells where strips of fish lay smoking. In one corner of this room, opposite the fire, stood Sam George's longboard.

---

[1] Where is it written that surf films have to be cheesy?

Chano produced a photo album, a worn book of plastic sleeves with pictures of Shun's hand-hewn board. We sat around a small table in the main room and looked at the book. There were pictures of surf canoes. There were pictures of Joe Curren and Holly Beck.

"How often do they see foreign surfers?" I asked Quintino.

"Not very often," he translated. "Most tourists and European surfers go to Rolas."

Ilhéu das Rolas is an islet just off the coast from Porto Alegre with a new Pestana-group hotel called the Equador. Rolas had surf: In fact Shun and his family had once lived there. But the owners of the Pestana Equador had displaced them to Porto Alegre to make room for their resort.

"Before Sam came, you surfed on your bellies?"

"Yes. And on surf boats."

"Made from what?"

"*Gofi.* It is a tall tree," said Quintino, "with light wood that floats."

Gofi was the slender white tree I'd noticed beside the highway. They lashed three of the slim trunks together to make a sit-down boat, which kids could paddle with a stick of bamboo halved lengthwise.

"How do you make the bellyboards?"

"When they have broken canoes, they carve them out of the bottom."

A board cut like that was called a *tambua* (tam-BOO-a), which, according to Quintino, was the local pronunciation of *tábua* (TAB-wa), or board. It had a lateral curve from the canoe bottom and even a scoop in the nose.

"But you never rode them on your feet?"

Here Chano interrupted. "Only after Sam came. He taught them to ride on their feet. And when he left, my son made a long tábua so he could stand."

Chano said the kids sometimes fished from the surf rafts, but the tábuas were just for fun.

"How many modern boards do you have here now?"

Five. Just the boards Sam and his crew had brought. Shun said he rode Sam's board every day.

"Who rides the others?"

He started listing names. It was a small group, maybe seven kids.

"All boys?"

"Yes."

I'd wondered whether the appearance of Holly Beck on the beaches of São Tomé had inspired a few girls to pick up a tábua.

"He says the boards have a kind of rope you put around your leg?" said Quintino.

"A leash?"

"He wants to know if you have any more of those."

"I should have thought about leashes."

"And a kind of soap that you put on the board?"

"Wax, of course. I brought plenty of wax."

Sam had absorbed a huge amount of detail about the islands—more than he lets on in the film—and before my trip he was both helpful and generous. He gave me ideas for presents. "You know what they'd like?" he said. "A chain saw. I tried to get them a chain saw, but I couldn't get one on São Tomé. And then people were telling me, well then they'll need fuel, and to buy fuel they'll need money." So he recommended surf wax, clothes, and pocketknives.

I asked Shun how long people on São Tomé had ridden tábuas and surf boats. He shook his head.

"Since before he was born," Quintino translated.

"What does Chano say?"

Chano shook his head and waved over his shoulder.

"Since before he was born," Quintino said. "There's no way he can tell."

In most parts of Africa the traditional response to the rolling sea was no different from the fear and mistrust in Morocco. In 1834, though, a

British officer called James Edward Alexander toured European colonies in West Africa for the Royal Geographical Society and went to Accra, the capital of Ghana, which in those days was a colonial outpost on the Gold Coast. He noticed a "surf game" that he'd obviously never seen before. "From the beach," he wrote in his *Narrative of a Voyage of Observation among the Colonies of Western Africa,* "might be seen boys swimming into the sea, with light boards under their stomachs. They waited for a surf; and then came rolling in like a cloud on the top of it. But I was told that sharks occasionally dart in behind the rocks, and 'yam' them."

Accra was dusty, hot, and short of water in those days, "a collection of brown thatched roofs, without streets, consisting only of irregular lanes," but nevertheless "the Montpellier of the western coast." Alexander sailed from there to Príncipe, which he called Prince's Island. "St. Thomas" he saw only from a distance. The tropical lushness and virgin quality of the island impressed him. He noticed women bathing half-naked in rocky streams and washing clothes, as well as a louche odor of corruption among the white slave traders. "I have seldom seen such a disgusting specimen of humanity as the American merchant to whom we were now introduced," he writes.

> He appeared in torn shirt sleeves, black vest, and striped long drawers, with his swelled feet in yellow slippers. His eye was blood-shot, his mouth foul from the effects of mercury, his arms and hands a mass of sores, and his knees and ankles swelled. He seemed to take a pride in showing us the consequences of fever; but if he had said of intoxication, he would have been nearer the mark. He invited us to take "gin sling," or "cock-tail" at the side-table.

Americans were here specifically to trade slaves. The British Empire had banned the business a year before, and Alexander abhorred it (even if he approved of the way his imperial government looked after the natives in far-flung parts of the world). "Slaves cost three musquets, or fifteen dollars, about Cape Lopez [now in Gabon], and when brought over to Prince's Island they sell for thirty dollars," he wrote, "but when transported to St. Thomas's produce eighty." In Cuba, "the average price this year is three hundred," which explained the American business. "In this accursed trade the slaves are packed with their knees bent and laid on their sides below, in a hold two feet high."

Alexander makes no other mention of the "surf game" on the Gold Coast. If he saw it on Prince's Island, he never said so. But children may have played in the waves along West Africa for as long as their fathers have fished in canoes. "These kids [in São Tomé] loved to surf before we got there," Sam told me. "That's the thing I love about this, is that we didn't introduce surfing to them. We found a surfing culture."

The first-ever Western description of wave riding comes from Cook's first voyage in 1769, ten years before Cook and his men saw stand-up surfing in Hawaii. Cook's botanist Joseph Banks noticed a sport in Tahiti that sounds like tábua riding:

> In the midst of these breakers 10 or 12 Indians were swimming who whenever a surf broke near them divd under it with infinite ease, rising up on the other side; but their chief amusement was carried on by the stern of an old canoe, with this before them they swam out as far as the outermost breach, then one or two would get into it and opposing the blunt end to the breaking wave were hurried in with incredible swiftness.

Some researchers have puzzled over the meaning of "stern of an old canoe," but after a visit to São Tomé it's clear to me what the Tahitians were doing.

Stand-up surfers in Africa, for a long time, had nothing to do with local kids on ragged slabs of wood. The modern sport arrived in South Africa in 1928, when the Australian showman Charles "Snowy" McAlister gave a surfing demonstration near Durban. By then white locals were bodyboarding, like their peers in Britain. Anne Bedding-feld, Agatha Christie's narrator in the 1924 novel *The Man in the Brown Suit,* refers to the sport as "surfing":

> I had never fully realized that Cape Town is on a peninsula, consequently I was rather surprised on getting out of the train to find myself facing the sea once more. There was some per-fectly entrancing bathing going on. The people had short curved boards and came floating in on the waves. It was far too early to go to tea. I made for the bathing pavilion, and when they said would I have a surf board, I said "Yes, please." Surfing looks perfectly easy. *It isn't.* I say no more.

Lifesaving clubs started to build their own hollow boards in South Africa during the '30s, keeping pace with Australia and Great Britain. A Durban pioneer named Fred Crocker invented a wooden-framed boat with paddles on it, attached to ropes, which a stand-up rider could use to steer. People still ride "Crocker skis" in South Africa now, but the spiritual father of modern surfing was an abalone diver and Volk-swagen salesman from Cape Town named John Whitmore. He learned about the sport from a photo of Hawaiian big-wave surfing in the early '50s. The sheer exoticism and thrill of the photo led him to experiment with his own boards before he met Dick Metz, a wandering American, in 1959. Metz had started a world hitchhiking tour the previous year by strolling out of his house in southern California and holding up his thumb.

He'd served in the Korean War, stationed in Hawaii with other Californian surfers like Bruce Brown (the filmmaker) and Grubby Clark. His hitchhiking odyssey took him from Central America to Southeast Asia, from India to the African coast. By the time he reached Cape Town, he was a dirty protohippie with long hair, a beard, and a Hawaiian print. He noticed a lone surfer in the water at Glen Beach, and when the man's board washed in on a wave, he "instinctively" ran to rescue it from the rocks. Whitmore swam in. "I told him it was one of the strangest boards I have ever seen," Metz wrote to Whitmore's biographer, Paul Botha. "He said, 'Well, what do you know about surfing?' . . . That very day I moved in with John and his entire family and lived with them for the next few months, much to Thelma [Whitmore]'s dismay."

Metz had worked for Grubby Clark in California, so Whitmore gained a connection for modern foam. He founded Africa's first board company in 1963. Metz also sent his friend Bruce Brown to Africa, and Whitmore guided Brown's film crew to the unforgettable final scene of *Endless Summer*. The gemlike, impossibly long tubes at Cape Saint Francis publicized by the movie in 1966 excited every surfer who saw them, and since then South Africa has been world renowned for its waves.

The sport was "white" in South Africa at first, but some of the world's most powerful professionals had brown skin. Naturally, there was trouble. The Hawaiian big-wave surfer Eddie Aikau was turned away by a whites-only hotel in 1971 when he arrived for the Durban 500. The contest's organizer, Ernie Tomson (father of Shaun), made a point of letting him stay in his beachfront apartment. This spirit of resistance coalesced in the '80s, when a handful of young South African pros formed a group called Surfers Against Apartheid to boycott home contests. By then the sport belonged to South Africa's self-image the way it belonged to Australia's, and the nation had enough talent to dominate the professional world tour. But the boycotts hobbled its standing until apartheid fell in 1994.

Intriguingly, Nelson Mandela has a surf spot named after him on Robben Island. His nickname has been applied to a pair of rough storm-surf breaks, Madiba's Left and Madiba's Right, because he used to do prison labor nearby. In the '70s a longtime editor of the *Cape Times* newspaper, Tony Heard, had the nutty idea of liberating Mandela with his surfboard. "The prisoners would often harvest kelp on the shoreline," he said. "I thought, hey, why not paddle quietly through the water, camouflaged by the kelp, get him to climb on the board and paddle two-up out into the shipping lane to be picked up by a foreign freighter?"

Morocco and South Africa became staging points for the spread of modern surfing to other parts of the continent. French surfers found their way south to Senegal and other French-speaking nations; South Africans roamed up to Angola and the diamond-rush ghost towns of Namibia and the Skeleton Coast. Californian and Australian "surf explorers" also pioneered parts of the coastline in the '70s. One of them was Randy Rarick, who went with Sam George on his first trip to São Tomé. Rarick surfed in the Durban 500 in 1971—the same year Eddie Aikau was turned away from his hotel—and wandered north. Later, of course, Angola, like Liberia and Sierra Leone, would be off-limits because of a brutal civil war. But Westerners stationed there in the '90s rediscovered the waves reeling off Angola's coast. "When I was there the entire surfing population was about fifteen people," Richard Norris, a former oil worker from Britain, told me. "They were a mix of people working in oil, NGOs, the UN, and diamonds. The civil war was still on, and although this didn't affect the area around Lunada [the capital] at the time, it did mean that you had to be careful driving to the beaches."

But very few parts of West Africa besides São Tomé have thriving indigenous surf communities. Even the African bodyboarders spotted by James Edward Alexander have disappeared. "I went surfing in Ghana," Sam George said, "and I went to the exact same spot that was described in Alexander's book in 1835. The villagers there freaked out when they saw me surfing. They'd never seen anything like it. It caused a huge stir. So, why they stopped is another fascinating question."

❦❦❦❦❦❦❦❦❦❦❦❦❦❦❦❦❦

Oddly, Sam was scrupulous not to expose the kids in Porto Alegre to surf videos. Of course he was *filming* a surf video, but he wanted to follow "the old *Star Trek* prime directive of, you know, not interfering in the culture." Videos caused trouble. "Somehow that really communicates the obsessive nature of surfing," he said. "Videos left behind in other countries."

"Like where?"

"Well, one place is British Columbia. People have surfed in Canada for years—it kinda got started with American guys going up there and dodging the draft." But some Canadians in an isolated town, blessed with excellent waves, learned to ride from high-performance surf videos. "So when the first visitors went there and saw 'em surf, they were doing aerial three-sixties and lay-back backside tubes. All they knew was Kelly Slater.

"Anyway, on São Tomé they're pretty self-sufficient. I bet you'll find that not much has progressed. The only way it'll change is if surfers go there, stay in the village, and live there just to surf. But these guys were more surfers than I am. I mean, *my* dad didn't surf. So I think you'll find not much has changed."

Sam did write an illustrated feature on São Tomé for *Surfer's Journal*, which I had with me in the village. It included photos of Shun in the water. I gave him my copy and he flipped quietly through the pages.

"*Que es esto libro?*" he said.

"*De Selmo,*" I said, which was his name for Sam.

"*Muchas gracias.*"

What I had seen of the ocean so far looked untroubled by waves, but I suggested going for a surf. He said it would get better around high tide. When? He discussed it with his father and a few other men.

Around three?

Good, I said. I'll bring the soap.

We drove out of Porto Alegre and into the rain forest in search of my lodging on the other side of a small isthmus. Praia Jalé, or Jalé Beach, was supposed to be "a fair walk," according to my guidebook, "or a short 4WD drive." This mattered because Sean and Quintino were taking the truck away that night; I would stay the weekend without transportation.

The muddy forest trail wound through damp clusters of banana trees and past clearings for corn or cassava. Light gray doves with rust-tinged wings stood in the mud, feeding, until our truck scared them off in parallel blurs of gray, soaring into the trees. It was a discouragingly long way. Walking with luggage might take an hour.

The "Ecolodge" at Praia Beach consisted of wooden huts built under palms and caroceiro trees. An old black man in a flat-brimmed cap waited for us. His name was Domingo. His domain here was the remotest stretch of sand I'd ever seen. Grilled-fish meals would arrive from Porto Alegre by motorcycle. For three days, Shun's village—a few miles distant—would be my metropolis.

I asked Domingo if taxis ran between here and Porto Alegre. No, he said, no cars. If I wanted to see Porto Alegre, after tonight, I'd have to walk.

"Look," said Sean, pointing under one of the shacks. "A surfboard."

We pulled it out. Domingo watched us carefully.

"Who does this belong to?"

Quintino translated. "It belongs to a Frenchman who lives in São Tomé city."

So Jalé was a surf spot. A left-handed wave broke just outside the door of my shack. It was crumbly, but it might improve.

"No one would argue if you took this out for a morning surf," said Sean.

"I was thinking the same thing."

But the board was too short. I considered shoving my own board back into the car after our surf session and for the next few days facing the forest trail with only a shoulder bag; the lack of transportation had started to bother me. But I knew it would be a lifelong regret if I woke up the next morning with a beautiful left outside my door and no decent thing to ride.

We returned the Frenchman's board to its hiding place. Domingo visibly relaxed.

When we returned to Porto Alegre for high tide, rain poured from the sky like a river and the village streamed with mud. People stared from their shacks. Shun appeared with his board, apologizing for the rain—he said it would keep the surf small. He handed me a note to give to Sam, and I noticed that we had been wrong about his name all along. It was spelled *Chum,* not Shun. Pronounced *shoom.*

He came off as a serious young man. With the needs of other people swirling around him in the village, he could be stolid and truculent, unsmiling, but when we carried our boards past the dugout canoes on the beach and started to paddle, he changed. He led Sean and me through a channel in the currents, a path of least resistance to what he said would be *las ondas grandes,* the big waves. (So far I'd seen nothing but slop.) In the water he was an anxious host. He apologized again for the rain. He wanted us to be impressed.

Out here, in the deep water, las ondas were about shoulder high. Dugout fishing canoes moved in and out of the bay and the fishermen hollered at Chum. Rain pelted the waves, but the equatorial water felt like a lukewarm bath.

"*Esta frio,*" Chum said after a while, smiling.

"*Não, esta caliente,*" I said.

He had a lump of scar tissue on his shoulder that might have been from a bullet or a knife. But he said it was from a fin on Sam's longboard. Someone had run over him in the water. The scar was like a coin-sized blister. The wound must have hurt, but he laughed.

We surfed for two hours. In spite of the rain it was terrific fun. A kid about Chum's age named Diviño paddled out on another modern board, and then a boy about twelve years old came out with a tábua. He was mischievous, round-headed, with a quick, brilliant smile. I recognized him from the film. The tábua was a narrow rough piece of timber, almost seven feet long. He tried to ride it on his feet, without much luck, but Chum swapped boards with him and showed us how it was done. He charged down the face of a waist-high wave.

"Jesus," said Sean.

"He's good," I said.

During a lull I asked the boy to swap boards. Chum told him to cooperate in the tone of an older brother saying, from personal experience, *You're crazy if you don't. He might give you that board.*

This had not been the idea. My thruster from Berlin surfed beautifully well; it wouldn't be easy to replace. I'd also started to plaster it with stickers from every part of the world, like a suitcase in a Warner Brothers cartoon. I was fond of it. But I was also curious about the tábua.

We switched, and I immediately realized that surfing on a soaked piece of timber would be hopeless. It sank low in the water, and the first waves I attempted just washed over me. The board was a curved, splintery, waterlogged beam.

"How is it?" asked Sean.

"Like being shipwrecked."

Sean was lighter and shorter, so I thought he might do better.

"Nope, you're right," he said after a few attempts. "It's just a log."

But Chum could ride it. And when the boy, whose name was Dende, had tried both of our boards, he made a point of saying he preferred mine. (It must have been easier for him to ride.) To make sure I understood I pointed to Sean's board while we all floated in the water.

"It's better, or no?"

Dende said instantly, like a cat complaining, "*Não.*"

It was impulsive and affectionate, with a gentle aggressive mischief that stayed on my mind.

Quintino and Sean left me at Praia Jalé that evening and drove along the potholed forest highway in what must have been constant rain. When they came to the first of the two fords on the river, they discovered the true purpose of the low-slung concrete: it wouldn't wash out. Floodwater was meant to flow across. Which, at the first ford, is just what the water did.

I heard this story later.

"It was dark out," said Sean, "so Quintino and I stopped the car at the river's edge, put the lights on full beam, and looked at the water. It was at least two feet over the bridge and chugging along."

They figured the truck had enough weight and suspension to cross. The puzzle was finding the edge of the ford. The curve of the flowing water showed them the downstream ledge; the other side was guess-work. Quintino decided to allow for some push from the river by over-compensating upstream. "In about four seconds we knew we'd made a big mistake," said Sean. With a crunch of metal they dropped both wheels of the truck off the ledge, "right in the middle of the river."

Now they couldn't move. They opened the doors, and the river flowed through the truck.

Soon four villagers found them and called their friends. Before long a group of about twenty-five people climbed into the water to try rocking the truck back onto the ledge. "We were lucky this happened in the south of the island," Quintino said. "On the north end people aren't so generous." But the scene was chaotic—"the typical African confusion," said Sean—and rocking the truck only tilted it farther off the ford. After a lot of yelling and screaming, Quintino decided to leave with some of the men to find a lever strong enough to move the truck. Sean waited in the passenger seat. "I wasn't sure about being a Portuguese-illiterate white dude alone among forty very poor villagers in the middle of nowhere," he said. But he was fine.

Quintino and the others returned with a heavy steel bar. The villagers used it to pry the truck back onto the ford, one tire at a time. A front blinker popped out from the pressure from the bar; otherwise the truck survived intact. The villagers swarmed around for a reward. Sean emptied his wallet, though he said that for services rendered it wasn't enough, "about 250,000 dobras, or nineteen dollars cash." But they could see it was all he had.

Now, delayed by two hours, they set off again, only to realize that a second ford was still ahead. This time they vowed to sleep in the truck if it was impassable. But the river turned out to be wider, meaning shallower and less powerful, and the only crisis was a massive clump of bamboo caught by its root mass on the edge of the concrete, with the long trunks lying in the path of the truck. Quintino and Sean waded out to release it, then drove across.

"We were soaked to the bone on our way home," said Sean. "We got back two hours later, and I went to bed and slept the best I had since being on the island."

Meanwhile I was having grilled fish in a shack at Praia Jalé. The meal came with cassava, fried banana, and wedges of spongy smoked breadfruit. But the fish had an undertone of African earth, of mold and dirt. I sat there by the glow of a candle, trying to get used to the taste and thinking Domingo had retreated to his shack. Then a cat came to the window. Domingo's voice made it scram. He was still in the room, I realized, folded into a low chair and obscured by deep shadow.

I said, "*Quieres comer?*"

"No, no," he said. "*Más tarde.*"

When I pushed everything aside to write in my journal he stood heavily and delivered my fish bones to the cat. Then he ate the leftovers.

By now I'd decided to give my board to Dende, assuming I saw him again. I would leave it up to fate. If he surfed with us the next day, I would trade him the board for the tábua. If not, no big deal. The main idea was not to embarrass him. I was extremely rational. Western toys could help people or insult them, I thought, and Africans needed other stuff besides surfboards. In Africa the thing to do was to spend money in the local economy and give to decent charities.

But I didn't see Dende. I surfed again with Chum, stayed another night, then surfed in front of my shack in disappointingly messy waves. After a great deal of walking on the trail—through dark thickets of forest rustling with monkeys and birds—I said good-bye to Chum and caught a public taxi up the coast.

This van rocked with African music. Passengers swapped in and out all day long. There were people with sacks of vegetables, people with tins of oil, women with babies in slings, men with sharp machetes. A public taxi was an event on the road, a vital catalyst of change, and kids on porches or on the roadside would dance to the blaring music while their parents gossiped with the driver. I imagined an African version of Steinbeck's novel *The Wayward Bus*.

Ninety minutes north of Porto Alegre we came to the coastal town of São João Angolares. "Angolares" referred to descendants of Angolan slaves who had revolted aboard a ship bound for the Gold Coast. Historians who accept this story set it around 1544. The ship wrecked on some rocks, but a number of slaves survived and founded a colony of free Africans on the beach near São João. Plenty of Santoméans believe the Angolares arrived even before the Portuguese landed in the 1480s; but either way, "there is little doubt that by 1550 there was an Angolar presence in São Tomé," according to a literary historian named Donald Burness, and that the Angolares have "managed to survive more or less independent of the tides of slavery and forced labor that [have] characterized São Tomé's history for more than five centuries."

One mark of independence was fishing. The Angolares were fishermen who had never worked the land. Quintino said Chum and his family spoke an Angolar dialect, and they were obviously proud of the fact that their ancestors had worked and played in the sea. "People in Porto Alegre are divided between fishermen and farmers," Quintino said. "The fishermen speak mostly the Angolar dialect and the farmers, who are mostly of Cape Verdean descent, speak Cape Verdean creole." Everyone also speaks an island-standard Portuguese.

Thinking along these lines, in the taxi, it occurred to me that surfing is still connected with freedom, on an island half a planet away from California.

≈≈≈≈≈≈≈≈≈≈≈≈≈≈≈≈

The plantation house at São João Angolares was a white wooden mansion with fanlight windows perched on a hill over the town and sagging in the rain. When I walked in, a young woman with long, braided hair was sleeping on the sofa on the lobby.

"*Desculpe*," I said, but the woman didn't stir.

I had no reservations. I was soaking wet. I'd hauled my baggage and surfboard up the hill from a bus stop. After two nights in the forest, this plantation represented comfort, civilization, rest.

"*Desculpe*," I said again, looking around for anyone else.

The old timber floors of the house were damp and pliant, oddly soft, like turf. Everything about the place felt both durable and evanescent. It seemed as if it had always been there, like a house in a recurring dream. As if you could arrive without warning, move into a room, sleep under the mosquito net, eat a multicourse meal on the verandah, and leave without meeting a stern hotelier demanding cash. You couldn't, but the strange stillness of Angolares was part of its charm. People would always be sweeping the yard or laying laundry out on the grass to dry, uselessly because of the constant rain.

Soon the woman stood up—young, offhanded, tall, and very pretty. I asked for a room and she led me upstairs to a wooden verandah, where six empty rooms were lined up behind French doors overlooking the jungle. She asked if I wanted lunch. Sure, I said. She disappeared. I seemed to be the only guest.

It bothered me that I still had my surfboard. After an hour I went downstairs for lunch on a wooden-floored terrace where the young woman introduced me to João Carlos Silva, the plantation owner. He is a famous artist and TV chef on the island, a large man with a small gray beard sitting behind his table with a drink and a slow-burning cigarette.

"*Bienvenue*," he said. We spoke French. With a few gestures he made it apparent that the plantation was his. He invited me to sit at any of the tables—all empty, but laid with white cloths—along the terrace, which overlooked the smoking, clamoring village of Angolares and a valley of bananas and palms.

From his table, Silva made executive decisions in a low voice, meditatively smoking, sometimes addressing pleasantries to me in French while the kitchen staff cooked and the young woman slept in a hammock.

"Why São Tomé?" he asked, but it was more than I could explain in French. I gave him an abbreviated version.

"I didn't know the surf was good on this island," he said.

"It's better in the dry season, during the southern winter. Then storms send waves up from the south."

He nodded. "The Portuguese come here to relax. The hiking and bird-watching can be very good. But we don't see so many surfers. Tourism is not what it could be."

Which meant Dende might not see another modern board for years.

I finished lunch and watched rain drip from the banana leaves. The village of Angolares smoked and clamored down below. Almost every town in São Tomé except this one had started as a slave plantation. There was nothing you could do about that; no amount of charity could make up for it.

"The way I met Chum," Sam George had told me, "was this: We spent like a week on the island and couldn't find waves. Then we went over to Rolas, that little island off the coast, and stayed in the hotel they had before they built the big resort. We said, 'Wow, there's waves.' So I got my board and paddled out, and when I did of course a crowd gathered on the beach. All these kids, mostly. And based on what had happened in other countries, when I rode my first wave, I rode it all the way to the beach, and I expected everyone to, you know"—he meant cheer—"be amazed. Well instead, they all turned and ran away.

"I thought gosh, maybe I've done something horrible here. Maybe I've done something bad. I should have asked permission. So I got out of the water and ran back to where we were staying in this little storeroom, and I said, 'Guys, there's rideable waves.' They got excited and ran to surf it. I stopped to get some water and sunscreen. But when I went back I saw the water was full of people.

"I thought, 'What the heck?' It turned out, the kids all ran to get their boards. I thought they were running away from me, but they were just running to get their stuff. One kid came up smiling, so I put him on my board, and he stood up immediately. That's how we got to be friends. He was like the ringleader, he was the most bold of all the kids. He attached himself to me. And that's how I met Chum."

"When you went back to make the film," I had said, "the whole village on Rolas had moved to Porto Alegre?"

"Not the whole village, but most of it. They'd built a giant resort, and they didn't want an African village on the beach. As the lone European manager told us the first time we were there, 'You might enjoy playing with dirty African kids, but I don't think our customers are going to.'"

Golf-course pirates.

I looked over at Silva, still smoking a cigarette at his table. "Is it possible to order a taxi to Porto Alegre?" I said.

He said, "But you just came from there."

"Yes."

He watched me for a minute, then nodded. "Of course." He asked the young woman to make a phone call. "It will be here in ten minutes."

It was ninety minutes to Porto Alegre, and I found Chum almost right away, coming down the muddy road in dark shorts and an open shirt. I told him in broken Portuguese that I wanted to trade boards, and we went searching for the boy he thought I wanted, trailed by a growing crowd of children. I realized there would be no way to do this without making a spectacle. But the first boy we found was about six or eight, and I didn't recognize him. I said something like "*O ninho com a tábua en el día primero*"—a mangled sentence that made no sense to Chum.

Back in the main part of the village I saw the board in question, a long plank with a burnt patch on the rail. It leaned against a dried-frond shack in the shadow of the Portuguese barracks. Was it Dende's shack? No, it didn't belong to Dende. In fact, the board seemed to belong to a man with graying hair who resembled a car salesman from Florida. He had no use for my board. But he did want to know how much I'd pay for his tábua. Not the point! I just wanted Dende to ride my board.

What started then was "the typical African confusion." Everyone yelled. Children stared and milled; someone brought a tábua that was almost as long but with a big notch in the side. Was this okay? Another kid ran up with a short bellyboard. How about this one? They were all okay. I just wanted to make sure the right boy took primary ownership of my board. And finally I saw Dende, watching shyly from the crowd of kids.

"I want to exchange my board for your tábua," I said, *Quero trocar ma prança por ta tábua.* He smiled. I felt compelled to add, "*Habes uma tábua?*" Do you have a tábua?

He shook his head.

Aw, crap.

But he went away and returned with the one I meant. Is this yours? I said, glancing around. Do you own it?

Dende shook his head again.

Now what? The crowd was very large. It would have included any disgruntled owner of the board. Anyone with a claim to it would lodge a protest. The Florida car salesman watched without saying a word. Dende was smiling. Apparently he'd made some sort of deal. Naked boys, girls in soiled skirts, wary-eyed parents, a one-legged man with a crutch, the drunk who'd found Chum for us two days before—everyone watched. Chano was there, too. I asked him if it would cause trouble to swap these boards. He looked concerned but shook his head.

We leaned the two boards next to each other, against the wall of a shack. Now there was a positive feeling of celebration. Chum took a machete and started to trim some dirt and black scum off the tábua. When it wouldn't quite fit in my board sack, he trimmed the tail, and (to my horror) the pointed nose. Then we zipped up the sack and five people helped me load it into a waiting taxi. A dozen other people helped Dende with his new acquisition, and I took a picture of my cream-colored epoxy board floating away down a muddy path on a parade of African children's hands.

The damp tábua was ten times as heavy; I wondered whether it would get through customs. Maybe I was about to introduce a terrible tree disease to the heart of Europe. Or maybe Dende was now in some complicated debt. Maybe there would be a feud over ownership of the board and I would return to São Tomé after a couple of years and hear legends about the white man with his evil plastic tábua who had corrupted Porto Alegre and started a series of civil wars.

My taxi set off with the heavy board in the back. African pop music started to blare. I saw Dende on the muddy road, boardless, and I must have looked troubled or questioning. I should have just *given* him my board. Maybe coming down here with buckets of cash and strewing it in the wind would have been more appropriate. Or pens, like the ladies from the plane? Or expensive pharmaceuticals?

No. In the water we'd simply made a deal. Now the circuit was complete, and Dende smiled and raised his thumb.

9

JAPAN:
PLASTICS

IN 1543, A junk from China wrecked on the Japanese island of Tanegashima, bearing a crew of Chinese merchant-pirates and three Portuguese rovers. While the boat was fixed, the Portuguese went duck-hunting. Their flashing arquebuses baffled the Japanese, and Lord Tokitaka, the island's feudal master, asked for shooting lessons. At that moment, wrote Noel Perrin in his excellent little book about firearms in Japan, the gun entered Japanese history. Lord Tokitaka bought the Portuguese weapons and ordered his chief swordsmith, Yatsuita Kinbei, to copy them. "There is a sad story that Yatsuita, unable to get the spring mechanism in the breech quite right, gave his seventeen-year-old daughter to the captain of a Portuguese ship that arrived some months later, in return for lessons in gun-smithing from the ship's armorer," wrote Perrin. "Whether that is true or not, it is certain that within a year Yatsuita had made his first ten guns, and that within a decade gunsmiths all over Japan were making the new weapon in quantity."

This was three centuries before American steamships arrived in Tokyo Bay under Commodore Matthew Perry, offering gifts and emblems of American culture meant to impress the Japanese—a miniature railway, a brass band, a book of congressional debates, a minstrel show—with the ambition to break open Japan "like an oyster"[1] to the glories of international trade. The Japanese, in other words, already had their own idea of international trade when Perry arrived. Those Portuguese sailors were the first white people they ever saw, and for a while European traders were called "southern barbarians," because they always seemed to come up from the south. "They eat with their fingers instead of with chopsticks such as we use," one chronicler observed. "They show their feelings without any self-control. They cannot understand the meaning of written characters."

Japanese gunsmiths mass-produced and even improved on the European arquebus. The proliferation of guns helped bring a long era of shogun wars to a quick and bloody end, and soon one clan, the Tokugawa, started to preside over a golden age in Japan. They continued to do business with ships from Europe into the 1600s, but the Tokugawa soon balked at Christian missionary behavior and decided to reseal the archipelago. They restricted trade with Europe to a trickle of ships, which had to land at coastal enclaves not completely unlike Essaouira in Morocco. They also quit sending orders to gunsmiths and started collecting Japanese firearms in government storehouses. The shoguns considered the gun a dishonorable and savage weapon.

After its first taste of world trade, in other words, not only did the oyster close; it also decided that guns were a form of foreign butchery and returned to the art of the sword for almost two hundred years.

𝄢𝄢𝄢𝄢𝄢𝄢𝄢𝄢𝄢𝄢𝄢𝄢𝄢𝄢𝄢

Osaka, more than three hundred miles southwest of Tokyo, is a rough commercial center, not as proud or refined as the capital but just as tirelessly urban, sitting at the far end of a sprawling bay—Japan's "inland sea"—with no hope of decent surf. I went there to see a high school friend named Brian, who grew up with me in southern Cali-

---

[1] "Old Japan was like an oyster; to open it was to kill it," said an early British Japanophile named Basil Hall Chamberlain.

fornia. Now he was a video game designer in Osaka. I hadn't seen him in twenty years, but he was still burly, with now-receding reddish hair and a short goatee on his squarish wrestler's jaw. To Japanese people he looked like Arnold Schwarzenegger. We met not on a street corner or a subway platform, but in a subway *car,* a moving target, which he directed me toward in a stream of precise phone messages. I found him in a thick crowd as the doors closed, smiling from behind a surgical mask. About a third of all Osakans wore face masks that spring because of swine flu. It was like San Diego when George Freeth died.

We found a restaurant in the blazing, high-roofed arcades of Kanda, a downtown district that resembles a triumphant American shopping mall. Whole buildings flashed with electric billboards. Giant blowfish, advertising multistory fugu restaurants, dangled like leviathans in the neon fog. It astounded me that a fish requiring expert chefs to carve away the lethal liver without poisoning the rest of the meat should be served in places with all the subtle charm of an Italian restaurant in Atlantic City.

Brian said he liked Japan because the people were so tolerant of outsiders mangling their language. "Japanese can be easy to speak," he said. "It's not easy to read or write, but when you talk, all you really need is a verb and an object. You could step into a restaurant and say, 'HUNGRY. WANT COW,' and they would give you something reasonable to eat. Then you could say, 'THANK YOU FOR COW,' and they'll be polite. When I first moved here it was a big relief from the attitude in America, which is 'Speak English! And if you cain't speak English, git the hell out!' English is a hard language to learn."

We decided against cow that evening. Brian found a sushi bar instead. We had *nihonshu,* the brewed rice liquor we call sake, along with a still-moving mackerel, speared with a slim wooden stick and bowed like a harp. Most of its side meat was filleted on the plate next to some glass noodles, a lump of horseradish, and a dandelion.

"That's fresh sushi," I said.

Brian pressed on the mackerel's fin. "You can still feel resistance," he said.

"Is it watching us?"

He touched a drop of *nihonshu* to the mackerel's small gaping mouth. "Ow!" said Brian. "Fuck."

"It just bit you."

"Yeah."

"This is strange."

Brian explained the difference between nihonshu and sake. "'Nihonshu' is more specific," he said. "'Sake' generally just means alcohol. But good nihonshu is never served warm." When he first moved to Japan, about fifteen years before, he ordered sake at a bar. "The bartender said, 'What kind? We have beer, whiskey, plum wine . . .'

"I said, 'SAKE'—with attitude." To Brian it was like an American bartender not understanding the word *Bud*.

"We sort of went back and forth like that for a while, and then finally the bartender said, 'Okay. Would you like that warm?'

"I said, 'Of course.' And I was thinking about the way they heat sake in the States, the whole ceremony, with a small ceramic pitcher in the boiling water, served in a warm towel and little ceramic cups. This guy put some sake in a water glass and popped it in the microwave."

We were sitting in front of a glass case of exotic fish. Brian examined the inventory. He asked one of the chefs a question in Japanese, and the smiling old man nodded. Soon a small dish of a soft white meat soaked in soy sauce and green onions was in front of us.

"What is it?"

"Try it," said Brian.

"Don't tell me later that it's some kind of mountain oyster."

Brian said nothing.

I took a slice of the soft pale meat and chewed. It was delicate but a little bland. The soy sauce and onions improved it.

"What are they?"

"Fugu testicles."

"Jesus!" I flooded my tongue with nihonshu. "Since when do blow-fish have balls?"

"Well, the milt. The seminal vesicles."

The sushi chef, who looked highly amused, said something in Japanese.

"He says it's good for virility," Brian translated.

"Can you ask him to say that in English?"

"What?"

"Never mind."

Osaka was an adventurous place to eat, not just because of the fugu balls. On another night I wandered the dark neighborhood near my hotel in search of a bowl of noodles and found a dingier maze of arcaded streets than the one in Kanda, an older system of high, girdered passageways with the lights quenched in all the restaurants, on the monstrous dangling puffer fish, on grinning giant gold-painted Buddhas, and on pink plastic boughs of fake springtime trees. Nothing was open except an occasional karaoke bar. These narrow, fluorescent-lit spaces seemed to ooze desperation: middle-aged men would croon into a sound system while a couple of hostesses behind a counter looked bored. I resolved to avoid them. Behind the drapes of one corner bar I heard raucous laughter and poked my head in, since no one was singing. The surprised guests insisted I sit down. The hostess, Rose, set me up with a tray of soybeans and a beer.

The guests included two glamorous-looking women and two men who might have shuffled in from nearby business hotels. Now and then they took a microphone from Rose, called up a song on her machine, and started to sing. It was, of course, a karaoke bar. A swooning music video would play on a ceiling-mounted TV and the guests would clap for each other like mad. Rose pointed at posters hanging around the room to indicate that I was in the presence of some semiprofessional artists. "Velly famous!" she said, and it was true that the singing sounded practiced and smooth. But these crooning, high-pitched songs were beyond my appreciation. Japanese pop relies on melodic structures that Yoko Ono used to be vilified for attempting in the West. Between performances, the screen showed a menu of songs, and only three titles appeared in English: "Maybe Someday," "MOON," and "Sadistic Desire."

All I really wanted was a bowl of noodles. When Rose realized I was hungry she swung into action, and soon I had a soup of broth, scallions, and egg. Perfectly tasty. She added to the meal as ideas occurred to her. Triangles of rice, then a hot red Korean sauce. (Rose herself was Korean.) The sauce had squid tentacles in it. I dabbed them on the rice and ate them with the savory soup. "Is good?" said Rose. "Mmmm," I said. She added chunks of cucumber, cubes of tofu, and some anis-tasting clover as a condiment. The singers at the bar poured glasses of cloudy but potent *shochu,* and soon it was a party.

"Did you sing?" asked Brian at the sushi bar.

"No."

"They would have loved you if you had."

I shrugged. "Karaoke's another part of Japan I've never understood. And I couldn't have done those songs."

"Well, every karaoke machine has 'Stand By Me.' And if you sing it in English, they'll be amazed you can pronounce all the words."

I never expected to love Japan. As a kid I never had much use for manga or anime, never learned a single character of kanji, and I still hate the taste of seaweed. I'd always assumed Tokyo was an impenetrable pop-culture dystopia, a city of suicidal salarymen in dark suits and brooding manga-dressed teenagers. But on the surface it's cheerful and welcoming; colors in the capital seem to range from slate gray to gleaming white. It has its share of dinge and dirt, naturally, but for me the tone was set by the girls in baby-doll outfits, by public TV screens advertising sweet drinks from the top of white office towers, by sunlight reflected in great warm panes off the glass department store windows in Ginza, and by the unexpected lightness of Japanese manners. Tokyo crowds have the same urban intensity as London or New York crowds, but they feel frothier, more exuberant, less depressive and sullen. In Tokyo everyone seemed to be lightly aware of everyone else—just enough to avoid collisions—so the bewildering masses of quick-footed people in train or subway stations seem to be injected with air.

Efficiency, of course, is a Japanese cliché. But so is German efficiency, and Germans aren't efficient. (Germans are thorough.) In Japan it's real. People stand in two lines at specified marks on Tokyo's subway platforms, waiting for the trains to glide into place, and when the doors open the people part in unison, like square dancers, to let the passengers out. *That's* efficiency. The day a German lets me out of a train without standing truculently in the way promises to be an unseasonable day in hell.

Efficient, fine. But efficient must mean bloodless, right? A young rail-office clerk in Tokyo looked at first like a bureaucrat beaten down by his job, all thick glasses and greasy hair. My paperwork raised a small battle cry in him and he ran the forms through a gauntlet of thumping red stamps and scribbled authorizations. He observed all the niceties, asking permission to take my passport after I'd laid it on the counter, offering it back with two hands. Performing his job seemed to fill him with pleasure. When I asked for a train-system map he hurried to a far end of the office to fish one out and handed it to me with genuine grace. I noticed this more than once. The frantic, detailed helpfulness had energy and warmth. It wasn't drudgery; it was a way of expressing love.

"They're old-school here in the sense that anything less than one hundred percent isn't good enough," said Rob Newman, the British host of a surf lodge I visited on the Chiba peninsula, southeast of Tokyo. Rob was absurdly tall, meaning taller than me, with a goatee and wraparound sunglasses. A former military man in his early forties, he'd lived in Japan for two decades. "I came when I had hair," he said, "and I never left."

We drove past sparse buildings and mirrorlike rice paddies. The Japanese use the wrong side of the road, which suited Rob. "It's because the Meiji emperor sent a delegation to the most advanced countries in the world," in the nineteenth century, "which at the time were Germany and Britain." The British helped Japan build its rail system, setting a precedent for driving on the left. "They've fucking surpassed us, though. Have you taken the Shinkansen yet?" The bullet train. "If you take the Shinkansen, time it, because if you're a minute late, they'll reimburse you." He shook his head. "They haven't gotten used to fucking up here yet. In America and Europe, we tell kids, 'Just do your best.' Fucking up has become part of our culture—it's almost expected. And the result is, over the last twenty, thirty years, we've educated a bunch of morons."

His lodge was a shambling surfer's crash pad at the base of a tree-grown hill. It had fake wood paneling, a number of bunk-bed rooms, and a bachelor's kitchen. A wide-screen TV had pride of place in the living room. Pictures of a surf trip Rob had taken to Sakhalin Island hung on the walls. "You want a beer?" he said, and told me about a group of surfers who came down from Tokyo every weekend, Americans and Brits with their Japanese girlfriends. "One thing I love about this job," he said, "is having bikinis hanging around the house when the women are here." But he didn't host many male Japanese surfers. "I don't get along with 'em. You get 'em in a group and they start drinking, they start complaining," and, he implied, ordering him around.

The Chiba peninsula, or more accurately the Boso Peninsula, which takes up most of Chiba Prefecture, still felt sleepy and rural. The coast highway ran past Rob's house and wound through surf towns like Taito and Katsuura, past seafood restaurants and car dealerships, and into rock tunnels blasted through lush green hills. Rob said American planes had "bombed the fuck" out of Chiba during World War II because kamikaze pilots had trained at local airstrips and because "fire balloons" had sailed for America from here. These were experimental bombs tied to hydrogen balloons made from tough paper or silk and set free to ride jet-stream currents across the northern Pacific. Most wound up in the sea. But up to a thousand fell in Kansas, Nevada, Wyoming, California, Canada, Michigan, and even northern Mexico. They killed a total of six people, all of them picnickers in Oregon who found an unexploded bomb in the woods.

Rob found himself in Japan almost by accident. He seems to enjoy being a gaijin, a foreigner. But he never intended to live here. He first applied for a job through the Japanese embassy in Britain "for a bit of a laugh. . . . Quite why I decided to actually go to Japan in the final instance is maybe down to the fact that I didn't want to make my bed to the standards at Sandhurst. I didn't mind learning to kill, but it was the part about making your bed so the sheet is so taut a coin will bounce, I forget what it is, either three or four centimeters in the air. It's like, 'Fuck off.'"

A Californian surf explorer named Tak Kawahara had explored this peninsula during trips to Japan in the mid-'60s. Tak was a large guy with receding gray hair, pushing seventy, given to wearing billowing Hawaiian print shirts. I met him in California. A point break south of Rob's house had been called Malibu ever since Tak had given it that name.

"I think the Japanese more recently have been startin' to call the break by its Japanese name, maybe because of pride. But way back when, I called it Malibu, and then it was known as Malibu for a long time," he told me. "I saw it breaking maybe a couple feet overhead, and obviously I grabbed my board. I couldn't get out there fast enough. A bunch of fishermen stopped me—actually grabbed me—from going in the water, because the day before, they had launched their boats to go fishing, and the boat capsized, and I think three fishermen died. So they thought, if I paddled out, there'd be instant death."

He paddled out anyway. "After I caught three or four waves, they figured, 'Oh, I guess he knows what he's doing.'" And a crowd of about fifty people gathered on the beach to watch.

"The problem was, back in those days, the roads in the country were all dirt and unpaved. It was real difficult to go along and check out the coast like you can do here in California. You'd have to park your car somewhere, hike over a very big hill through dense forest, and peer over. We never got that adventurous."

He came to Japan for the first time in 1964 with a friend named Ted Chihara, in search of business opportunities. He'd written to a number of Japanese companies to investigate large-scale surfboard manufacture; he thought using a Japanese factory to make modern boards might cut costs. "Labor at that time was like China," he said.

The most promising reply came from Yonezawa Plastics, in Tokyo, and Tak eventually convinced them to build the first commercial line of modern boards in Japan. The resulting brand—Malibu—was aimed at Americans. "I didn't realize there was anybody who surfed in Japan," he said. "Mainly 'cause I never saw anybody. A lot of times I was just on the beach by myself. Just talkin' to myself, like, 'Wow, did you see that wave I just caught?'" He laughed. "But Yonezawa Plastics decided for promotional purposes to put on kind of 'Meet Tak' kind of thing. They laid out a buffet and they had the media there, and all that. When that all came together, there were maybe a couple dozen guys who showed up. That was the first time I saw local guys, Japanese, who surfed in Japan."

"When was this?"

"I wanna say '66, '67—maybe a year or two after I went there the first time."

By then there were considerably more than two dozen surfers in Japan.

A friend of Tak's, Hiromi "Doji" Isaka, introduced me to a representative sample of Japan's first surf generation. The sheer flow of information was intimidating at first—visitors to Japan sometimes feel bombarded by information—but soon a few patterns emerged.

First we met Takao Kawana, in Tokyo, the sometime head of the Nippon Surf Association. He was a large man with plump, almost pink skin who walked with a limp and looked surly but in fact had the humor of a little boy. He started surfing in 1963 on Kamogawa Beach. He said an American serviceman had handed him an issue of *Life* magazine with a spread of thrilling surf pictures—probably the 1961 issue of *Life* that helped fuel the post-*Gidget* boom in the United States. Takao cofounded a surf club at Kamogawa called the Dolphins. "The air force people just lived next door," said Doji, who translated. "His father rented a house to them. His father liked American people."

"Why did the Japanese like Americans in those days?" I said.

"They were kind," Doji translated. "They gave out all kinds of candies and foods and sweets. Crackers and jam. Peanut butter. Everything new."

Doji himself grew up in a coastal town called Chigasaki, on the Shonan coast, south of Tokyo. Now it's a suburban jumble of 7-Elevens, bike-rental stores, noodle restaurants, and occasional surf shops, not unlike Redondo Beach. Doji said that in the 1940s there was nothing in Shonan but fishing towns and geisha houses. Then American bases arrived. The geisha communities, he said, "were probably more accepting of American culture." But only after surfers from Tokyo started flooding the coast did the coastal towns grow restaurants, hotels, convenience stores, even apartment blocks. It felt astonishingly like southern California, with winding coastal roads and bright-lit plastic signs, or flashing neon, burning against a soft dull overcast sky.

"I was just raised by the beach, so from elementary school, walking by the shoreline, it was natural to play on the sand and go swimming. Then 'surfing sounds' started coming in—Beach Boys, the Ventures. At middle school parties, girls started to say, 'Oh, surfing is fantastic.' So we said, 'We can do surfing.' That's how we got the idea."

Doji was an often terse but good-humored man with a mustache who walked with a shoulder bag weighing down his side. As a boy in Chigasaki, he had taught himself English as well as the craft of making surfboards from an American book he found in a Tokyo shop. By the late '60s, he was one of Japan's most accomplished surfers. "'Doji' means 'mistake,'" he said. It was a nickname with an epic story attached. In 1969 he learned about an international contest in Baja through *Surfer* magazine and decided to fly there with Takao. But in those days communication was less than instantaneous, and Doji never heard the news that the contest had been rescheduled. "He came to the attention of the California surf media later that year when he turned up in the offices of *Surfer* magazine [in southern California], wondering where to check in for the World Championships," reads Doji's entry in *The Encyclopedia of Surfing*. "The bewildered surfer was told the event had months earlier been postponed until 1970, and moved to Australia."

"Takao named me because of that trip," Doji said. He growled, imitating Takao: "'*You, Doji.*'" He chuckled. "We tried to find English names, American names, so I tried to name myself Don or Donald. But all my friends were like, 'Oh, you're Doji.'"

He gave me a tour of the Shonan coast, from town to town and surfer to surfer. It was a pleasantly baffling experience. We took a train to Chigasaki, his hometown, and from the station we walked into a delicately colored shop filled with cakes of something indefinable, either soaps or sweets. The merchandise was laid out under crystalline glass and wrapped in pretty colored paper. Doji ordered some sort of housewarming gift—which most likely I should have thought to buy myself—and while they ran his payment a woman in a dark skirt served us lemon-curd jelly with basil tea. A sweet, refreshing snack. Then it was off to Tsugumitsu Saga's apartment. Saga had grown up on the beach at Kugenuma, just down the road, and learned about surfing, like Takao, from a *Life* magazine handed him by an air force officer stationed at Naval Air Facility Atsugi, a few miles inland. Saga thought it might have been the same officer who handed Takao his magazine.

In those days, the way for a soldier to travel from Atsugi to Kugenuma Beach was by train. But the train operators didn't understand surfboards, so Saga's first board was a gift from another American who wasn't allowed to load his longboard onto the train that had carried him to the beach in the first place.

This second serviceman had a name. "He was Garth A. Jones," said Saga, with admirable precision. "He worked for the American newspaper, *Stars and Stripes*. He wanted to become a professor at the University of California, for oceanography."

Saga gave me a T-shirt with the name of his surf-clothing shop, Honolua Surf. It read ALOHA 49, ONE MORE YEAR TO GO UNTIL 50 YEARS SURFING. So Japanese surfing—according to the shirt—had started in 1960. But both Saga and Doji were noncommittal about both the true date and the true pioneer.

"It's difficult," said Doji. I had heard the Japanese never say "no," but take on a vague expression and say "It's difficult." "We were all surfing separately in those days, in separate towns. There's all different stories. If you say you were the first, someone else might say, 'No, I was surfing before that.' So we made an agreement, to never claim we were the first. Also, people's memories are getting weak. So who can really say it was this year or that? It's very difficult."

Some Japanese rode waves on inflatable rafts in the '50s. Some kids learned to spring to their feet on these rafts. Others rode Australian-style surf skis, essentially flatboats shaped like broad surfboards and turned not with a fin or keel, but with a pair of ropes like horse reins. ("It didn't work," said Doji.) "There are even stories that some people surfed on Hokkaido," the northern island, "in the Sea of Japan," he said. "But they don't get surf in the summer. But our weather makes the waves for Hawaii," meaning a low-pressure system moving up the Sea of Japan in the winter might kick up rideable surf in Hokkaido, too. "But it would be very cold. Sometimes it snows. So, it's difficult."

We talked to a lean and garrulous man in his early seventies, Osamu Sakata, who saw nameless gaijin (in this case, American servicemen) surfing near his home in Oiso, west of Chigasaki. But he learned to surf by studying an Australian woman who lived with a family near his beach. She was young, he said, "a student," and apparently beautiful. The sight of her walking in the waves was impressive to Mr. Sakata. Soon Oiso had a club called the Big Wavers, though Oiso rarely gets big waves.

Mr. Sakata had learned to shape boards as early as 1962. I asked him how. "The library," Doji answered. "He worked in the library to research how to make this kind of stuff."

"So it was just like you. He found it in a book."

"Hm," said Doji, meaning yes.

"Did you know each other at the time?" I said.

"No."

"So up and down the coast, everyone was doing the same thing. All these towns had people who were surfing and making boards."

"Hm," said Doji.

The coastal clubs were holding contests by 1964. One photo from that year shows the Kamogawa Dolphins outfitted in uniform windbreakers, custom-made for the team. By 1965 the clubs were arranged under the Nippon Surfing Association, with Osamu Sakata as the first president.

The marvelous Mr. Sakata also handed me a wooden board, called an *ita-go*, which he said had been used locally for bodyboarding since about 1914. It was a perfectly rectangular, sanded slab of plywood with a handle cut through it near the top, to grasp it with one hand and lie on in the turbulent surf. The board looked as if it had started life as a shutter, or the side of a handled crate. Maybe it had; ita-go turns out to be "an Edo period [1603–1868] term for wooden planks with a rectangular cross-section," according to a dictionary of Japanese architectural terms. Mr. Sakata had a magazine with a photo of four people on the waterline in 1925, two boys and two shirtless, aggressive-looking young men, wearing traditional *hachimaki* headbands. They were Shonan fishermen. "The fishermen ruled the beach in those days," Doji explained. "There was no one else here." One of the boys in the photo held an ita-go painted with kanji characters.

"What does it say?" I asked.

"Oh," Doji said, after he studied the photo. "It's an advertisement for a publishing company."

Finally, Kazumi Nakamura, small-boned but dignified, about seventy years old, had a short, sparse mustache and the careful manner of a cancer patient. (He had terminal stomach cancer.) I met him in Chiba with Rob, rather than in Shonan with Doji. He ran the largest surf shop on the peninsula, a freestanding wooden building with plate-glass windows called CHP Surfboards. A shop with the same name existed in Redondo Beach. Tak had founded an export business called California Hawaii Promotions in the '70s, opened the shop in Redondo, and later lent the name to Kazumi. In the meantime Kazumi and his sons had become one of the first families of the Japanese surfboard business.

Kazumi grew up in Kamogawa, like Takao Kawana; in fact they were childhood friends. The first surfboards he ever saw were used by American soldiers at their local beach in 1963. "The servicemen surfed at lunchtime," his son Daisuke translated, "then dug a hole in the sand to put the boards in. Then he waited for a full-moon night, climbed the fence, dug up a board, and went surfing."

It was the most colorful variation on a theme: the American base, the excited boy, the exotic vision of men walking the waves. After a while Kazumi taught himself to shape crude wooden boards by working from templates in American magazines. "In those days it was feet and inches for surfboards," translated Rob, "but Japan was metric, so they had to change it all over. And they didn't have calculators, so they used an abacus."

Kazumi gave Tak credit for introducing the business of surfboard manufacture to Japan. "He was the guy who brought the American technology and science involved to Japan," he said. Tak had worked for a number of shapers in California, like Dewey Weber and Greg Noll, but he'd never built a factory. "Without any architectural background at all—and it wasn't very sophisticated—I took ruler and pen in hand, and drew the first factory out," said Tak. "The whole thing, down to the minute details. It went from blowing foam to shaping and glassing and sanding." Yonezawa Plastics manufactured Tak's designs under the Malibu name until about 1971. But Yonezawa himself was another aspect of the postwar rush to be modern that had swept up the surfers in Chiba and Shonan. He'd built his postwar empire on disposable packing material. "At the time I met him," said Tak, "every time you walked into a market and saw, like, flour wrapped in plastic, that was Yonezawa. That's how he made his fame and fortune."

Chigasaki Hall, a hotel not far from the ocean, was one of those low-slung Japanese structures with a front door hidden by a few cloth banners. It sat in a quiet, tree-shrouded corner of Doji's hometown. The young owner, Katsuyuki Mori, met us in the wooden entryway as we took off our shoes. An old surfboard stood just inside the door. It was a curiosity: a heavy redwood board, seven feet long and cut in the shape of a blade. Katsuyuki said his grandfather had brought it from Hawaii in 1928. A gift from Duke Kahanamoku, carved in about 1920.

I asked the obvious question. "Did your grandfather surf?"

"He brought it back for the hotel," which had been founded around the turn of the century. "For the guests."

Katsuyuki had raffish black hair, a light pink dress shirt, and a darker pink tie. He was young, slim, formal, and flawlessly polite. We retreated to a sort of smoking room with a long table and sliding wooden doors. Katsuyuki showed me a photo of his grandfather, Noboyuki Mori, standing beside a tree in military uniform. Long boots, an officer's cap held at ease by his waist, clipped mustache, dress blade.

"His grandfather brought over all classic things for the hotel," said Doji. "An Indian motorcycle, too."

"So the board was just to decorate the hotel."

"Or to use for activities."

"Did guests ride that board?"

"Yes," Katsuyuki said.

"But, actually, you'd have to be tough to carry it," Doji interjected quickly. "Very heavy wood. It had to be carried by two people."

"Who rode it regularly?" I asked Katsuyuki.

"Just clients," Doji translated. "Guests. It wasn't private equipment."

"Could your grandfather surf?" I asked Katsuyuki again.

"On a kiddie surfboard," Doji translated.

"On his stomach, or on his feet?"

Katsuyuki said something that sounded like a demurral. "All depends on surf conditions," Doji translated.

No one, in other words, became such an accomplished surfer on this old redwood log that it had entered Mori family lore. On the other hand, no one can say for certain that Noboyuki Mori or any of his guests had never managed to stand on the board in mild or favorable surf.

Soon a woman old enough to be Katsuyuki's mother served us three glasses of iced green tea. Hospitality was impeccable and swift. The woman set down each glass with a deep bow, then moved around to Katsuyuki and *knelt,* holding the tray until he finished a sentence and was pleased to take the glass. That boggled me. I'd heard of these old-fashioned Japanese manners but never seen them in action. I was glad she didn't walk on her knees.

"We were just discussing," Doji said, "—if it was redwood, it might be from California."

"I was thinking the same thing," I said.

"And in those days they would have needed the whole piece of the tree, so the board would have its own power. You can't glue it together [from finished redwood lumber]. So it would have been a very special person to have this board."

"Is there any chance it came from California?"

They deliberated.

"With his grandfather," said Doji, "there's no report that he went to the United States. Maybe they just brought the wood from California."

"Or someone else brought the board."

Katsuyuki showed us an early photo of the board with a dapper

Japanese man in a boater hat and bow tie, a friend of Noboyuki Mori's, holding it up. It bore three distinct white initials, PCM, which must have belonged to the original owner. These letters had long since rubbed off, because the board had since led an ignominious career as a garden bench. It had spent about fifty years under a shade tree behind the hotel.

I laughed. "Who turned it into a bench?"

"Probably his father."

Some surfers drifting through the garden had made remarks about the shape. "When I saw it in the '70s, I thought, 'Oh. Looks like a surfboard,'" Doji said. "But I didn't take any interest." In the '90s the picture with the bow-tied man surfaced in a municipal yearbook, from someone's old photo collection. The family has no idea what "PCM" stands for, or even what the bow-tied gentleman's name might be; but by 2004 they decided to unbolt the slab of wood and prop it near the entrance, because they realized that the weathered bench was not just a surfboard, but the oldest surfboard in Japan.

Rob's lodgers from Tokyo arrived on a Friday afternoon. Gareth, or "Gaz," worked for a London-based headhunting firm called Robert Walters. So did his girlfriend Mariko, and so did Mike, his little brother. They came to Chiba every weekend. Another British-Japanese couple named Jesse and Satomi were also down, along with two other friends. Gaz joked that Mike was leaner and stronger at most sports because of the way he'd abused his younger brother when they were kids. "I used to say, 'Hey Mike, ready for a race? First one across the street and back with a Pepsi, wins.' And off he'd run. But the result is, he's skinny and athletic, while I'm a lazy bastard."

We went to the Topanga House for a drink. The Topanga was a roadside bar with a jukebox and a clacking pool table. The affable owner's name was Toshio, but most people called him Bob. He had a mustache and a drunken smile, and in the humid island weather he wore a Hawaiian print open to his chest.

I wanted to know why the place was called Topanga House. "Because I love Topanga Beach!" Bob said over a glass of wine. Malibu and Topanga were the epicenter of southern Californian hedonism in the '70s, which was very much Bob's era. He also ran a taco joint down the road.

Rob told a story about the dutiful tendencies of Japanese women. He said girlfriends would carry surfboards for their boyfriends from a parked car to the beach—just a handful of yards—but the subservience could be deceptive. A Japanese woman has her own mind, he said, but she won't embarrass a man in public. Honor and image are all-important. Once a Japanese girlfriend of Rob's had found him in bed with another woman, also Japanese. "I left the room and sat out on the patio with a glass of whiskey, thinking, Okay, now the shit's gonna come," Rob said. "But they stayed inside and talked about which one was gonna have me for a boyfriend. They worked it out between themselves. And I was thinking, 'I love this country.'"

Why did Japanese people imitate Americans? They had a strange, distinct culture of their own. Why, come to think of it, didn't they hate us? We are the only nation in the world (so far) to have dropped nuclear munitions, and we did it right here in Japan. Yet the Beach Boys were cutting-edge cool in Japanese coastal towns only twenty years later.

Maybe that was somehow the idea. Pico Iyer noticed a general instinct in Japan to mimic foreigners, not limited to Americans. "In its relations to the world at large," he wrote in the '80s, "Japan reminded me . . . of a tribal conqueror who dons the armor, or even eats the heart, of a defeated opponent, so that his enemy's strength will become his own." He noted that 64 percent of all Japanese had said in a 1980 poll that they wanted nothing to do with foreigners. "In ancient times, people who committed the crime of being foreign were beheaded; nowadays, they were simply placed before the diminishing eye of the TV camera (entire shows were devoted to portraying the stupidities of gaijin). In the Japanese context, imitation was the insincerest form of flattery."

I happen to think Bob's Topanga Beach style was a sincere form of dropping out, the remains of a rebellion in the 1960s and '70s when some Japanese kids, like their Western contemporaries, tried to be less formal and striving than their parents. But Iyer had a point. Mimicry, in Japan, might be a form of national defense.

We retired to Rob's house and got up at five the next morning to beat the weekend crowds at Ichinomiya Beach. Even at that hour the sky was bright. We walked down an overgrown trail and into the beach parking lot, which was already half-full of cars. Some surfers had stands for their boards to keep them safe from abrasion on the asphalt; others were already done for the day and hosing off with portable plastic showers. Every car had a pair of sandals or shoes waiting on the pavement for its owner to return. It made me think of something Doji had said in Tokyo. He and his friends had spent their lives on the beach in the '60s, but now surfers drove to the coast for a few hours and went home. "The automobile is the base of activity," he said. "Surfers bring equipment with them in the car—a bucket with water, a bucket for changing clothes, dressing room, everything." The era of surf clubs and beach parties was over. "People only surf for themselves. No communication—just facing the water. I think it's very bad."

The surf at Ichinomiya broke under a soft morning haze to the left and right of a jetty composed of concrete tetrapods. These enormous weights fit together like Legos. They line the parking-lot edge of the beach in place of wild rough rock. You can walk right over them without cutting your foot. The government has strewn Japanese beaches with hundreds of thousands of tetrapods to armor the homeland against sand erosion, but like most public-works projects of this kind—the breakwalls in Tel Aviv, the jetties in Sylt—they have been a ponderous failure. Tetrapods can worsen coastal erosion far more efficiently than they prevent it; they can also ruin the surf. Ocean currents are too subtle for government initiatives.

On this particular morning the waves were smooth and shoulder-high, slow but beautiful, with a few quick glassy sections. Dozens of locals were out—at five a.m.—spread over a long gray stretch of shore. Some were eager and skillful; others just sat in the water. A surprising number were women. Japan may have a higher proportion of female surfers than any nation in the world. One woman credited *Blue Crush*. Some people said it was a natural progression from bodyboards, which saw a huge resurgence a few years ago. But Doji pointed to Japan's slightly insane-seeming surf magazines. One of them, *Oily Boy*, was packed with photos of deck shoes, beach guitars, portable grills, tanning oils, fitness drinks, and radio-controlled cars. (My issue happened to advertise a plastic toy of Doji himself, on a surfboard—Doji had been a TV sportscaster and still had a national profile.) It was labeled MAGAZINE FOR ELDER BOYS, but in its earlier incarnation as a 1970s youth magazine, *Oily Boy* had built momentum for the Japanese surf craze of the '80s. The newer, analogous magazine for girls, *Fine*, was even more frenetic. Page after page had variations on the summer skirt, the carefully torn pair of jeans, the Ugg boots knockoff, and the T-shirt printed with some near-meaningless slogan (SURF SOUND, BEACH BEACH BEACH, IN THE WATER SINCE 53). It gave four-step surf tutorials. It recommended the right kind of boyfriend.

"Japan has always had female surfers," a South African named Terrence Charles Lotter told me later. Terrence was a friend of Rob's who'd lived in Chiba since about 1983. "If the boys can do it, the girls wanna try. It's always been like that. Japan has the largest proportion of female surfers in the world."

He also said the influence of American soldiers wasn't the whole story. "The Japanese have an affinity for Hawaii," he said. "It's like the Promised Land to them. A lot of Japanese descendants live in Hawaii, and it's another island culture, so they naturally idolize Hawaii, and surfing has a more positive image here than in other countries."

But the feeling in Japan was far mellower than in Hawaii or California. Ichinomiya had an easy, sandy-bottomed wave, and we surfed for two hours without hassle. In spite of the crowds in the water no one seemed cranky or aggressive. The locals were considerate. Some just floated in place.

"That group thing is in them," said Terrence. "They can't help it. Even when there's no surf, it's still crowded. A lot of them come and just zone out to the horizon. If they catch anything, they're lucky— the bonus is if they catch a wave. But that's their special time. Some foreign guys come here and say, 'The surf's shit, but look at all the people in the water. What are they *doing*?'" He laughed. "Well, I know what they're doing, but it's hard to explain."

Satomi and Mariko went off to surf by themselves, but I talked to Mariko later, during a barbecue at Rob's house. She was an energetic young woman with large, impassive eyes who denied there was tension in the water for female surfers in Japan. But I couldn't tell if she was telling the truth or saving the reputation of the Japanese male.

We talked around a raging fire on the dark and crowded patio. The conversation turned to ghosts, and a British expat said his house in Japan was haunted—not according to him, but according to every Japanese person who had ever stepped foot inside. "It's only the big stupid gaijin who can't understand," he said. "Apparently the Japanese feel ghosts more than we do."

"That's true," Mariko said. "I used to talk about ghosts openly until I moved to Canada," where she'd lived for six years. "But everyone there made faces at me."

There followed a completely unscientific discussion of whether the bathroom of a certain house had "bad energy" or not. To me it was a mystery that the Japanese could mix so much rational technical sophistication with such colorful Asian superstition. Maybe I was a stupid gaijin, too; maybe the right word for both aspects of Japanese-ness was "sensitivity." Mariko chalked it up to Shinto and Buddhism. Both traditions cultivate a belief in spirits.

She also said Zen Buddhism became "Japanese" after it arrived from China. It never imposed a foreign system, in other words, the way Christian missionaries after Perry had tried to do. Japan had absorbed

Buddhism and changed it. I said: Wasn't that the whole idea? To absorb other cultures, figure them out, and make them Japanese, i.e., better?

Mariko didn't say yes or no. She said Japanese kids were schooled to be mimics—teachers drilled them to give back precise and literal answers. "In North America you push students to create things and think for themselves," she said. "The first time a teacher did that to me in Canada, it was hard." She also saw Westerners who lingered in Japan lose their spontaneity. "I think, in Japan, we aren't very creative. But all we need is a spark. If you give us an idea, something new, we can learn how to do it. We're good at figuring things out."

Surfing came to Japan in two great surges, first in the '60s and again in the '80s, but the first wave corresponded with a period of furious national change. "For a good time after the war," Tak told me, "they were rebuilding. The Japanese are a very industrious people, so to go off and goof around on the beach was really not thought about." But by the '60s the bomb-flattened cities had risen from the cinders; the economy had turned around. The Olympics came to Tokyo in 1964, the same year the Shinkansen started bulleting to Osaka. "Surfing was part of the young culture," said Doji. "It was combined with the hippies. Medication. Drugs." He laughed.

"So it was Japanese hippies who surfed?"

"We had no background for real hippies in Japan," he said, "because they're already here—in the mountains!" He laughed. The word *sanka*, or mountain people, has an ancient resonance in Japan. "It wasn't like European culture, going back to the forest—they were already there. 'Back to the mountains' means going back to the real Japanese. Not hippies! But the beach, nobody had used it before. That was new."

"So it was a combination of a couple of Japanese elements," I said.

"Right. And free sex."

But the hideous plumes over Hiroshima and Nagasaki had alienated Japan from itself. Doji said his postwar generation questioned the group ethic that had contributed to wartime fascism. "The Japanese love to go in one direction," he said. "That's part of Japanese culture. Fascism just matched to that part. But after the Second War, we said, 'No. We don't have to follow.' Maybe we can work on a team, in a company, but after work—no.

"Your country has a base of religious Christians, and they have a community," he said. "The people are working together—at any age, they can get together and work, volunteer. They know how to do it. I really feel that way. But in Japan, we've lost real community. After the Second War, we said, 'No, we are free.' But free means, we threw everything out."

An American businessman in Tokyo, Bill Totten, gave me more detail. He grew up in California but now owned a large software company in Tokyo called K. K. Ashisuto. He wore natty blazers and bow ties, had crew-cut gray hair and a sarcastic knowing smile—central casting couldn't have ordered a more traditional gaijin—but he was quiet-voiced, thoughtful, fluent in the nation's politics and history and, for the last three years, a Japanese citizen. He said Japan had maintained a tradition of moral education for about two thousand years before General MacArthur arrived in 1945. "Buddhist temple schools taught a little arithmetic and ethics and reading and writing," he said, "but it was mostly moral education. The natural Shinto, like the Tao of China, basically says: 'God didn't create the world for us; we're part of the world and we have to live in harmony with the gokiburi, with the cockroaches and everything else.' Buddhism teaches you to lower your greed. Confucius basically said to kings: 'Why are you so powerful? Isn't it mostly luck? You were born strong, you were born healthy, so recognize that your power comes from good fortune, and use that power to help other people, rather than use it greedily.' Put all those together, it becomes what all Japanese call Bushido, and that's the way the Japanese were trained until about 1945.

"There was a lot of corruption—during the war they corrupted it to make Japanese the master race and stuff like that. But over a period of two thousand years, it worked real well. Then MacArthur came in, and since they had corrupted a lot of that for the war effort, he said, 'You can't teach that shit anymore.' But they didn't replace it with any other moral education. And the people who had a moral education until 1945 kept leading the country until about 1990. So you've got an entirely different country since then."

So Japan's Western orientation had strengthened since then, I said. It hadn't peaked in the '60s but rather had grown more intense.

"Yeah. Basically it's a colony, a US colony now."

Totten was very cut-and-dried. He used the word "indoctrination" to describe the influence of American pop culture on Japan. But he reminded me that the Meiji leaders, after Commodore Perry twisted open the oyster, had sent their delegations to Europe to learn about trains and factories and Western life. They wanted to see what Japan had been missing.

"When the Meiji people overthrew the government here [in the 1860s], they basically said, 'Everything about Japan in the past was backward, and what we have to do is copy the West.' They spent eighty years teaching the people to wear shoes rather than clogs. They started dancing parlors to teach Western dancing, they taught English and all this stuff. But they also brought back the emperor—some people say a phony emperor—and said, 'He's god. All of you are his subjects. And he's so powerful that Japan cannot lose any war. You're a subject, so you have to die for him.' They taught that for about eighty years. Even after Hiroshima and Nagasaki were A-bombed, the Meiji were still saying, 'We're winning the war, you have to keep fighting for the emperor.'

"All of a sudden, the government gave up. The emperor came on the radio and said, 'Hey, shucks, I'm not a god, I'm just a normal guy like you. I'm just a normal person!' The Japanese had never heard his voice. That must have really shocked people. Suddenly you can't believe in your own country. And the average American serviceman is pretty nice—they came here and saw people who needed a cigarette, so they gave them a cigarette; they saw people who needed chocolate, so they gave them chocolate. All of a sudden you see you've been lied to by your government for eighty years, you were told these barbarians, when they came in, would rape everybody and hurt everybody, but when they came in they were friendly! That really screwed up the Japanese psyche. A lot of the people who had been educated by the Japanese moral code until 1945 also lost a lot of confidence. What they had been taught was a losing affair; so they lost the confidence to pass on their values to their children, and the institutions basically threw out that moral teaching."

The Yasukuni Shrine, just a few hundred yards from Totten's office in Tokyo, sits in a placid garden behind a series of magnificent wooden torii gates. It's a peak-roofed, Meiji-era monument to the spirits of Japanese soldiers. Most of Japan's neighbors have bitter memories of the Meiji era, when Japan returned to the gun, and the subsequent years of imperialism, but Yasukuni treats the two-million-odd martial souls enshrined here as nothing less than divinities. It's a busy place. Tour buses disgorge in the parking lot; old people shuffle up to the shrine to light candles and incense, and a war-history museum—with a full-size Zero fighter plane parked in the lobby—does brisk business. This museum refers to the Rape of Nanking as the "Chinese Incident" and World War II as the "Greater Pacific War." Yasukuni is such a powerful site in Japanese politics that some prime ministers feel obliged to pay their respects in August, on the anniversary of Japan's surrender to the United States. They normally attend as private citizens, not prime ministers, to avoid outraging nearby governments; but the neighbors complain anyway, arguing that Yasukuni promotes a nationalistic and spiritual worship of Japanese war criminals.

Here and there, in hard-to-reach corners of former German military bastions, you find a marble wall hung with a grim iron cross and the names of soldiers. But they're secretive and guilt-ridden affairs. A German memorial like Yasukuni would be impossible. The nimblest explanation I've heard for Japan's failure to exhibit much regret for its wartime aggression is that guilt itself has no currency. Japan has a culture of shame, of reputation and face. The way to recover from the horrors of the war in the second half of the "American century" was to build Japan into a respectable economic power.

"People don't talk about the war here," Brian had said in Osaka, lowering his voice to keep from offending the sushi chefs. "Their memories of it are different from ours." He said his mother-in-law had commented on his hairline sometime before he married his Japanese wife, Yoshie. "She pushed back my hair and said, 'Oh look, you have two little Pearl Harbors there.'" He widened his eyes. "Yoshie noticed I was upset. She said, 'What's wrong?' and I said, 'What does she mean by that? It would be like me finding a bald patch on a Japanese person's head and saying, 'Oh look, it's a little Nagasaki!'

"But Yoshie calmed me down. Her mother wasn't trying to offend me. She was just trying to find a reference we would both understand. To the Japanese, Pearl Harbor wasn't pivotal. They don't think of it as the attack that brought us into the war. They think of it as one event in a long series of escalations."

The Pacific war, officially, was a struggle to win freedom for the so-called "greater East Asia Co-Prosperity Sphere." In practice this meant wresting European colonies from their traditional masters, for the benefit of Japan. Indonesia, Malaya, the Philippines, and Burma were "liberated," and for a while the Japanese government could believe it had a European-style empire of its own.

The United States resisted this expansionism in a series of steps before 1941, much to Japan's irritation. And it ended Japan's militant imperialism altogether with a pair of nuclear bombs. Hiroshima . . .

Hiroshima—like Cologne, Dresden, and parts of Berlin—is now a hypermodern city because it was flattened in the war. Photos from the aftermath show the remains of a few sturdy brick structures on a charred and desolate plain. Tens of thousands of people died instantly. Some left just black scars on the ground. "The sinking sun made everything around us look pale, and both on and beneath the [river] bank there were pale people who cast their sinister shadows on the water," wrote a Hiroshima survivor named Tamiki Hara, in a short story from 1947, four years before his suicide. "Their faces were so puffy and swollen you could hardly tell whether they were men or women, with eyes that were mere slits and horribly blistered lips. They lay on their sides, their painful limbs exposed, barely breathing. When we passed before them, these strange people spoke to us in faint, gentle voices, 'Give us some water.'"

I spent an afternoon at the museum in Hiroshima, and buses from at least three separate schools unloaded hundreds of schoolchildren, who clustered like iron filings near two exhibits: the paper cranes folded by Sasaki Sadako, a twelve-year-old girl who died of leukemia in 1955 because of radiation from the bomb; and the wrinkled brown remnants of a schoolgirl's skin and fingernail, which had flaked off in the immediate aftermath. Interest in the skin was morbid curiosity; stories about it must have circulated at school. Interest in the cranes was the result of Sasaki's heartbreaking story, which has become a national myth memorialized in children's books and TV specials and a monument in the park outside. Sasaki started folding small origami cranes after she fell ill, believing she would heal once she had folded a thousand. She died first. The story, like the whole museum, is used eloquently by the Japanese government to argue for nuclear disarmament. But it's also a central part of the story Japanese tell themselves about World War II. Sasaki has become a sort of Anne Frank, which is strange, since Anne Frank's people hadn't taken up arms in a war of regional conquest, like the Germans and the Japanese.

The Meiji era was the crucial period when an archipelago of antiquated shogun warriors tried to compete with Europe and take what its leaders considered Japan's proper place in the nineteenth-century world. Old arquebuses came out of storage and were "converted to percussion rifles for the new national army," according to Noel Perrin. "They performed admirably." Thousands were converted again to bolt-action rifles for the Russo-Japanese War. Robert Kimbrough, an American firearms expert, wrote at the time (around 1904) that some bolt-action rifles he saw "carried names and dates from the mid-1600s, and weapons so converted were for use with modern powder without blowing up! No higher praise can be given the workmanship of the old Japanese craftsmen."

The Meijiera gave way to more militant nationalism, and by 1945—not even a full hundred years after Commodore Perry opened Japan to international trade—we would punish the Japanese horribly for their sudden taste for colonial wars. At least that's one way of looking at the bombing of Japan.

"We only did that because they bombed us first," a Hawaiian woman said to James D. Houston in Waikiki during the 1990s. "The feeling is that Pearl Harbor was an act of aggression," she said, "and the Japanese still have not shown sufficient regret."

> "But maybe we shared some of the responsibility there,"
> [Houston] said. "We may have brought it on ourselves."
> "What do you mean?"
> "If we hadn't taken Hawaii away from the Hawaiians back in
> 1893 and then turned it into a military arsenal, maybe there
> wouldn't have been anything to attack."

One morning in Chiba I saw a man walking back and forth in the shorebreak at Taito Beach with a strange sticklike contraption. He used it almost like a pair of enormous knitting needles, to squeeze and impale the wet sand. I asked Rob what was going on.

"Ah, Mr. Yoshida," he said. "He's trying to save the surf. He's laying down fishing nets."

"Excuse me?"

"He's spreading fishing nets and ropes out there. He says he hopes it'll bring back the sandbar. Terrence can tell you about it."

Terrence Charles Lotter—who had elucidated the strange habits of Japanese surfers for me—was a burly, round-headed artist with piercing blue eyes, farmer's forearms, and a boyish smile. He used to be a surfer on the Japanese circuit; he was the first foreigner to pass a test once administered to would-be pro surfers in Japan. Now he ran a gallery stuffed with his own paintings on the two-lane highway through Taito. He'd moved to Japan in the early '80s, as I mentioned—just before the South African government imposed a travel ban on its citizens. In those days the Pretoria government was busy retaliating against anti-apartheid bans imposed by other countries.

The fishing net project, said Terrence, belonged to an old obsession of Yoshida's. The idea was to reclaim the sandbars eroded in currents misdirected by the tetrapods and other local improvements. "He does it all day, every day. Even at night," said Terrence. "He moves with the tides. His whole life is dedicated to it. He's got this little surf shop, where he makes surfboards, right over there. Sea Eagle. That blue building. He's like a Japanese hippie. Eccentric; he doesn't give a fuck what anybody else thinks. And he's got his crew of loyal fans, guys who've bought a surfboard off him, who come down here and park in front of his shop," which he rarely opens for business. "There's two T-shirts from fifteen years ago in there, a couple of bars of wax. He's like, 'I'm not a surf shop guy.' And he makes the worst surfboards I've seen. Bumps everywhere, just terrible. The most terrible surfboards on the planet. He only makes about twelve of 'em a year, but he's still got this loyal crew, they've grown old with him.

"He's trying to build a sand bank. First he put out big sandbags, tried to sink those and build a reef. Then he got the idea of using tires, so he had all these tires strung out there, but the city hall came down on him. So he had to drag all these tires out of the water. Now he gets old fishing nets, the nets fishermen don't need anymore. He twists them up in long ropes, so there's a spiderweb of nets and ropes out on the sand. When the waves hit the ropes, it causes enough resistance that the sand actually builds up. It's started to work, just in the last four or five years. He keeps adding, and pulling, adjusting. He's actually managed a good wave. That resistance to the natural flow and the water, it's built up sand.

"About two years ago he had this major tragedy, which sort of spurred him on. That's when the nets started getting better, too. He was tying the ropes out there, standing waist-deep in the water, and as he was bent over the wave came and hit him from behind. He went head-first into the sand. It fucked up his neck, so he can't surf anymore. He was devastated. He's almost seventy now, and he got a full-on neck injury two years ago, so he says his legacy has to be this wave."

I was curious about Yoshida, so we walked across the road to his vacant shop and looked through the dusty windows. One of his hangers-on said the old surfer was napping in his sanding room; that was where he slept. So we walked to the beach and sat on a bench to wait. But soon he appeared, wearing a dark blue sweatshirt and rubber wading boots. Yoshida was a wrinkled, bantamweight man with short white hair. His gear on the beach consisted of fishing floats, long delicate nets, a few tires, and a lot of rope. He pointed out at the water and over at a concrete parking lot at the base of a cliff. "He says the water used to come all the way in," said Terrence, "—right up to the cliff. Now with all the construction, the wave's been destroyed. But it's coming back." We watched the surf for a while. "When the tide goes out again, he'll go back in."

"I see."

Yoshida belonged to the first generation of Japanese surfers, and his story followed the now-familiar pattern. He grew up here in Taito and heard about surfing from magazines. In those days, a few finished modern surfboards were available from Seibu department stores, but they cost the equivalent of a year's salary. So he tried to make his own. But it sank. At last he found an affordable wooden board by a local shaper. "He talked to one of the military guys," Terrence translated, "who could speak a little Japanese. He said, 'Teach me,' and the guy said, 'Okay, just watch.' Then he had it. He thought, Oh, you're supposed to move sideways," on the wave. "But a while later, further down south, he saw slightly more advanced human beings who could walk to the nose." These soldiers were much better surfers; but he wanted to know why they moved up and down on their boards. "They said, 'If you move in this way, you get more points [in a contest].' So he taught himself to do that."

He started to surf at the age of twenty-five and became one of Japan's top professional surfers. When he retired at forty-five, Terrence said, his ability was still astonishing.

But the most intriguing surfer I met in Japan was Taro Takahashi, who picked me up at the Taito train station the following day in a rattling, miniature white pickup. The tiny cab contained an orange woodsman's helmet as well as a small copper wind chime tinkling from the rearview mirror. Taro chain-smoked. He had white bristles on his chin, glasses, and salted black hair pulled back in a ducktail. We drove on narrow roads between sprouting rice paddies, around sundown, while he apologized for his English; he said he normally woke up at one thirty in the morning to run a paper route, so—at five thirty or so in the evening—he was tired.

He lived just down the road from Terrence's studio; there had been no need for me to get on the train. His overgrown yard hid the house almost completely from the road. A few squat wooden pillars in the pavement had been tumbled into a bush under his bedroom window. He waved dismissively. A car had run into the bush, he said. It had barely missed cracking the house. Now red lights, like runway lights, blinked nervously along the curve.

Inside, the cluttered small house had faded surf pictures hanging on the wood-paneled wall. Taro's wife was gracious and thin, with glasses; she made green tea. Taro had to move a stack of papers to let me set my teacup on a sort of metal barrel. A TV nattered during our conversation, and he spoke in urgent bursts, full of deep-voiced emotion. "I lived in downtown Tokyo, before," he said. "In young time. High school. Every summer I went to Hayama Beach. Shonan. Camping. One month, summertime. Diving, and fishing, and swimming. And— cooking. Sometimes, cooking, I made a fire, with wood and lots of magazines, old magazines. Once I looked at a magazine," a Japanese children's magazine, "and I saw Hawaii pictures. And surfing! *Whoo!*"

He estimated the year at 1959. Japanese kids were riding ita-gos. "But we didn't stand. Just imagine—an older guy, standing on a wave!" He brightened. "*Whooo!*"

At the fireside he had slipped the magazine page in his pocket, then returned to Tokyo and tried to build a board from plywood. His first two attempts failed, but the third board floated so well that "everybody" who tried it could stand on a wave. "I like everything handmade," he said. "This house, too. I am very poor. No money. But I want everything. So I think, 'All right, I can make this.'"

He finally had a chance to inspect American-made boards, first an expensive import that someone in Shonan had purchased from the Seibu department store, then a board belonging to the son of an American serviceman. "He was a young American, taking his board to Hayama Beach, and riding. He gave me a present—a surfing magazine. A soldier's son. His name was Mark. But Mark died in the Vietnam War."

The longer I talked to him, the more I suspected that Taro was Japan's first homegrown stand-up surfer. He wasn't a mimic, for one thing. He had the original mind and abiding curiosity of someone who picks up a new idea for its own sake. By 1963 he'd learned to shape urethane and fiberglass boards using material scrounged from factories around Tokyo. He went up to total strangers and said, as he put it, "'Please, I want to make a surfboard.' 'What, surfboard?' 'Please, I need fiberglass and polyester resin and urethane foam.' And finally [they would say], 'All right! You're a funky boy.'"

At Hayama Beach he formed Ducks Surf Club. Their symbol was Donald Duck. On the first several boards for his friends, he put Donald's face. "And then the people knew—'Duck, Duck, Duck.' But Donald Duck is patented," he said, so he couldn't use the image to sell his boards. "So then I designed a decal," which to this day is the logo for the Ducks Surf Shop, run by his son in Tokyo. "After that, a little fame, lots of friends."

"You built a business."

"Mmmm, but I didn't want a business," he said. "Forty years, surf-board making. I don't like it. Very bad and unhealthy." So he quit in the mid-'90s and built this house in Taito—near one of the best surf breaks in Japan—to become a farmer. "Rice, and vegetables, everything," he said. "Four years later, the government wanted forest workers." From the top of the TV he grabbed a framed wooden slate with lots of writing. It was his forestry certificate. "School—one year. Japanese Forest Keepers' Association." At his age, pushing seventy, he climbed trees with a chain saw. He cleared and trimmed and picked up trash. A cleaner forest led to cleaner streams, which led to a cleaner ocean. "A long time ago, Japanese beaches were *very* dirty," he said. "Lots of gar-bage. But now it's mountain cleaning [for me]. Very nice time. I help on the mountain to clean the ocean. *Very* happy! Somebody asked me, 'Mr. Taro, why don't you surf on the beach?' But I'm surfing now on the mountain. Very dangerous. Lots of good sweat. Like a big wave." He laughed.

I thought of the plastic stew in the middle of the northern Pacific, a sort of toilet bowl for deathless modern junk from both Asia and North America. The soup consists of two patches, east and west of Hawaii, shaped by the swirling currents. These vast fields of plastic bottles and bags, Lego blocks, syringes, cotton-swab shafts, and probably fragments of urethane surfboards have collected in a total area estimated to be more than twice the size of France. An American oceanographer named Charles Moore discovered the mess in 1997, when he aimed his boat through the North Pacific Gyre, a doldrum at the heart of the turning Pacific currents, which sailors normally avoid. Since the plastic is trans-lucent and sparse and floats just under the surface, and a lot of the volume consists of flakes and tiny beads, satellite photos have never picked it up. "These pieces never go away," Moore told *National Geo-graphic*. "Here we've invented a material that for all practical purposes lasts forever, and instead of using it on products we want to last a long, long time, we're using it on products that we may only use for seconds."

Taro had dedicated his strength to opposing this abomination. He would never make much of a difference, or not on his own, but it was important to labor in the right direction.

****

A more evanescent sport than surfing is hard to imagine. In the '60s it may have looked like a whirlwind fad, like Hula-hoops, but it's proved to be at least as durable as a plastic bag. And the world has changed so quickly since the first pop explosion of surfing that images and stories from that time seem almost antique. Even Mike Purpus, in Redondo, sounds like a hopeless old-timer. "The good thing about surfing [in the '60s] was, parents had more control over you," he said in his reedy surfer's voice. "The first thing they'd say if you did anything wrong was, 'You can't go surfing.' It was worse than taking away sex. Now parents punish their kids by takin' away their video games and their cell phones, so they have to go outside and play. When I was a kid, you got grounded. You had to stay in, and the only way to get out was to drive your parents nuts, so they'd throw you out. That's what's happening now. Video games have killed the surf star." He glanced around the trophies in his room. "I can't even *believe* it."

Not long ago a San Diego real estate consultant told the *New York Times* that he had no shame about trying to sell homes to strangers at his local break. "I'll sit in the water and listen to conversations," he said, "and if someone says something about real estate, I'll find a way to interject." A public prosecutor from San Diego told the same reporter that surf lessons had boosted her legal career. Surfing had "opened so many doors to meet people, network and just enjoy being a woman interacting with other professionals on a social level. . . . Judges I appear with surf, opposing counsel surf, my colleagues surf, and [I've] made so many friends who surf as well."

A new breed of American surfer, in other words, goes *looking* for crowds. Very strange. Surfers once took to the ocean to get away from bosses, judges, colleagues, opposing counsel, and consultants with their idiot sales pitches. The Japanese coast since the '80s has been a reliable glimpse of the sport's future—throngs of people in the water who may or may not really surf—which is why Taro Takahashi is so interesting, with his crops of vegetables in the yard and his quixotic enthusiasm for cleaning the ocean by trying to scrub the mountains. He's an individualist, an enthusiast with the boyish impulses of George Freeth or Duke Kahanamoku. At the same time he seems more intensely Japanese than the crowds of weekend surfers from Tokyo. He designed one of Japan's first modern surfboards, and while other pioneers from his generation have grown famous and rich as founders of major brands, Takahashi lives a bit like the mountain people Doji mentioned, the ancient Japanese hippies.

Maybe more than other nations, Japan adopted surfing in conscious imitation of American style; and maybe more than other nations, Japan has made surfing its own. It's hard for me to think of the spread of the modern sport now as a sign of world cultural domination by the United States—of "California Über Alles" or Western pop hegemony. Too much else is going on. Each country has absorbed surfing in a different way. The British Empire brought soccer to Africa and Asia, and no one calls it a British schoolboy sport anymore. Surfing might be the American analogy. Finding the heart of a wave with your feet on a board has an elemental logic, like kicking a soccer ball. It may be simple enough to outlive the muscular forces that moved it around the world.

"Surfing has taught me many things," Taro said. "It has good energy. Longboard surfing. *Very* peaceful!" The sport was in tune with nature, in his opinion. "Shortboard surfing, very aggressive—I don't like it. But surfing has been very instructive."

How?

He thought for a moment. His answer was as quotable as a proverb from Duke.

"Well, one thing," he said. "It's like work. Paddle, paddle—and sometimes, big wave come!"

BIBLIOGRAPHY

Alexander, James Edward. *Narrative of a Voyage of Observation among the Colonies of Western Africa*. London: Henry Colburn, 1837.

Angelo, Claudio. "Q&A with Iconoclast Who Makes First Contact with Amazonian Tribes." *Scientific American*, April 2007.

Baker, Christopher P. *Cuba*. Moon Guidebooks Series. Berkeley, CA: Avalon Travel, 2006.

Beaglehole, J. C., ed. *The Journals of Captain James Cook on His Voyages of Discovery: The Voyage of the* Resolution *and* Discovery, *1776–1780, Part Two*. Cambridge, UK: Cambridge University Press, 1967.

Bellow, Saul. *To Jerusalem and Back*. New York: Penguin, 1998.

Berry, Andrew, ed. *Infinite Tropics: An Alfred Russel Wallace Anthology*. New York: Verso, 2002.

Bingham, Hiram. *A Residence of Twenty-One Years in the Sandwich Islands*. New York: S. Converse, 1847.

Bowles, Paul. *Their Heads Are Green and Their Hands Are Blue*. New York: Harper Perennial, 2006.

Boyer, Sam, Sam George, and Paul Taublieb, directors. *The Lost Wave: An African Surf Story*. VAS Entertainment, 2007.

Brennan, Joseph L. *Duke: The Life Story of Hawai'i's Duke Kahanamoku*. Honolulu: Ku Pa'a, 1994.

Burness, Donald. *Ossobo: Essays on the Literature of São Tomé and Príncipe*. Trenton, NJ: Africa World Press, 2005.

Carroll, Corky. "The Totally Unofficial History of the Modern Surfboard." www.corkycarroll.com.

Colas, Antony. *The World Stormrider Guide*, Vol. 1. Cornwall, UK: Low Pressure Publishing, 2000.

———. *Stormrider Guide Europe: Atlantic Islands*. Cornwall, UK: Low Pressure Publishing, 2007.

Dana, Richard Henry, Jr. *Two Years Before the Mast*. New York: Signet Classic, 2000.

Davis, Robert C. *Christian Slaves, Muslim Masters: White Slavery in the Mediterranean, the Barbary Coast, and Italy, 1500-1800*. New York: Palgrave Macmillan, 2003.

Doyle, Mike, with Steve Sorensen. *Morning Glass: The Adventures of Legendary Waterman Mike Doyle*. Three Rivers, CA: Fuyu Press, 1993.

Duane, Daniel. *Caught Inside: A Surfer's Year on the California Coast*. New York: North Point Press, 1996.

Eisenstadt, David. "Surfing Whodunit." *Los Angeles Times*, October 11, 2005.

Finnegan, William. "Blank Monday." *New Yorker*, August 21, 2006.

Finney, Ben R., and James D. Houston. *Surfing: A History of the Ancient Hawaiian Sport.* San Francisco: Pomegranate Artbooks, 1996.

Friend, Theodore. *Indonesian Destinies.* Cambridge, MA: Belknap Press of Harvard University Press, 2003.

Gault-Williams, Malcolm. "Oom: John Whitmore." *Legendary Surfers* Web site, March 15, 2008. www.legendarysurfers.com.

George, Sam. "Pre-Contact: The Surfing Tradition of São Tomé." *Surfer's Journal* 16, no. 3, Summer 2007.

Ghazvinian, John. *Untapped: The Scramble for Africa's Oil.* New York: Harvest Books, 2008.

Gordon, Andrew. *A Modern History of Japan: From Tokugawa Times to the Present.* New York: Oxford University Press, 2009.

Gott, Richard. *Cuba: A New History.* New Haven, CT: Yale University Press, 2005.

Halliday, F. E. *A History of Cornwall.* London: Gerald Duckworth, 1959.

Hara, Tamiki. "Summer Flower." Anthologized in *The Crazy Iris and Other Stories of the Atomic Aftermath.* New York: Grove Press, 1985.

Heine, William. *With Perry to Japan.* Honolulu: University of Hawaii Press, 1990.

Hitchens, Christopher. "Can Israel Survive for Another 60 Years?" *Slate,* May 12, 2008. www.slate.com/id/2191193.

Holmes, Rod, and Wilson, Doug. *You Should Have Been Here Yesterday: The Roots of British Surfing.* UK: Seasedge, 1994

Houston, James D. *In the Ring of Fire: A Pacific Basin Journey.* San Francisco: Mercury House, 1997.

Iyer, Pico. *Video Night in Kathmandu and Other Reports from the Not-So-Far East.* New York: Vintage, 1989.

Johnston, Tim. "We Saw a Fireball 10 Storeys High." *Times* (London), October 14, 2002.

Kampion, Drew, ed. *Dora Lives: The Authorized Story of Miki Dora.* Santa Barbara, CA: D.A.P./T. Adler Books, 2005.

Kingston, W. H. G. *Captain Cook: His Life, Voyages, and Discoveries.* London: Religious Tract Society, 1871.

Kinzer, Stephen. *Overthrow: America's Century of Regime Change from Hawaii to Iraq.* New York: Henry Holt, 2006.

Koke, Louise G. *Our Hotel in Bali.* Wellington, New Zealand: January Books, 1987.

Lane, B. A. *Time and Tide Wait for No Man on the Severn.* Coleford, UK: Douglas McLean, 1993.

Leonard, Alex. "Learning to Surf in Kuta, Bali." *Review of Indonesian and Malaysian Affairs* 41, no. 1 (2007): 3–32.

Lewis, Bernard. *The Middle East: A Brief History of the Last 2,000 Years.* New York: Scribner, 1995.

Lewis, Norman. "Hemingway in Cuba." *Granta,* Summer 1985.

Mansfield, Roger. *The Surfing Tribe: A History of Surfing in Britain* Newquay UK: Orca Publications, 2009.

Martin, Andrew. "Surfing the Revolution: The Fatal Impact of the Pacific on Europe." *Eighteenth-Century Studies* 41, no. 2 (2008): 141–7.

Miller, Tom. *Trading With the Enemy: A Yankee Travels Through Castro's Cuba*. New York: Basic Books, 1992.

Milton, Giles. *White Gold: The Extraordinary Story of Thomas Pellow and Islam's One Million White Slaves*. New York: Farrar, Straus and Giroux, 2004.

Morris, Jan. *A Writer's World: Travels 1950–2000*. London: Faber and Faber, 2003.

Moser, Patrick, ed. *Pacific Passages: An Anthology of Surf Writing*. Honolulu: University of Hawaii Press, 2008.

Neely, Peter. *Indo Surf and Lingo*. Bali, Indonesia: Peter Neely, 2002.

Pappé, Ilan. *A History of Modern Palestine: One Land, Two Peoples*. Cambridge, UK: Cambridge University Press, 2003.

Pennell, C. R. *Morocco Since 1830: A History*. New York: New York University Press, 2001.

Perman, Stacy. "Hang Ten for Ha-Shem." *Guilt and Pleasure*, no. 5, Summer 2007.

Perrin, Noel. *Giving Up the Gun: Japan's Reversion to the Sword, 1543-1879*. Boston: David R. Godine, 1988.

Rensin, David. *All For a Few Perfect Waves: The Audacious Life and Legend of Rebel Surfer Miki Dora*. New York: HarperEntertainment, 2008.

Richie, Alexandra. *Faust's Metropolis: A History of Berlin*. New York: Carroll and Graf, 1998.

Ricklefs, M. C. *A History of Modern Indonesia Since c. 1200*, 3rd ed. Stanford, CA: Stanford University Press, 2001.

Schroeter, Daniel J. *Merchants of Essaouira: Urban Society and Imperialism in Southwestern Morocco, 1844–1886*. Cambridge, UK: Cambridge University Press, 1988.

Seibert, Gerhard. *Comrades, Clients and Cousins: Colonialism, Socialism and Democratization in Sao Tomé and Príncipe*. Boston: Brill Academic, 2006.

Shanks, Hershel. *Jerusalem: An Archaeological Biography*. New York: Random House, 1995.

Stokesbury, James L. A Short History of World War II. New York: Harper Perennial, 2001.

Toer, Pramoedya Ananta. *The Mute's Soliloquy: A Memoir*. New York: Hyperion, 1999.

Twain, Mark, *Letters from Hawaii*. Honolulu: University of Hawaii Press, 1975.

Verge, Arthur C. "George Freeth: King of the Surfers and California's Forgotten Hero." *California History*, Summer–Fall 2001.

Vidal, Gore. Introduction. In *Tennessee Williams: Collected Stories*. New York: New Directions, 1985.

Viertel, Peter. *Dangerous Friends: At Large with Hemingway and Huston in the Fifties*. New York: N. A. Talese, 1992.

Von Rohr, Mathieu. "Oil Speculation in São Tomé: How to Rob an African Nation." *Spiegel Online International*, April 18, 2008. www.spiegel.de/international/world/0,1518,548272,00.html.

Wade, Alex. *Surf Nation: In Search of the Fast Lefts and Hollow Rights of Britain and Ireland*. London: Simon and Schuster, 2007.

Warshaw, Matt. *The Encyclopedia of Surfing*. Orlando, FL: Harcourt, 2003.

Weller, Sheila. "Malibu's Lost Boys." *Vanity Fair*, August 2006.

Wright, William. *Fishes and Fishing: Artificial Breeding of Fish, Anatomy of the Senses, Their Loves, Passions, and Intellects, with Illustrative Facts*. London: Thomas Cautley Newby, 1858.

ACKNOWLEDGMENTS

Special thanks to Susanna Forrest for urging me to write this book (in a slightly different form), and for suggesting it to my excellent agent, Elizabeth Sheinkman; to Elizabeth for all of her hard work; to David Rensin for letting me use material he'd gathered but never published about Miki Dora; and to Malcolm Gault-Williams for his collected histories of surfing at Legendarysurfers.com.

Thanks also to Karen Rinaldi, my enthusiastic editor, who surfs the frigid Jersey shore, and thanks to Greg Villepique and Nancy Elgin, my sharp-eyed copy editors.

The following people were also immeasurably helpful in various unsung ways:

Indonesia: Samuel Indratma, Mark Hanusz, Aji Ramyakim, Tim Johnston

Germany: Nicole Busse, Gregor Kolmar, Charles Hawley, Daryl Lindsey, David Gordon Smith

Morocco: Hakim Meskine, Omari Boumediene

United Kingdom: Robin and Rosemary Forrest, Roger Mansfield, Chris Jones, Alex Wade

Israel and Gaza: Christoph Schult, Mohamed Alwan, Yisroel Pensack

Cuba: Eduárdo Valdés, Tom Miller, Chris Baker

São Tomé and Príncipe: Guitola Doria at Navetur-Equatour, Quintino Quade, Sean Buckley, Ned Seligman, David Hecht, Mathieu von Rohr

Japan: Tak Kawahara, Hiromi Isaka, Takao Kawana, Rob Newman, Brian Wanamaker, Tierney Thys, the Nakamura family

INDEX